Lauther's

Complete

Punctuation Thesaurus

Of The
English Language

By

Howard Lauther

Branden Publishing Company
Boston

Library of Congress Cataloging in Publication Data

Lauther, Howard. 1935-
   [Complete punctuation thesaurus of the English
   Language]

   Lauther's complete punctuation thesaurus of the English
   language / by Howard Lauther.
      p. cm.
   Includes index.
   ISBN 0-8283-1945-6 : $19.95
   1. English language--Punctuation. I. Title.
PE1450.C74 1991
428--dc20   91-14703
                                        CIP

BRANDEN PUBLISHING COMPANY
17 Station Street
Box 843 Brookline Village
Boston, MA 02147

How to Use This Book

① Begin by finding your problem in either the **Punctuation Categories** at the front of the book or in the **General Index** at the end, which lists the categories in alphabetical order. Here are examples from both sections:

Punctuation
Categories

Indirect Quote

37.1 Examples
37.2 Preceded by *like* or *as*
37.3 Preceded by *that*

General Index

quote (indirect)

Examples 37.1
Preceded by *like* or *as* 37.2
Preceded by *that* 37.3

② Whether using the category listing or the index, observe the number which precedes or follows the punctuation problem. Next turn to that rule number in the book, which will supply you with the answer, and note any exceptions which are provided. Example:

37.2 Indirect quote is preceded by "like" or "as." This is one of those rare instances when the indirect quote should be encased in double quotation marks (" "). When there are two or more quotes in succession, double quotations marks will follow one another.

1 QUOTE: He would always say things like "I didn't see anything. I didn't hear anything."

2 OR MORE: They said things like "I didn't see anything." "You'll have to talk to my lawyer." "I was out of town at the time." "I don't recall."

Exception: **Indirect quotes are questions.** Omit the quotation marks and capitalize the first word of each.

People who come into the store ask such questions as How

Punctuation Categories

Word

Begins a Sentence
1.1 Unimportant to sentence
1.2 Natural pause follows it
1.3 Provides essential information
1.4 Interjection or acts as one
1.5 Needs emphasis
1.6 Confusion is possible
Followed by...
1.7 Identical word
1.8 Strong pause
1.9 Interrupting word or phrase
1.10 Series of words or phrases
1.11 Add-on word or phrase

At Midsentence
Interrupts...
2.1 The sentence
2.2 Phrase within a sentence
2.3 As a comment, explanation, identification, etc.
2.4 As an interjection
Followed by...
2.5 Identical word
2.6 Word spelled phonetically
2.7 Duplicate pronoun
2.8 Another verb
Other
2.9 Confusion is possible
2.10 Showing sarcasm, doubt

Ends Sentence
Preceded by...
3.1 A light pause
3.2 A strong pause
3.3 An identical word
3.4 *And* (missing)
Other
3.5 Repeats sentence's meaning
3.6 Easily removed

In Pairs or Series
Pair of Words
4.1 Identical
4.2 Descriptive
4.3 More than one pair
4.4 Strong pause follows
Series of Words
4.5 When to separate
4.6 When NOT to separate
4.7 Emphasizing each
4.8 Identical
4.9 Adjectives/adverbs as nouns
4.10 Nouns are identified
Introduces Sentence
4.11 Followed by adverb, verb
4.12 Strong pause follows
Midsentence
4.13 Cannot be removed
4.14 Interrupts
4.15 Followed by a question
End of Sentence
4.16 Cannot remove
4.17 Strong pause precedes
Miscellaneous
4.18 Words are numbered
4.19 Words and phrases in series

Stands Alone
5.1 One stand-alone word
5.2 Two or more in succession

Highlighted
6.1 Alphabetic letter as a noun
6.2 With one-letter prefix
6.3 Unofficial definition follows
Preceded by the words
6.4 *By-word*
6.5 *So-called*
6.6 *Word*
6.7 *Called, marked, labeled,* etc.
Represents
6.8 Irony
6.9 Sarcasm
Other
6.10 All letters capitalized
6.11 Technical or unfamiliar word
6.12 Nouns in a legal document

Phrases & Adverbial Clauses

List of Full and Partial Phrases

List of Opening Words

Sentence

Simple Sentence

Joining Two Sentences

Joining Three Sentences

Joining Four+ Sentences

Quote

Motto, Epitaph
Follows...
34.1 Noun or pronoun
34.2 Verb
Interrupts
34.3 Follows a pronoun

Dialogue
Accompanied by...
35.1 *Said, asked*, etc.
35.2 List of verbs used
35.3 Preceding noun or pronoun
35.4 Conjunction & new sentence
35.5 Nondialogue phrase
Showing...
35.6 Dramatic pause
35.7 Hesitation, uncertainty
35.8 Quick transition of thought
35.9 Unfinished line of dialogue
35.10 Stuttering
35.11 Thinking dialogue
35.12 Remembering words spoken
Dialect
35.13 Adding to dialogue
35.14 Omitting first letters
35.15 Omitting middle letters
35.16 Omitting last letters
35.17 Omitting first and last letters
35.18 Combining words
35.19 Showing pronunciation
Miscellaneous
35.20 Joining related sentences
35.21 Follows one word
35.22 Strong pause after introduction
35.23 Person is being addressed
35.24 *Hello* and *good-bye*
35.25 Actor's directions in a script
35.26 Stage directions in a script
35.27 Making a request
35.28 Nonwords
35.29 Changing the spelling

Direct Quote
Preceded/Followed by...
36.1 *Said, replied*, etc.
36.2 Noun or pronoun
36.3 Preposition
Long
36.4 Three typed lines or more
36.5 Spans paragraphs
36.6 Full letters or telegrams
Short or Shortened
36.7 Succession of short quotes
36.8 Shortened
36.9 Acts as an add-on
Interrupted by...
36.10 Comment, explanation
36.11 Another quote
36.12 Notation of error in quote
Miscellaneous
36.13 Exclamation/ question mark
36.14 Naming the source of quote
36.15 Common expressions
36.16 Emphasizing some words
36.17 Foreign words
36.18 Successive, from same source
36.19 Court testimony
36.20 Precedes/follows *was, is*
36.21 Remembering a quote

Indirect Quote
37.1 Examples
37.2 Preceded by *like* or *as*
37.3 Preceded by *that*

Cliché (Old Saying)
38.1 Explanation
38.2 Subject of sentence

Proverb, Principle
39.1 Synonyms explained
39.2 Capitalization
39.3 Quotation marks and italics
39.4 Follows a strong pause
39.5 Follows word like *proverb, principle, axiom*, etc.

Poetry
40.1 Quoting a poem as seen
40.2 Quoting in paragraph form
40.3 Omitting one or more lines

Time

In a Sentence

Time Elements

Time Span

Question

Direct Question

Indirect Question

List

In a Paragraph

Vertical

Number

Appears before...

Large Number

Small Number

Monetary

Measurement

Miscellaneous

Title

Literary Title

Bibliography

Footnote

Person's Title

Other Titles

Name

Person's Name

Company's Name

Punctuation Marks

Hyphenating

Prefixes

Hyphemes/Solidemes

Other Words

Other

Referring the Reader

Headings/Captions

Military Commands

Capitalization

Closings in Letters

Trite Combinations

Incorrect Combinations

Abbreviations

First Word

1.1   **Unimportant to the meaning of the sentence.** Insert a comma (,) after the opening word. This is often the case when adjectives, adverbs, and interjections introduce a sentence.

Obviously, it's not the sort of thing you should practice.

Exception: **Exclamation mark used.** Comma may be omitted when an exclamation mark (!) is placed at the end of a short sentence. This is frequently the case when the first word is an adverb which ends in "ly."

Obviously he didn't care about her!

Exception: **No pause.** Comma may be omitted when there is no pause after the word, particularly if the sentence is short.

Frequently she would.

1.2   **Natural pause follows introductory word.** Insert a comma (,) after the introductory word.

Sure, we can go there if you like.

1.3   **Provides essential information.** When the introductory word allows the reader to better understand what follows, no punctuation is needed. In the first example, the word *suddenly* appears to be removable because the rest of the sentence would still make sense without it; but in fact it adds crucial information by telling us HOW he moved and, therefore, should not be isolated. The importance of the word may be tested by simply placing it at the end of the sentence, instead (*see* second sentence).

BEGINNING: *Suddenly* he moved in front of me.
END: He moved in front of me *suddenly.*

However if the first word is followed by a long, unpunctuated sentence, a comma (,) will be needed after it, even though the word adds important information. And should a phrase be added to the end of a long sentence, the comma after the first word may often be retained, although in most cases it would be omitted.

Suddenly, he stood up in the crowd with all the cockiness of a young man who wanted them to know that he was as tough as they come and as mean as they get.

1

<table>
<tr><td>Exception:</td><td>**Conjunction joins two related ideas.** Insert a comma (,) after the opening word. In this example the conjunction is "and."</td></tr>
</table>

Suddenly, he stood up and began shaking my hand.

1.4   **Interjection—or a word which performs as one—leads off a sentence.** Insert a comma (,) to set it apart. Except when the interjection is not being used in a dramatic way—in which case the sentence would end in a period (.)—insert an exclamation mark (!) after the sentence, or use a question mark (?) if a question is being asked.

<table>
<tr><td>INTERJECTION:</td><td>*Wow,* this is the hottest day ever!</td></tr>
<tr><td>ACTS AS ONE:</td><td>*Man,* what I wouldn't give for a pizza!</td></tr>
<tr><td>UNDRAMATIC:</td><td>*Good,* I'm glad you're going.</td></tr>
</table>

<table>
<tr><td>Exception:</td><td>**Side-by-side interjections.** They will probably need to be distinguished from one another by punctuation. Many pure interjections require a hyphen (-) between them; but when the interjections can perform as other parts of speech as well, the comma (,) is usually the correct punctuation unless there are three in a row (*see* last example).</td></tr>
</table>

<table>
<tr><td>HYPHEN:</td><td>*Oh-oh,* we're in for it now.</td></tr>
<tr><td>NOUNS:</td><td>*Boy,* boy, what a shame.</td></tr>
<tr><td>NONE:</td><td>*Boy oh boy,* what luck.</td></tr>
</table>

1.5   **Needs emphasis.** When a strong pause is needed after the opening word, insert a dash (—) after it. Note: do not overuse this punctuation mark.

Camille—it was a name that kept spinning in my head.

1.6   **Confusion is possible.** Lack of a comma after the first word may sometimes confuse the reader. To prevent that from happening, force a pause by inserting a comma (,) after it. If a comma did not force a pause after *before* in the first example shown below, one could easily think that more information is forthcoming after *Navy*. But the problem may also be solved by inserting another word rather than a comma, although the comma is usually preferable.

<table>
<tr><td>NO COMMA:</td><td>*Before* he was a sailor in the Navy.</td></tr>
<tr><td>COMMA USED:</td><td>*Before,* he was a sailor in the Navy.</td></tr>
<tr><td>WORD ADDED:</td><td>*Before that* he was a sailor in the Navy.</td></tr>
</table>

2

1.7   Followed by an identical word. The two words may be separated by several different punctuation marks, depending on the effect you wish to achieve.

PERIOD (.):   *Fine. Fine.* If that's what you think.
COMMA (,):   *Slowly, slowly* he began to move.
EXCL. MK. (!): *Hear! Hear!* I'm all for that!

COMBINATION: *Yeh, yeh,* I know.
                Yeh, yeh—I heard you the first time!
                Easy. Easy! You'll break it.

1.8   Followed by a strong pause. It is likely that some type of elaborating information follows it, perhaps in the form of an explanation, definition, summary, or question. Insert a colon (:) after the word. The first word following a colon is rarely if ever capitalized, for the information is wholly dependent on the other opening word for its existence.

DEFINITION: *Sit:* used by people to make a dog behave.
SUMMARY: *War:* that will be the result of it.
EXPLANATION: *Greed:* you will find this trait in all of us.

Exception: **Question follows.** Capitalize the question.

                Love: Is that what is missing in the world today?

1.9   Interrupting word or phrase follows. Do not place a comma after the first word, even though it usually requires one. The interruptions in the sentences below are preceded and followed by commas.

WORD: *Next* the government, unbelievably, voted a tax increase amid one of the worst recessions ever.

PHRASE: *Next* we hear, if I'm not mistaken, that the city is going to raise our taxes.

Exception: **Interruption is emphasized.** Precede and follow it with a dash (—), and return the comma (,) to its rightful place following the introductory word.

            Next, they said—and I hope for our sake that I am wrong about this—that the city is going to raise our taxes.

1.10   Followed by words or phrases in a series. The introductory word does not need to be set apart by commas, for the sentence already has ample punctuation. In this example, the series ends the sentence.

Next we decided to have lettuce, onions, and tomatoes.

Exception: **Lengthy information after the opening word.** If the information between the introductory word and series is lengthy (shown below in italics), the comma can often be inserted after the introductory word, because the possibility of confusing the reader is highly unlikely.

Next, we drove down to that place where Edna and Billy Bob got married on a Monday morning and had ourselves some lettuce, onions, and tomatoes.

1.11   **Followed by a word or phrase which is added to a sentence.** Instead of placing a comma (,) after the introductory word, insert it before the word or phrase which has been added to the sentence. In this example, the common expression *you know* is being added.

Actually it wasn't his, you know.

Exception: **Add-on phrase is emphasized.** Insert a dash (—) before it and return the comma (,) after the first word.

Actually, he tried—for all the good it did.

Exception: **Lengthy information after the opening word.** If the information between the opening word and the add-on word or phrase is long, or if the sentence has no other separating commas, return the comma (,) after the first word.

Still, I don't think Jerry meant to hurt anyone with that remark which he made about fast food restaurants, if you want my personal opinion.

Midsentence Word

2.1   **Interrupts the sentence.** If a definite pause can be detected before the word is read, insert a comma (,) before and after it. In the examples which follow, various parts of speech are shown as interruptions.

ADJECTIVE: But Little Edith, *trustful,* didn't see through it.
ADVERB: All of them, *undoubtedly,* are going to play poker.
INTERJECTION: And then, *golly,* what a time we had.
NOUN: It was Bloomfield, *Secretary of State,* who said it.

Exception: **No pause detected.** The comma is usually omitted before and after the word. Of all the parts of speech, it is perhaps the adverb—particularly one which ends with the letters "ly"—that most frequently falls into

4

this category. In the third example the comma AFTER the interruption is not removed, because the pause can be detected; therefore, the introduction and interruption join and form an introductory phrase. Still there are some introductory words, such as *now* and *well*, which are used as pauses themselves—however subtle—and must be followed by a comma (,), as displayed in the last example.

NO COMMAS: Yet *surely* you know its importance.
She then *finally* decided she would go.

ONE: But *really*, it wasn't what I expected.
TWO: Well, *really*, I didn't know.

Exception: **Interruption + add-on.** If the interrupting word is an adverb which ends in "ly" and it is soon followed by an add-on phrase, it is usually not necessary to set it apart with commas.

ORIGINAL: Then Wilma, *fiercely*, ran out of her room.

+ADD-ON: Then Wilma *fiercely* ran out of her room, *demanding to know who had fired the shots.*

But another speech part, such as a verb ending in "ing," might well retain its preceding and following commas.

Then Wilma, *choking*, ran out her room, gasping and hacking her way toward the bathroom.

Exception: **Ample punctuation before interruption.** The interruption may not require commas before and after it. Commas around the word *therefore* in the example shown below would overload the sentence and give it a choppy look, which could lead to confusion.

Given those circumstances, choices, and potential results, I *therefore* would be afraid to do anything.

Exception: **Interruption refers to time.** If it follows a phrase which relates to a geographical phrase, the two are often combined into one phrase. Below, *in Cincinnati* is the phrase, and *recently* is the interrupting time element.

5

In Cincinnati *recently,* there was a bank holdup and they only got away with a coupon for broccoli.

2.2   **Interrupts an interrupting phrase.** With the addition of an interrupting phrase, the sentence already has ample commas and more could prove to be confusing. Therefore, a word which interrupts an interrupting phrase will need something more powerful than a comma to set it apart, and the dash (—) is usually the punctuation mark that can do that. In the first example below, *however* does not need to be isolated; in the second sentence, *obviously* is given special emphasis in order to draw special attention to the subject's lack of ability when playing the piano.

NOT ISOLATED: He played every instrument, except *however* the piano, with perhaps more enthusiasm than anyone I've ever seen.

ISOLATED: He could play every instrument, except—*obviously*—the piano, with more enthusiasm than anyone I've ever seen.

Exception: **No pause before the one-word interruption.** Eliminate the commas before and after the word. In this example, *indeed* is the interrupting word.

I discovered that the train was to arrive, coming *indeed* from the west, on the fourth day of February.

2.3   **Interrupts as a quick identification, personal comment, or explanation.** Encase the word in parentheses. For special effect, a question mark (**?**) or exclamation mark (**!**) may be inserted before the last parenthesis as well. Use the parentheses sparingly.

IDENTIFIES: The home team (Bedford) won the game in the ninth.
EXPLAINS: It's a sweaty (humid) day.
COMMENT: He said he had a degree from Boston College (unlikely) and that he was a millionaire (hah!).

Exception: **Interruption needs emphasis.** Use the dash (—), instead. Here is a one-word personal comment.

They thought—*honestly*—that it was he who had been writing the plays all along.

2.4   **Interrupts as an interjection.** The word may be followed by an exclamation mark (**!**). However, this is only acceptable in informal writing (novels, plays). Lewis Carrol used it to great effect in his book, *Alice in Wonderland.* In the example below, the word *crash*—which can easily be removed—is not really an interjection, but it performs as one.

6

Then it went *crash!* into the wall.

2.5   **Followed by an identical word.** When no pause can be detected between the two words, or the removal of one of them would hamper the meaning of the sentence, no separating comma is needed. In the following examples the duplicate words are necessary.

    VERB: They *had had* more than their fill of trouble.
    PREPOSITION: Then they came *in, in* their swimsuits.
    CONJ.-PRON: It was obvious *that that* was him.

    Exception: **One word can be removed.** In this situation the conjunction "and" is usually implied between the two words, and the comma (,) is used to represent its absence.

                       It went *up,* [and] *up* into the clouds and was never seen again.

    Exception: **Second word needs emphasis.** If removable, insert a dash (—) before and after it.

                       The protagonist is almost—*almost*—certainly not to be suspected as having anything to do with it.

2.6   **Word is phonetically spelled.** The phonetically spelled word acts as an interruption and needs to be placed between brackets.

It happened in the capital city of Yinchwan [yin´shwaän´] about two hundred years ago.

2.7   **Followed by duplicate pronoun.** No comma is needed between them when neither can be removed.

They told *you you* had to do it or leave?

2.8   **Two verbs are in a row.** If the first one is in the form of the verb *to be,* a pause is usually noticeable and a separating comma (,) is required to prevent confusion.

I think whatever *is, should* have been.

2.9   **Confusion is possible.** If it is necessary to force the reader to pause, a comma (,) is employed to force that pause. For example, if a comma did not precede the word *to* in the example below, it would be easy to think that the stock market jumped over 1900 points rather than 100, even though the word "from" does not appear.

The stock market jumped one hundred points, *to* over two thousand to-day.

Exception: **Pause needs more emphasis.** Insert a dash (—).

The simple fact *is*—not one of them had taken the trouble to see for themselves.

2.10   **Showing sarcasm or doubt about something.** An exclamation mark (!) is normally used to show sarcasm; the question mark (?), for doubt. Both are encased in brackets and placed immediately after the word to which they refer.

SARCASM: The car is more reliable [!] than the Henderson Bullet.
DOUBT: He said he took the thiggermajig [?] and tossed it into the bag.

Exception: **Questioning the proper use of a word.** In brackets, insert what you think is the correct word, followed by a question mark (?).

She said, "I've got an ax to sharpen [grind?] with you."

Last Word in Sentence

3.1   **Light pause precedes last word.** Insert a comma (,) before it.

So there they were, *falling.*

3.2   **Strong pause precedes the last word.** It is likely that it is being used as a one-word explanation, summarization, conclusion, confirmation, etc. which supports the information preceding it. It should follow a colon (:), and the word need not be capitalized.

ELABORATES: He was only afraid of one thing: *fear.*
SUMMARIZES: So that's all it comes down to: *money.*
CONCLUDES: There's only one thing left to do: *hope.*
CONFIRMS: Yes, that's what I'm going to do: *operate.*

Exception: **Pause needs emphasis.** Use a dash (—) instead of a colon. Keep in mind, however, that not all words lend themselves well to having a dash precede them.

That's all it comes down to—*money.*
Exception: **Last word followed by related phrases.** When a colon precedes the last word and highly related phrases follow, the phrases may be dramatized by iso-

8

lating them and capitalizing the first word of each. (*See* first example below.) Some, however, may be strung together in a series, separated only by commas as you see in the example below.

A raw emotion is seeping into their lives: *fear*. Of loneliness. Of sickness. Of indifference, poverty and hunger. Of an end to precious life.

A raw emotion is seeping into their lives: *fear*—of loneliness, of sickness, of indifference, poverty and hunger. Of an end to precious life.

3.3 **Preceded by an identical word.** No punctuation will be needed between the last and preceding word when both are essential to the sentence.

When is enough *enough?*

Exception: **One word needs to stand alone.** Punctuation depends on the effect you wish to achieve. In the first sentence example below, the stand-alone word restates the meaning of the word before it; in the other, it repeats and shows disbelief. Furthermore, notice how the exclamation mark (!) follows the question mark in the second example, to provide more drama.

The marriage is *over. Over.*
They said they *wouldn't? Wouldn't?!*

Exception: **Both words are easily removed.** Punctuation depends on the nature of the words and how they are being used. In the first example are interjections which are easily removed; in the second, the identical words are showing agreement; in the third, the words provide comfort; and in the last example, the words function as verbal pauses.

INTERJ:	Won't you, *huh? Huh?*
AGREEMENT:	I'm all for that! *Hear! Hear!*
COMFORT:	Of course you're scared. *There, there.*
PAUSE:	So that's the way they feel about it. *Okay. Okay.* Well, I hope they don't want any more favors from me.

3.4 **Conjunction "and" is removed from between two words.** Its absence should be represented by a comma (,).

9

| 2 ADJECTIVES: | The dinner was *tasteless, disastrous.* |
| 2 VERBS: | The group *acted, danced.* |

3.5   **Last word repeats the meaning of the preceding sentence.** Use the comma (,) to set the last word apart, unless the relationship is very close and no pause can be detected (*see* second example).

It was done, *over.*
The realization exploded in my mind *suddenly.*

3.6   **Easily removed.** The last word should be preceded by a comma (,). This is frequently the situation when some adverbs are the last word—unless, of course, other commas precede them in the sentence, in which case the comma is waived—the prime example being those which end in "ly."

ADJECTIVE:	There he was busted, *broke.*
ADVERB:	I thought he was telling the truth, *naturally.*
INTERJECTION:	You said she didn't call, *huh?*
NOUN:	It was the one thing that always eluded him, *success*
PRONOUN:	I find it quite entertaining, *that.*

| Exception: | **Add-on phrase follows adverb.** In most cases, the phrase is set apart rather than the word; but if the phrase is emphasized with a dash (—), the comma is returned before the word. |

| NORMAL: | She did her best *though,* recognizing that she might never win first prize. |

| EMPHASIZED: | She did her best, *though*—even while recognizing that she never had a chance. |

| Exception: | **Two short sentences are joined.** Most add-on words do not require a preceding comma. In this sentence, the conjunction "and" connects the two thoughts. |

She couldn't say anything, and I found that I couldn't *either.*

Pairs & Series of Words

4.1   **Pair of identical words.** Insert a comma (,) between them. In the second example provided below, the word *sure* would normally be set apart by commas; however, since there are two of them, only the first one receives that treatment.

INTRODUCES:	*Sure, sure* that was true then, but how about now?
MIDSENTENCE:	It was *many, many* years ago when I was rich.

Exception: **Pair is often seen together.** Using punctuation to separate them is usually not necessary, for the comma is implied. Here is an example of two words that fall into this category; the conjunction *and* is missing between them.

We knew this was our *last best* hope to win.

4.2   **Pair of descriptive words immediately precedes a noun.** They need to be separated by a comma (,) when the conjunction "and" can be inserted between them without disturbing the flow of the sentence.

It was a *warm, humid* day on the island of Bono Bono.

Exception: **Can't remove word before the noun.** The comma is NOT used to separate the descriptive pair. While the word "bad" is removable from the sentence which follows, "romantic" is not, for the latter is linked to "poets" and tells the reader what *kind* of poets are being written about.

All of the *bad romantic* poets wrote sonnets about her.

4.3   **More than one pair of words in succession.** Place a comma (,) between the words within each pair and separate the pairs with periods (.). In the example which follows, the pronoun "he" is implied before each word in the series, and the comma represents the conjunction "and."

Is, isn't. Was, wasn't. Could, couldn't. It's the story of his life.

Exception: **Reducing the strength of the pauses.** Insert semicolons (;) between the pairs.

Is, isn't; was, wasn't; could, couldn't. It's the story of his life.

4.4   **Strong pause follows a series of pairs.** Insert a colon (:) after the last pair, for a summarization, explanation, elaboration, etc. is no doubt following them; but use a dash (—) when more drama is desired. Only capitalize the word after the colon when it begins a question, or the information does not need the series to make sense. (*See* third and fourth examples below.)

DASH: *Is, isn't; was, wasn't; could, couldn't* —what a display of decision-making!

11

COLON: *Is, isn't; was, wasn't; could, couldn't:* The argument
                continued to swirl regarding who he really was and what
                he was capable of doing.

Question: *Is, isn't; was, wasn't; could, couldn't:* Why don't they
                make up their minds about him?

4.5   **When to separate words in a series.** If the conjunction "and"
            can easily be inserted between the words, separate them with commas
            (,), and insert a conjunction before the last word of the series, placing a
            comma before it as well. Some insist that a comma is not needed before
            the conjunction. But not doing so may sometimes confuse the reader,
            making him think that the last two elements of the series belong to-
            gether, when in fact they are separate. For example, take a look at the
            second sentence example below: without a comma before "and," it
            would be easy to assume that the farmer had a little restaurant business
            on the side. Omitting the comma before the conjunction is simply a
            bad habit which can lead to a lack of clarity.

            Cheat, fight, drink, and *bellow* as long as you wish.
            Farmer John sold *corn, potatoes, beans, beef, ham and eggs.*

4.6   **When NOT to separate words in a series.** If the conjunction
            "and" cannot be placed between words in a series, no punctuation is
            necessary. For instance, placing "and" between the italicized words be-
            low would make the sentences quite awkward.

            Rich chocolate marshmallow sundaes are delicious.
            What I want is a *big coconut cream* pie and a glass of milk.
            I think my favorite is *baked round yellow* cornbread.

4.7   **Each word in a series is emphasized.** Insert a conjunction be-
            tween each of them. This creates a singsong redundancy and dramatizes
            each word through a series of slight pauses. However, it is not a tech-
            nique that lends itself to frequent use.

            Packing and *unpacking* and *traveling* and *waiting* is tiring.
            I love her because she is *cute* and *smart* and *warm* and *rich.*
            You may *cheat* or *fight* or *drink* or *bellow* as you wish.

Exception: **Last word emphasized.** Capitalize the last conjunc-
                tion and precede it with a period (.), which will set the
                last word apart from the other words in the series.

                It was *short* and *sweet.* And *frightening.*

4.8   **Identical words in a series.** They need commas (,) between them,
            and the last word is not preceded by a conjunction.

BEGINNING:	*Blow, blow, blow* your horn, Gabriel!
MIDSENTENCE:	I'm going to *eat, eat, eat* until I can't eat any more.
END:	The Cat of Canterville fell *down, down, down.*

Exception:	**Words convey a sound.** In this instance, commas are rarely if ever used between identical words in a series.
	Squish squish squish was the sound he made. I heard his shoes go *click click click* in the hall. All night I heard the faucet go *drip drip drip drip drip.*

4.9   **Adjectives or adverbs used as nouns in a series.** Place double quotation marks (" ") before and after them, making sure to *follow* each closing quotation mark with a comma. A preferable option is to italicize each word (*see* second example).

When you use the words "up", "down", "right", "left", what meanings are you giving them?

When you use the words *up, down, right, left,* what meanings are you giving them?

Exception:	**Series ends the sentence.** When using double quotation marks around each word in a series, the period (.) is placed *before* the last closing quotation mark ("). But if it is a question, it *follows* the quotation mark.
	He gave vague meanings to the words "up", "down", "right", and "left."
	What meanings are you giving to the words "up", "down", "right", and "left"?

4.10   **Nouns in a series are identified.** Insert a comma (,) after each, and begin the identifications with *who* when it is a person; *which,* if it is not. In the first example, the series prior to the dash (—) is not part of a complete sentence. (Note: a colon could have been used rather than a dash.) In the second example, the series not only precedes a full sentence but is part of it as well. For your convenience only, the nouns have been italicized for quicker identification.

Johnson, who wrote the script; *Barber,* who got the money together and hired the actors; and *West,* who directed it and delivered it under budget—they were responsible for the movie's success.

The list included *Johnson,* who wrote the script; *Barber,* who got the money together and hired the actors; and *West,* who directed it and delivered it under budget: all were responsible for the movie's success.

4.11 Opening series is followed by an adverb, preposition, or verb. Such a series does not require punctuation after its last word.

ADV: Fighting, drinking, burping and lying *forever* seems to be that gang's only goal.

PREP: Fighting, drinking, burping and lying *at* the drop of a hat is that gang's primary action.

VERB: Fighting, drinking, burping and lying *are* about the only things that gang knows how to do.

4.12 Strong pause follows the opening series. An explanation, summarization, conclusion, or some kind of elaborating information usually follows such a pause; therefore, a colon (:) should be inserted. Do not capitalize the word after the colon, for the information is dependent on the series for its existence. In the first example below, a summarization follows the series; in the second, it explains; in the third a question is posed, but it needs the series to make sense and is therefore not capitalized.

SUMMARIZATION: Eating, drinking, sleeping: *remember to keep these in mind if you want to stay young.*

EXPLANATION: Deception, thievery, and destruction: *these represent the key activities of street gangs.*

QUESTION: Cheating and lying and stealing: *is that all you know how to do?*

However, if the information after the colon can easily stand alone despite the absence of the series, leaving no doubt in the mind of the reader, capitalize its first word. Here are two examples, the second one being a question:

Cheating and lying and stealing: *The* gang knew and practiced every vice known to man.

Cheating and lying and stealing: *How* long are we going to tolerate corruption from our Congressmen?

Exception: **Series needs more emphasis.** Replace the colon with a dash (—), and do not capitalize the word following this dramatic punctuation mark.

Arguing, begging, crying—these are her tactics.
Argue, beg, cry—you're still not going to the movies.

> In the next example, the information following the series is what could be called a "throwaway" phrase.

Look at her argue, beg, cry—*as if it's going to help.*

4.13 **Series of words cannot be removed.** This means the series is an integral part of the sentence. Although the words themselves are separated from one another by commas (,), no punctuation precedes or follows the series itself.

I think my *arms, legs, feet, neck, ears,* and *neck* hurt from early that morning until late in the evening.

Exception: **Words need emphasis.** Insert the conjunctions "or" or "and" between each word and omit the commas.

They said it was written by *Bibbs* or *Swearingen* or *Jelineck* or *Henderson,* I think.

Exception: **Confusion possible.** If the information after a series could possibly be confusing if not set apart, insert a comma (,) after it. Without a comma after "cats" in the following example, it could easily be read as if the dogs, birds, and cats had the writer's binoculars.

I saw their *dogs, birds,* and cats with my binoculars.
I saw their *dogs, birds,* and *cats,* with my binoculars.

4.14 **Series interrupts the sentence.** Insert a dash (—) before and after it. In the first example, a conjunction precedes the last word in the series. In the second one, however, the conjunction is eliminated; moreover, word combinations rather rather than single words comprise the series.

He—*bold, cunning,* and *patriotic*—was responsible for the victory.
There I sat—*white shirt, new tuxedo, freshly shined shoes*—waiting for her to appear in all her glory.

Exception: **Quick explanation, identification, or personal comment.** An interruption of this type should be placed it inside a parentheses. In the examples which follow, the first is an identification; the second, a comment; the third, an explanation.

IDENTIFIES: Those three (Felix, Sarah, and Bart) had been getting on his nerves for a long time.

15

<table>
<tr><td>COMMENTS:</td><td>Her manner wasn't ingratiating (argumentative, accusatory, and egotistical is more like it), and I knew it would be hard getting the truth from her.</td></tr>
<tr><td>EXPLAINS:</td><td>That supposed cure (liniment, heat, aspirin, and tea) will in no way solve the problem.</td></tr>
</table>

4.15 **Midsentence series is followed by a question.** Insert a comma (,) after it when it is the last part of an introductory phrase, to indicate a pause. Do not capitalize the question.

Recognizing that they want *money, fame,* and *revenge,* is there anything they do not want?

4.16 **Series of words cannot be removed from the sentence.** A sentence-ending series which cannot be removed is an integral part of the complete thought. The words are separated them from one another with commas (,), but no punctuation immediately precedes the first one.

These eggs should be *fried, scrambled,* and *boiled.*

4.17 **Strong pause precedes a sentence-ending series.** Insert a colon (:) before it, because it is acting as an explanation, summary, conclusion, confirmation, or an elaboration of that which precedes it. In the third example, notice that no conjunction precedes the last word of the series.

<table>
<tr><td>EXPLAINS:</td><td>In college, he was involved in many sports: baseball, football, basketball, and hockey.</td></tr>
<tr><td>CONFIRMS:</td><td>We agree with Professor Perk's analysis of our curriculum: what we need are more *language, mathematics,* and *gymnastic classes.*</td></tr>
<tr><td>ELABORATES:</td><td>They were the most tender of plants: *sheltering, cooling, calming.*</td></tr>
<tr><td>SUMMARIZES:</td><td>Their key virtues, once again, are as follows: *imagination, compassion,* and *a thirst for knowledge.*</td></tr>
<tr><td>CONCLUDES:</td><td>Therefore, we have only three things left to do in order to make it work: *analyze, plan, participate,* and *produce.*</td></tr>
</table>

16

Exception:	**Needs more emphasis.** Precede it with a dash (—). A conjunction may or may not precede the last word of the series.

It has created these dangerous precedents—*nationalism, terrorism, prejudice.*

Give me what he's having—*love, luck,* and *liquor.*

4.18 Numbers before each word in a series. To precede each word in a series with a number, place the number in parentheses and insert commas (,) after the words; also, a conjunction should be inserted before the last parenthesized number.

The Burt Company is (1) old, (2) bankrupt, and (3) closed.

Exception:	**No conjunction before last word.** Replace all of the commas in the series with semicolons (;).

The Burt Company is (1) old; (2) bankrupt; (3) closed, which also reflects the town's character.

4.19 Words and phrases intermixed in a series. Separate each with commas (,).

It was the first time I heard him speak his mind in a manner that was *straightforward, quite candid, highly personal, caring,* and *exciting.*

Exception:	**One phrase is longer than usual.** Separating the words and phrases with commas will probably not do; instead, use semicolons (;) as a punctuation division .

It was the first time I heard him speak his mind in a manner that was straightforward; *oddly apolitical;* caring; *highly personal for someone in his position;* and exciting.

Word Stands Alone

With the exception of prepositions and conjunctions, most parts of speech can be made to stand alone. They are followed by a period (.), question mark (?), or exclamation mark (!).

5.1 One stand-alone word. It usually needs clarifying information to precede or follow it, in order to make its isolation credible. Here are examples of different parts of speech which are separated from the other information by a period (.), exclamation mark (!), or question mark (?).

ADJECTIVE:	*Beautiful.* It's just beautiful
ADVERB:	They're here. *Finally!*
INTERJECTION:	*Alas!* What else can I do?
NOUN:	Who do I love? *Emily.*
PRONOUN:	Not her. *Her!*
VERB:	*Jump?* Did you say jump?

5.2 **Two or more stand-alone words in succession.** They may be followed by exclamation marks (!), question marks (?), or periods (.).

Quiet! Silence! How many times must I tell you?
Drunk? Disorderly? Well, if those are the charges, he should be jailed.
Greed. Scandal. Yes, I'd say that typified the 1920s and 1980s.

Highlighting Letters & Words

6.1 **Alphabetic letter acts as a noun.** Double quotation marks are not needed before and after an alphabetic letter when (1) reference is being made to it as an alphabetic letter; (2) the letter is substituting for a noun; or (3) the letter is part of a noun. However, the alphabetic letter should be capitalized. Another option is to type the letter in dark letters (*see* second sentence below).

LETTER:	I don't know when to put E before I.
Bold letters:	I can make out a capital **P** and a small **T**.

NOUN
Part of:	She lives on K Street.
Substitute:	If A sells to B, and B sells to D, where does that leave C?
Exception:	**Single letter could be misunderstood.** Then insert double quotation marks (" ") before and after it.
	Please remove "a" from that word.

6.2 **Word with a one-letter prefix.** The alphabetic letter requires capitalization, and a hyphen (-) is needed to separate it from the next word. In most cases it is performing as part of a noun.

He made a U-turn before I could do anything.

6.3 **Unofficial definition follows.** Double quotation marks (" ") should be inserted before and after the word when it is followed by an official definition. Another option is to italicize it (*see* second example)

18

"Testing" is how we find the source of the problem.
Testing is how we find the source of the problem.

> Exception: **Two definitions in a sentence.** Highlight the definition rather than the word, using *single* quotation marks (' ') instead of double. If the single quotation mark happens to fall at the end of the sentence, place the ending punctuation (such as a period or question mark) *after* it, not before.
>
> Do not confuse Jocko 'the umpire' with Jocko 'the father,' for they are not at all alike.
>
> Please do not confuse Jocko 'the umpire' with Jocko 'the father'.

6.4 **Precedes or follows "by-word."** Double quotation marks (" ") must be inserted before and after the word. But only use *by-word* when referring to something in a contemptuous manner.

"Parrot" is the by-word around here for anyone who talks and thinks like the manager.

6.5 **Preceded by "so-called."** When used in a sentence, this hyphenated word and the word which follows it are neither italicized nor placed between double quotation marks.

Their so-called business is something their management team apparently doesn't wish to talk about.

> Exception: **"So-called" is implied, not spelled out.** Return the double quotation marks (" ") before and after the word. Another option is to italicize it.
>
> But it seemed their "business" wasn't something their managers wanted to talk about.
> But it seemed their *business* wasn't something their managers wanted to talk about.

6.6 **Preceded by the noun "word."** *Word* itself is not highlighted in a sentence, but that which follows it should either be italicized or placed between double quotation marks (" "). Underlining may be used as a substitute for italics.

The word *amount* is frequently used in relation to money.

6.7 **Preceded by an action verb.** No quotation marks are needed around an action verb such as *call, labeled, marked.* Nor is it italicized.
The jar was marked Exhibit A.

6.8   **Represents irony.** Place the word between double quotation marks
(" ") or italicize it.

The "remedy" was infinitely worse than the disease itself.
The *remedy* was infinitely worse than the disease itself.

6.9   **Represents sarcasm.** It needs either an exclamation mark (!) or a
question mark (?) immediately after it, in brackets. Placing the word in
italics is another option.

His wealth [?] can be measured in memories only.
His *wealth* is not something I would want.

6.10   **All letters are capitalized.** When double quotation marks (" ")
seem inadequate in highlighting a word, consider capitalizing every letter. But mind you, this is a technique that should only be used once in
a great while. Reserve it for those special situations.

He may have lots of push, but I need someone with PULL.

6.11   **Technical or unfamiliar word.** Double quotation marks (" ")
should be inserted before and after it, or place it in italics.

To "robotize" the machinery will take careful planning and more than
five million dollars.

6.12   **Defining nouns in a legal document.** When establishing the
use of certain nouns at the beginning of a legal document, do not highlight them with double quotation marks; instead, capitalize every letter.
Thereafter the words are typed normally and without capitalization. In
this example, the words *buyer* and *seller* are defined for the reader.

For the sake of expediency, Ansul Whitlock shall hereafter be known as
the BUYER, and Carlos Cabalero shall be called the SELLER.

6.13   **Foreign word.** It requires no special treatment unless you wish to
highlight it for some reason, or if it is a word which might be unfamiliar to the reader. If highlighting is necessary, place the word between
double quotation marks (" ") or use italics. Foreign slang should always be highlighted with quotation marks (see Rule 8). However, if
you are quoting a passage that is comprised entirely of foreign words,
only use italics or quotation marks to draw attention to one or more
words.

ITALICIZED: It was truly *magnifico*.

6.14   **Philosophical term.** Use single quotation marks (') before and after
it. If it ends a sentence, insert whatever ending punctuation is appropri-

20

ate—that is, exclamation mark (!), question mark (?), or the traditional period (.)—*after* the single quotation mark.

Among religious philosophers there is considerable disagreement on what is generally considered to be *'the beginning'* and what will be *'the end'*.

6.15 **Word combination.** When drawing the reader's attention to a word combination, it should either be italicized or placed between double quotation marks (" ").

Before I learned to drive, I thought *fill'er up* meant getting your teeth fixed at the dentist.

Before I learned to drive, I thought "fill'er up" meant getting your teeth fixed at the dentist.

Words & Letters Missing

When omitting a WORD from a sentence, but you still want it to be implied, indicate its absence with a comma (,). But do not abuse this literary shorthand.

An omitted alphabetic LETTER is represented by an apostrophe ('). But this type of punctuation should be restricted to highly informal writing, such as when writing dialogue for novels, plays, and short stories.

7.1 **Conjunction is omitted, but is implied.** Insert a comma (,) to represent the missing conjunction.

BETWEEN...
Sentences:	You can see ~~that~~ she is fine.
	You can *see, she* is fine.
Adjectives:	It's scary ~~and~~ mind-boggling.
	It's *scary, mind-boggling*.
Nouns:	That's all they had: vanilla ~~and~~ chocolate.
	That's all they had: *vanilla, chocolate*.
Pronouns:	Her ~~or~~ him—it doesn't matter.
	Her, him—it doesn't matter.
Prefixes:	I guess he was about five- ~~or~~ six- years old.
	I guess he was about *five-, six-*years old

Exception: **Legal paper or technical report.** The virgule (/) may be used to indicate the absence of the conjunction. For example, *landlord and tenant* becomes *landlord/tenant*. However, strict grammarians aren't comfortable with using the virgule's in this manner.

7.2 **Preposition is omitted between two highly related words.** They are better represented by the virgule (/). In most cases this will occur when statistical or technical information information is being included, or when well-known terms can be reduced to, say, a couple of alphabetic letters. For example:

bushels per load = bushels/load
letter of credit = L/C

7.3 **Pronoun is omitted.** This is often done when the pronoun is the last word of a complete thought, and another complete thought immediately follows. In the first example below, a colon (:) is inserted after the pronoun; but with the pronoun's removal in the second example, both the pronoun and the colon can now be replaced by a comma (,). Observe, too, that the question loses its capitalization when it immediately follows a form of the verb *to be* (am, are, be, is, was, were).

ORIGINAL: What Osgood is simply trying to say is ~~this:~~ are you going to keep pretending?

FINAL: What Osgood is simply trying to say is, are you going to keep on pretending?

7.4 **Verb is omitted.** It should be represented by a comma (,). This is not commonly done, but it can be quite effective in the right circumstances and when it is the same verb. The verbs missing in the sentence examples below are indicated at the left.

IS: Our nation, under siege and weary.
JUMP: You think I can, over that?

7.5 **Two words are omitted.** They may be represented by a comma (,), as long as the information left still makes sense. In the example which follows, the words removed are not side by side; instead, they are the verbs of separate but highly related sentences.

His plate is half empty; his stomach is half full.
EDITED: His plate ~~is~~ half empty; his stomach ~~is~~ half full.
FINAL: His plate, half empty; his stomach, half full.

Exception: **Side-by-side nouns removed.** A longer-than-usual dash (printers call them em dashes), or underlining, should be used; but this, obviously, is a punctuation technique which should be used quite sparingly. An example of underlining:

She discovered that _____ had been cheating the company for nearly five years.

7.6 **Words are implied, not stated.** Implying several words in a sentence through punctuation is done in order to say as much on paper with as few words as possible. Below is an example of how a statement, which is now well-recognized as a cliché, might have been gradually edited until, finally, even the comma was dropped; because the pause which was once necessary between the two longer versions has long since vanished.

ORIGINAL: The more there are, the merrier it will be.
REMOVED: The more ~~there are~~, the merrier ~~it will be~~.
1st VERSION: The more, the merrier.
FINALLY: The more the merrier.

ORIGINAL: If you don't know, then you don't know.
REMOVED: ~~If~~ you don't know, ~~then~~ you don't know.
FINALLY: You don't know, you don't know.

7.7 **Removing one or more words to create a headline.** Because of little space and for more impact, words can be omitted from newspaper and magazine headlines, and punctuation is often used to represent their absence. In this example a strong pause is created after *poll*, requiring a colon (:), and the comma (,) indicates the conjunction is missing. Colons, semicolons, and dashes should be used sparingly in headlines, but a period (.) at the end of a headline should never occur.

ARTICLE'S
MAIN THEME: In a recent election poll, candidates George Williams and Tom Ivory are leading their opponents.

EDITING TO
CREATE HEADLINE: ~~In a recent election~~ poll, candidates ~~George~~ Williams ~~and Tom~~ Ivory ~~are~~ leading ~~their opponents~~.

FINAL HEADLINE: Poll: Williams, Ivory Lead

7.8 **Removing one or more words from a quote.** Full quotes can rarely be used as headlines, for they are too long. Whether using a shortened quote as part of or as the complete headline, the result is that a quote is being re-quoted; therefore, single rather than double quotation marks (' ') are employed. Colons, semicolons, and dashes should be used sparingly, and never insert a period (.) at the end of a headline.

INFORMATION IN ARTICLE:	Said Commissioner Sims today: "I've tried to be a gentlemen with these protestors, but I'm tired of being Mr. Nice Guy."
EDITED:	~~Said Commissioner Sims today: "I've tried to be a gentlemen with these protestors, but I'm~~ tired of being Mr. Nice Guy."
FINAL HEADLINE:	'Tired of being Mr. Nice Guy'
OTHER OPTION:	Sims: 'Tired of being Mr. Nice Guy'

7.9 **First letter(s) omitted from a word.** They should be represented by an apostrophe ('). In the first example, the letter A has been omitted from the word *above;* in the second sentence, the letters B and E have been removed from the word *between.*

> 1 LETTER: *'Bove* that picture is my daddy's Civil War gun.
> 2 LETTERS: He was *'tween* the devil and the deep blue sea.

7.10 **Middle letter(s) omitted from a word.** They should be represented by an apostrophe ('). In the first example, the letter O has been omitted from the word *frivolous;* in the second sentence, the letters S and I have been removed from the word *possibly.*

> 1 LETTER: Sort of a *friv'lous* way of doing things.
> 2 LETTERS: I think pos'bly that I might.

7.11 **Last letter omitted from a word.** It should be represented by an apostrophe ('). In this example, the letter G has been omitted from the word *running.*

That's the way my luck's been runnin' lately.

7.12 **Word's first and last letters are omitted.** They should be represented by apostrophes ('). In this example, the letters A and D have been omitted from the word *and.*

What I want is a big platter of bacon 'n' eggs.

Slang

8.1 **Explained.** Slang words are written the same as any other word and do not require quotation marks (" ") to set them apart. It may consist of more than one word and affect any part of speech except conjunctions, indefinite articles, and pronouns. In the examples below, they have only been italicized for your quick identification.

1 WORD:	That's a *cool* way of doing things.
2 WORDS:	Don't *choke up* when the going gets rough.
3 WORDS:	You're nothing but a *dirty old man*.
HYPHENED:	That *blankety-blank* tried to cheat me.

8.2 **Preceded by a verb like "called", "labeled", and "marked."** The slang word needs double quotation marks (" ") before and after it. Normally, though, proper nouns are not highlighted when they follow action verbs like these.

SLANG WORD:	She was a *called* a "dingbat" by just about everyone.
PROPER NOUN:	It was *labeled* candy, but it certainly didn't taste like anything I have ever had before.

8.3 **Foreign slang.** It needs double quotation marks (" ") before and after.

He called himself a "félouse," but I don't think he has ever handled a gun.

Curse Word

9.1 **Representing omitted letters from a curse word.** All of the letters except the first one may be omitted and replaced with underlining (__) when you do not wish to spell out the entire word; simply make certain that there isn't any doubt in the reader's mind about which curse word is being represented. Another option is to include the first and last letter of the curse word. Do not overuse either technique.

FIRST LETTER ONLY:	D____ you, John, will you shut up?
FIRST & LAST LETTER:	S____t, now what!

9.2 **Representing an omitted curse word.** An entire curse word may be represented with three asterisks (***). But do not overuse this punctuation technique; and, again, make sure the reader has a reasonable idea regarding which curse word is missing.

He said, "Move your *** feet or I'll move'em for you."

9.3 **Representing more than one missing curse word.** A series of cursewords may be represented by various symbols. If you use this technique, do so only once. These symbols can be found above the numbers on any typewriter or computer keyboard, and there is no particular order or kinds which should be used. Using this technique indicates that a series of curse words are being used. Their nature is left strictly to the reader's imagination.

Now what I want from you, you %#!@* crook, is an apology and my money.

Frequently Used Words

Here in alphabetical order are words which are frequently used. Many are supplied with definitions, and the definition(s) applied to a word is usually critical in determining what punctuation to use—if any. In some cases, guidance on how to use a word correctly in a sentence is provided.

10.1 **accused.** This word can serve as an adjective, noun, or verb. When it acts as a verb, it must be followed with the preposition *of* rather than *with*, although not necessarily immediately.

"OF" FOLLOWS
IMMEDIATELY: *Accused* of padding his own pockets with public funds, Abner Doohickey hired a lawyer.

"OF" FOLLOWS
SUBSEQUENTLY: Abner Doohickey was also brought to trial, *accused* for the fourth time of padding his own pockets with public funds.

10.2 **after.** If you are not using this word as a substitute for one of the definitions shown below, it is a preposition.

ADVERB
   at a later time: *After* Jean arrived, we all ate dinner.

   behind: *After* his horse came mine, some fifty lengths back.

CONJUNCTION
   following the
   time that: *After* I was informed about her deception, I began to set traps for her.

   I began to set traps for her *after* I was informed about her deception,

   Exception: **More emphasis is needed.** The dash (—) may be substituted for the comma .

   He said he didn't want to go—*after* he told everyone that wild horses wouldn't stop him

10.3 **albeit.** To the left of the sample sentences below are the meanings which this conjunction is capable of assuming in a sentence, which can be quite helpful when deciding when to use punctuation.

EVEN IF: *Albeit* the bank didn't grant the loan, I'll get the money someway.

ALTHOUGH: She said she would be here, *albeit* the weather may not permit it.

10.4 **alias.** This word, which may also act as a noun, is not accompanied by punctuation. But when the hyphenated adjective *so-called* is implied before it, it should be encased in double quotation marks (" ").

His name is Edward Socks *alias* Teddy Shoe.

SO-CALLED
IMPLIED: His "alias" was a total joke.

AS A NOUN: Do you think he should be given an *alias?*

10.5 **also.** Below are the meanings which this adverb and adverbial conjunction may assume in a sentence.

IN ADDITION: He had a great desire to play in that game; *also*, there was something he wanted to prove.
LIKEWISE: As it was done for her, it should be done for him *also*.

BESIDES: *Also*, what makes think you I care?

TOO: They *also* must be held accountable for their deeds during that time.

Exception: **Means "too" at the end of the sentence.** It will need a comma before it (see first sentence below). However if a comma is already present, as it is in the second example, it rarely needs to be set apart.

They found the note she had written, *also*.
In the attic, they found the note she had written *also*.

10.6 **although.** Below are the meanings which this conjunction is capable of assuming in a sentence.

GRANTING THAT: *Although* she's been meeting her payments, I doubt her ability to continue doing so.

THOUGH:	He volunteered his services, *although* he was hoping they wouldn't accept.

10.7   **amen** and **sobeit.** Whether at the end of a prayer or not, this word is always capitalized and isolated from the other information. Follow it with a period (.), although an exclamation mark (!) may be used when more drama is desired. When it is linked to and precedes a noun, a comma (,) should be inserted after it.

Well, we've lost all of our money. Sobeit.
Praise the Lord! Amen!

Exception:	**Linked to a noun and someone is being addressed.** A comma (,) after the word is essential.

Amen, brother. *Amen.*

10.8   **and.** This is perhaps the most popular and flexible of all the conjunctions, for it can join words , phrases, and sentences. Below are some of the ways it may be used and punctuated.

BEGINS....

sentence:	A cloud of suspicion hung over Charles, *and he didn't help himself by lying to Mrs. Fillibut.*
add-on phrase:	He felt more powerful than ever before, *and yet protective at the same time.*
consequence:	Do it *and you'll wish you had never set foot in my house.*

BETWEEN WORDS

verbs	I suggest that you try *and* make me, big shot.
adjectives	It seems that he was upset *and* jealous about Sheila dating someone else.

> If it is necessary to emphasize the second word, insert a dash (—) before it and another one after the word which follows it.

It seems that he has acquired—*and maintained*—a reputation for being a pain in the neck.

MEANS "ALSO":	*And,* there was something about her story that didn't jive.

Exception:	**Assumes the role of a noun.** Insert double quotation marks (" ") before and after it.
	What I don't want from you is a bunch of "ifs", "ands", and "buts."

10.9   **and/or.** While the use of the virgule (/), or slant, in the combining of these two conjunctions is not usually looked kindly upon by strict grammarians, its use is fairly widespread. In the first example shown below, this combination is used; in the second, a grammatical option is provided.

VIRGULE...

used:	There is apparently no ambition *and/or* pride left within the group.
not used:	There is apparently *neither* pride *nor* ambition left within the group.

10.10   **as** and **like.** These two words are frequently and erroneously substituted for one another. Here are some tips on when to use "as" and when is it proper to use "like."

1.   **"As" always introduces a full sentence, but "like" is only capable of leading phrases.** The quickest way to check which one should be used is this: when the words "similar to" can be substituted, then *like* is the correct word to use; otherwise, *as* should be employed. Note the first example below: "similar to" is used and it does not read well; therefore "as" is the correct word to use in this instance.

AWKWARD:	*Similar to* everyone else felt that day, he believed they should have won.
"as" used:	*As* everyone else felt that day, he believed they should have won.

If the verb "felt" is removed, then "like" may be used.

Like everyone else that day, he believed they should have won.

2.   **"As" can be used as a conjunction; "like" cannot.** The definitions which the former may assume are listed in the left-hand column below, and the type of punctuation often accompanying it can be seen at the right.

BECAUSE:	*As* it was starting to rain, the umpire ordered the infield to be covered.
	The umpire ordered the infield to be covered, *as* it was starting to rain.
CONSIDERING THAT:	*As* I hadn't done anything to be ashamed of, I didn't see any reason to apologize.
	I didn't see any reason to apologize, *as* I hadn't done anything of which I would be ashamed.
WHILE:	*As* she washed the dishes, I dried them. I dried the dishes *as* she washed them.
Exception:	**Writing dialogue.** *Like* may be used as conjunction when writing dialogue, if is important to capture the flavor of the character's speech, however ungrammatical it may be.
	Like I said, I'm just taking my time. I'm just taking my time, *like* I said.
Exception:	**The word "as" leads a quick explanation or personal comment.** Encase its group in parentheses.
	Then King Louie (*as* Marie's protector) told her that now was as good a time as any.

3. **Neither "as" nor "like" may immediately precede a colon (:).** Both words need one or more words after them to act as buffers. The first two examples use the word "as": one contains a vertical list; the other, a list within a paragraph. The third example uses "like."

AS:

first
example: The problem with the car is *as follows:*

1. It has two square tires and a round one.
2. There is no gas tank.
3. Someone forgot to install a motor.

second
example: Our food will be *as follows:* a tuna salad sandwich; a bowl of beet soup, laced with cream; three crackers, unsalted; and a jug of America's most popular soft drink.

30

LIKE: He said the painting reminded him of things *like this:* sunny Sundays, a day at the park, baseball, and porch swings.

Exception: **Phrase is inserted after the word "follows."** The colon (:) is delayed and placed after the phrase, instead. For quick identification, the phrase has been italicized in this example.

                   The recipe ingredients were as follows, *though not necessarily in this order:* chick peas, honey, okra, spaghetti sauce, and garlic.

4. **"Like" may be a part of a two-word description (adjective), but "as" cannot.** When "like" combines with another word to form a two-word description, it must be followed it with a hyphen (-). However, when it is the *second* word, no hyphen is needed unless the word before it ends with the letter L (*see* third example below).

DESCRIPTIVE: These *like-minded* women had caused trouble.
SECOND WORD: The antique had a *curvedlike* pedestal.
FOLLOWS "L":   Randy had a *barrel-like* shape.

10.11 because. Below are the meanings which this conjunction is capable of assuming in a sentence, including the punctuation which is demanded.

ON ACCOUNT OF
THE FACT THAT: I bought a soda *because* I was thirsty.

> But if you switch the two complete thoughts around, the comma (,) must be inserted between them.

                   Because I was thirsty, I bought a soda.

FOR THE
REASON THAT: It never happened, *because* he was never there.

> But if it leads a long statement which has punctuation, precede with a semicolon (;).

                   You're not going to get another chance at the big leagues again; *because* the last time you were there you didn't do one thing about improving your skills but just sit in the dugout, drink pop, and sweat.

Here are additional ways the word may be punctuated in a sentence. In the first example it is used repetitively, followed by short sentences, and commas (,) are needed to separate them. In the second sentence, however, the sentences are longer; for this reason, *because* needs to be preceded by a semicolon (;).

REPETITIVE

Short:	I did it *because* you ordered it, *because* I was afraid, *because* I had no personal convictions, *because* it seemed right.
Long:	I did it *because* you ordered it; *because* I was afraid of what you might do to me if I didn't; *because* I had no personal convictions about who should receive support; *because* for some weird reason it seemed right that the mission be completed.
AS A NOUN:	Insert double quotation marks (" ") around it.
	His "because" was weaker than I thought it would be.

10.12 **before.** This word is capable of performing as an adverb, conjunction, or preposition. As a preposition, it frequently precedes the indefinite articles "a" or "the."

ADVERB

ahead of:	Jasper got into line; *before* him was Orville.
previously:	*Before*, I was just a hungry man on the street.
sooner [than]:	*Before* we could think twice, the winds came.

CONJUNCTION

previous to the time when:	She was his friend *before* she was his wife.
sooner than:	*Before* I'll commit treason, I'll see you hanged.

PREPOSITION

awaiting:	Now *before* the Congress, this bill is overdue.
face to face with:	Carlos, *before* the judge, began to whimper.
in front of:	*Before* the mirror Junior flexed his muscles.
prior to:	Yancy, *before* the marriage, was a happy man.
Exception:	**Its group needs to be emphasized.** Insert a dash (—) before it.
	That's how much he made—*before* taxes.
Exception:	**Part of an oath.** When the oath introduces the sentence, a comma (,) follows it. As an add-on, however, the dash (—) is usually more

appropriate, including an exclamation mark (!) after the last word.

Before all that's holy, I swear I didn't know. I promise you—before God!

10.13 **but.** This versatile word may function as a preposition and help tie a phrase to the main thought (*see* last example); serve as a conjunction and link sentences together; or relate to the verb in a sentence and become an adverb. However, it performs awkwardly as an adverb (*see* first two examples), and you should consider using the word *only* instead. Below are the definitions it may assume in a sentence.

ADVERB

just: Had I *but* considered the consequence of my action, I wouldn't have done it.

merely: They are *but* human beings like the rest of us.

CONJUNCTION

yet: Bruce wanted to write the great American novel, *but* he didn't have any talent.

excepting: They would accept no excuse *but* the one Hortense gave them.

that: There is little hope *but* she will turn up.

unless: They can't win two games in a row *but* they lose four games afterwards.

who were
not: How many of us have read those words *but* not choked with memories?

which
were not: Are there any streets or buildings in the town of Shadrack *but* owned and dominated by Cabrielle?

PREPOSITION

save: He went to bed with everything on *but* his scarf.

Exception: **Acts as a noun.** Place the word between double quotation marks (" ").

There are no "buts" about it.

Exception: **Follows the words "doubt", "help", "else", or "not."** It is omitted after *doubt, help* and *not;*

but in the case of the word *else*, it, rather than *but*, is removed.

doubt: I don't doubt ~~but~~ you are right.
help: I couldn't help ~~but~~ notice that you laughed.
else: It was no one ~~else~~ *but* him.
not: I will not be ~~but~~ a minute.

However if it precedes "because," then "not" is acceptable, but insert a comma (,) before "but." And if it is preceded by "not only," insert a comma before it and add the word "also" after it.

The game is being delayed *not* for any specific problem, *but* because the umpire wanted it that way.

She wanted the dinner to be a success *not only* for his sake, *but also* because her reputation was on the line.

If "but also" is immediately followed by an interruption to the sentence, the comma before it is omitted and the interruption is set apart instead. The interruption in the following example begins with "if we can."

The team was not only ill-prepared to win for lack of practice *but also* because, if we can believe the circulating rumors, their trust had been shattered as a result of the coach's behavior.

Exception: **Introduces a contrast.** In this situation, other words are frequently implied before or after it. Knowing what and where the implied words are can be crucial to deciding what punctuation to use, if any. In the first example, the comma (,) is needed because it launches a complete thought; in second it is the second half of a phrase, so a comma is not required. In both instances, the implied words have been placed between brackets for your quick identification.

I found the wine to be quite delicious, *but* [it was] somewhat presumptuous.

Our house—[it was] professionally designed, [it is] unique *but* not ostentatious—is being featured in *Classic Home Magazine*.

Exception: **Means "had it not been."** In this situation it is the leader of a phrase that will need to be set apart,

34

unless it ends a sentence with no preceding pause. Here are three sentences:

But for you, I would still be back on the farm.
Our house, *but* for him, would have been sold.
I would still be back on the farm *but* for you.

Exception: **The combination "all but" is used.** It is the same as writing *almost*. Punctuation is not needed unless it leads a phrase (*see* the second and third examples).

He was *all but* exhausted from the ordeal.

All but exhausted from the ordeal, he still managed to make a pig of himself

There he was, *all but* exhausted from the ordeal.

Exception: **Noun or pronoun is implied after it.** If commas are included in the other sentence, the comma which normally precedes *but* in the sentence can be safely omitted.

She felt some compassion for him, a desire to help him in any she could *but* [she] wanted no physical contact.

Exception: **"But rather because" follows "not."** No comma is required before the conjunction.

It happened not because I wanted it to *but rather because* there was no other alternative.

Exception: **Precedes an interjection or a verb.** A comma (,) will have to follow the second word when a pause can be detected. However, insert a colon (:) or a dash (—) when the pause is strong.

INTERJ: *But hey*, who am I to say he's wrong?
But wow—what a difference!

VERB: Todd said that he went to bed early. *But wait:* Didn't he have dinner engagement at the Apollo the same night?

Exception: **Leads a stand-alone nonsentence.** No internal punctuation is necessary. Merely capitalize "but."

But jump into the bed he did.

Exception: **Follows "who."** No comma is needed before "but."

Then there was Homer, who not only could swim underwater *but* was able to sing as he did it.

10.14 centering. This word should be followed with "on," not "in on."

Centering on the bulls-eye, he let the arrow go and was sorry to see that it missed its intended mark by at least six feet.

10.15 consider. This verb may represent an entire sentence by itself and be followed by a colon (:). The first example shows it as part of a full sentence; the second is an edited, reduced version.

PART OF
SENTENCE: I think you should *consider* these possibilities: If he can play first base, then Orville can be the shortstop; and if we can teach Rolando to hit the curve, he can pinch-hit for Buford.

SENTENCE
REDUCED: *Consider:* If he can play first base, then Orville can be the shortstop; and if we can get Rolando to hit curves, he can pinch-hit for Buford.

10.16 considering. This word may serve as an adverb, conjunction, or preposition, and the meanings it can assume are listed below. The comma (,) is used to set the word or its phrase apart; but if more emphasis is needed, the dash (—) may be substituted.

TAKING ALL THINGS
INTO ACCOUNT: Things didn't turn out badly, *considering*.

IN VIEW OF: *Considering* what you said to Paula, I'm not at all surprised that she's angry.

Dramatic: I couldn't believe he actually said that—*considering* his abject fear of him, and all.

10.17 down. *See* "left" for punctuation guidance.

10.18 east, west, north, and **south.** When these words are part of a compass direction, join them to the other compass direction without a hyphen. But if they precede another compass direction which is already comprised of two words (e.g., *southeast*), insert a hyphen (-) them.

| NO HYPHEN: | They began to travel *east* during the summer of '44. |
| HYPHEN: | You can only get there by traveling *east-southeast*. |

10.19 **either.** This word may act as an adjective, adverb, conjunction, or pronoun. As the first or last word in a sentence, a comma (,) will be needed to set it apart when it can be removed without being missed.

BEGINNING

Pause:	*Either,* I don't care.
Strong pause:	*Either:* that means you can take the box on the left or on the right.
"Or" follows:	*Either* you do what I say <u>or</u> you're going to have to pay the consequences.
Leads a phrase:	*Either way*, it simply can't work.

MIDSENTENCE

Interrupts by itself:	None of these, either, have what it takes.
Phrase interrupts:	His choices, *either the throne or her*, were too few for his taste.
Add-on phrase:	He was free to go home or fly to Paris, *either of which seemed attractive to him.*

LAST WORD

| Removable: | I don't believe you should it take it, *either.* |

But if a comma (,) appears elsewhere in the sentence, omit the comma before *either*. In the first example below, the comma follows the first word; in the second, the opening phrase; in the third, an interrupting phrase is set off. In all three cases the comma is removed from in front of "either."

Well, I doubt if they thought so *either.*

She didn't go to London, and I decided not to fly to New York *either.*

Contrary to common belief, the Mayor wasn't in town *either.*

| STANDS ALONE: | *Either!* Neither! Both! Hell, I don't care! |
| Exception: | **The word "else" follows.** Omit *else.* |

37

He said that either you go or ~~else~~ I will.
He said that either you go or I will.

Exception: **More drama is desired.** Use a dash (—) to offset the word or its group.

Either—that's what I said.
His choices—*either* join up or shut up.
Sure—*either*.

10.20   **else.** This word primarily serves as an an adverb or conjunction. Below are the meanings it may assume in a sentence.

ADVERB
otherwise: He had no options, *else* why would he do it?

if not: You must be there by six; else, we might as well call the whole thing off right now.

CONJUNCTION
under other
conditions: The 16-inch rainfall caused the levee to run over; *else* it would have held and prevented the flood.

10.21   **ergo.** This is an adverbial conjunction, and typical punctuation situations where it may be used are virtually identical to those pertaining to the word *therefore*. *See* Rule 10.87.

10.22   **excuse** and **pardon.** There is a fine distinction between these two words which is worth noting. Basically, if the smallest amount of guilt is being recognized about something—however fleeting and short lived it may be—the word *pardon* should be used instead of *excuse*. That's why one hears that a prisoner has been pardoned rather than *excused*.

NO GUILT: *Excuse* me, I think you're sitting in my seat.

SOME GUILT: *Pardon* me, I thought this seat was going to be empty for the night.

SARCASTIC: *Excuse* me!
Well—*exCUSE* me!

WANTING SOME-
THING REPEATED: *Excuse* me?
Beg *pardon?*

10.23   **fancy.** This verb may represent an entire sentence by itself and be followed by a colon (:). The first example shows it as part of a full sentence; the second is an edited version.

SENTENCE: *Try to fancy this, if you will:* they're going to sell doughnuts at three cents apiece, with or without icing.

EDITED: *Fancy:* they're going to sell doughnuts at three cents apiece, with or without icing.

10.24 **for.** If this word substitutes for any of the meanings shown in the left-hand column below it is a conjunction, and a comma (,) will be needed before it when it is not the first word in the sentence. Otherwise it is a preposition; in that case, refer to Rule 17.2 regarding the punctuation of prepositional phrases.

BECAUSE: His argument that the world is round has thrown the scientific community into a turmoil, *for* it is contrary to accepted truth.

OWING TO THE
FACT THAT: It wasn't like they thought it would be, *for* there hadn't even been any fireworks.

SEEING THAT: You shouldn't eat so much at one meal, *for* it only gives you gas and makes you uncomfortable.

Exception: **Means "because."** If the information which follows is lengthy or is in the form of a question, capitalize it and insert a period (.) after the word which immediately precedes it; otherwise a preceding comma (,) will suffice.

              His theory that the world is round has thrown the scientific community into a turmoil. *For* how many experts now have their reputations on the line as a result of completely overlooking that one simple principle?

Exception: **Begins one of three highly related sentences.** A semicolon (;) should either be placed in front of it or before the first word of the last sentence.

              It had not been like they thought it would be; *for* no one in their right mind would have suspected such a turn of events, and you really can't blame anyone.

              It had not been like they thought it would be, *for* no one in their right mind would have suspected such a turn of events; and you really can't blame anyone.

Exception:	**Begins a common expression.** An exclamation mark (!) usually follows if the phrase stands alone; otherwise it is set apart by a comma (,). Use a dash (—) when more emphasis is desired. In the following examples, the expression stands alone, introduces a sentence, and is added to a sentence with and without emphasis.

For the love of Mike!
For Pete's sake, what are you talking about?
What are you talking about, *for* Pete's sake?
So, he said he'd have a drink—for old time's sake.

Exception:	**"For example" or "for instance."** Capitalize and follow either with a comma (,) when it introduces information which elaborates in some way on what precedes it.

There is increasing evidence of global warming. *For example*, it is now possible to fry an egg on your sidewalk in the dead of winter.

Another option is use a colon (:) and not capitalize it; and if more than one example follows, separate them with semicolons (;). The abbreviation *e.g.* may be used in place of "for example," but not in fiction.

There is increasing evidence of global warming: *for example*, it is now possible to fry an egg on your sidewalk in the dead of winter; people are going to work in their underwear.
There is increasing evidence of global warming; *e.g.*, it is now possible to fry an egg on your sidewalk in the dead of winter.

10.25 got. Grammatical reminder: Do not precede this word with a verb.

INCORRECT:	You *have* got to do better than that.
CORRECT:	You *have* to do better than that.

10.26 granted. Grammatical reminder: There is no need to place the word *that* after it when it leads a phrase, for it is already implied (*see* first example). This word may introduce, interrupt, or be added to a sentence.

PHRASE:	*Granted we didn't find gold,* but we were good sifters.
INTRODUCES:	*Granted,* it was more than I expected from him.
INTERRUPTS:	But, *granted,* he was taller than the others.
ADD-ON:	It was more than I expected from him, *granted.*

40

10.27 **had.** When this verb begins an introductory, interruptive, or add-on phrase, that phrase must be set part by a comma (,). Note: it must never immediately precede the preposition *of*, and do not follow it with *have* nor any contraction of it (e.g., *they've*).

INCORRECT: I would have told you, *had* I've known it.
CORRECT: I would have told you, *had* I known it.

10.28 **hear.** When not an integral, unremovable part of the sentence, this word is usually added to a full sentence and is preceded by a comma (,), period (.), or dash (—). Moreover, it acts as a one-word representative of a larger question, such as *Do you hear me?* It may also appear twice in a row, which indicates support of something, in which case it demands an exclamation mark (!).

Original: I'm coming over there. Do you *hear?*
Edited: I'm coming over there. ~~Do you~~ *hear?*
Stands alone: I'm coming over there. *Hear?*
Linked: I'm coming over there, *hear?*
Emphasized   I'm coming over there—*hear?*
Twice in a row: Hear! Hear!

10.29 **however.** This is an adverb and adverbial conjunction. If you are using the word to mean (1) *whatever extent*, (2) *in whatever manner*, or (3) *by whatever means*, it is an adverb, and below is an example of it being used that way. But if you are using it as a conjunction to link two sentences, it is synonymous with *still*. In that case, it will need a comma (,) after it when it is capitalized and removable; a preceding semicolon (;) and a following comma will be required when it stands between two highly related sentences.

ADVERB: *However* you want it done, that's the way I'll do it.
             I'll go *however* you want me to go.

CONJUNCTION: He wasn't afraid. *However,* he began to carry a gun when he walked that street.

             He wasn't afraid; *however,* he knew he should be.

Exception: **The "ever" part of the word means "in the world."** Separate *how* from *ever*.

             How ever will we pull this thing off?

10.30 **if.** Below are the definitions which this conjunction is capable of assuming in a sentence. Knowing the meaning you are attaching to the word is often important in determining what punctuation, if any, is needed.

41

ALLOWING THAT:	*If* they are the state spelling bee champions, why can't any of them spell that word?
	I'd say he is the better of the two, *if* everything is equal.
ON THE CONDITION THAT:	*If* you will pay me ten percent interest, I'll loan you the money.
	I will agree to those terms *if* you'll let me look at the contract first.
WHETHER:	How can you be sure *if* he's telling the truth?
Exception:	**Functions as a noun.** Put double quotation marks (" ") before and it.
	What I don't want from you is a bunch of "ifs," "ands," and "buts."
Exception:	**Launches an exclamatory sentence.** Place an exclamation mark (!) at the end.
	If only he had called before nine!
Exception:	**Begins an introductory or add-on phrase.** Set the phrase apart with commas (,). Use dashes (—) for more drama.
	If anything, I was hungrier than I was before. I think he owes about five dollars—*if that.*

10.31 imagine. This verb may represent an entire sentence by itself and be followed by a colon (:). The first example shows it as part of a full sentence; the second is an edited version. Notice, too, that the second sentence retains its capitalization, for it is not dependent on the word *imagine* for its existence.

ORIGINAL:	Can you imagine that? At one time he had over a million dollars.
EDITED VERSION:	*Imagine:* At one time he had over a million dollars.

10.32 inasmuch. Preceding "as," it means the same as *seeing that* and *because*, and the complete thought which it launches is always set apart by a comma (,).

42

SEEING THAT:	*Inasmuch as* you don't care if I stay or go, I am at a loss at what to do next.
BECAUSE:	I was kicked out of my office this morning, *inasmuch as* I couldn't pay the rent.

10.33 insomuch. As the first word of a group which supports a sentence, it is followed by "as" and its group is set apart by a comma (,). But if it immediately follows a verb, the comma is omitted. Below are the definitions it may assume in a sentence, which can helpful in determining when to use punctuation. The dash (—) may be used before the word when more drama is needed.

TO SUCH A EXTENT:	*Insomuch* as it ran over, my cup was filled to capacity.
TO SUCH A DEGREE:	My cup was filled *insomuch* that it ran over.

10.34 instead. When this adverb introduces, interrupts, or is added to a sentence, a comma (,) should set it apart from the other information; likewise when it leads a phrase that begins or interrupts the sentence. However, when it and its word group round out a complete thought by providing another option, no punctuation is required: it is, in that instance, a unremovable part of the sentence.

INTRODUCES	
By itself:	*Instead,* I thought she was one of them.
Part of phrase:	*Instead of playing the fool,* I proceeded to impress them with my knowledge.
INTERRUPTS	
By itself:	I felt, *instead,* like a bump on a log.
Part of phrase:	Edgar, *instead of taking more money out of his savings account,* went back to work.
ADD-ON	Why not sing this song, *instead?*
COMPLETES SENTENCE:	Would you like go there *instead of over there?*
Exception:	**Sentence already has commas.** Refrain from setting the word apart with commas.
	Though it should have been a happy time, I felt *instead* like a bump on a log.

43

Because the audience is becoming unruly, why not sing this song *instead?*

10.35 its and it's. When combining the pronoun *it* and the verb *is,* substitute the second "i" with an apostrophe ('); however, when showing the pronoun owns something, the apostrophe is omitted.

IT IS: *It's* the same dumb thing you did last week, Jethro.
OWNERSHIP: She painted one of *its* fenders pink.

10.36 leastwise. This is a colloquial word and should not be used in formal writing. But when writing dialogue, an uneducated character in a novel or play might well use it. It means *at least.*

Leastwise that's how I see it, Mr. Gumps.
That's how I see it, *leastwise.*

10.37 left, right, up, and **down.** What follows are some familiar punctuation situations which affect these words. All four share many similar punctuation possibilities, though not identical in every way.

NOUN: The *right* and the *left* of that political party have been at war with each other ever since Buster died.

PREPOSITION: *Up* the hill you can perhaps make out the enemy's bunker.
VERB: *Downing* his medicine, Michael tried to *right* at least one of the two wrongs he had committed.

RIGHT
    Pause follows: *Right,* as always.
                        Right—and don't make me say it again.

    "Or" missing: Go *right,* left—it doesn't matter.

    No pause: *Right* you are!

    Counting cadence: *Left, right! Left, right!* To the rear, march!

    Add-on word: Yeh, *right.*
                        Yeh—*right.*

    Leads a phrase: *Right for the first time in his life,* he nearly drowned in his own glory.

    Stands alone: *Right! Right!* Go left! Whoops!

LEFT

Pause follows:	*Left,* notice how the image fades out.
Leads a phrase:	*Left to his own devices,* he managed to get into deep trouble.
	And there's the Taj Mahal, *left of that building.*

UP

Pause follows:	*Up,* I finally made myself some breakfast. *Up*—not down!
Leads a phrase:	Then Jerry, *up to his old tricks again,* tried to borrow some money from me.
Stands alone:	You said it was which way? *Up? Down?*

DOWN

Pause follows:	*Down,* the stock market rallied later that day. *Down*—put it down!
Interrupts:	The stock market, *down,* caused a great ripple in the business world.
	The stock market, *down by a hundred points,* caused a great ripple in the business world.
Dramatic add-on:	He was down to pocket change—*down to his last shred of hope.*

10.38 lest. Below are the definitions which this conjunction is capable of assuming in a sentence. Knowing the meaning you are attaching to the word can be important in determining whether or not punctuation should accompany it. Note: the bracketed words in the first example are implied rather than stated.

SO THAT:	*Lest* they [will not] find it, we must hide it carefully.
IN ORDER THAT:	He asked for her hand in marriage, *lest* he could get his hands on her money.
FOR FEAR THAT:	*Lest* his crop would wilt in the drought, he prayed for rain.

Exception: Follows a sentence which indicates concern or alarm about something. No comma is needed before it.

We were at our wit's end *lest* we had done the wrong thing.

10.39 like. *See* the word "as" in this section.

10.40 likewise. Below are two definitions which this word can assume in a sentence. When it begins or ends a sentence, a comma (,) sets it apart; but if punctuation already exists, the comma is often omitted to prevent confusion.

ALSO: Freddy wanted to take Marcia to the prom, but he felt certain that he had an obligation to Sue *likewise*.

Simple
sentence: He felt certain that he had an obligation to Sue, *likewise*.

IN LIKE
MANNER: Freddy wanted to take Marcia to the prom. *Likewise*, Arnold had the same notions.

Freddy wanted to take Marcia to the prom; *likewise*, Arnold had the same notions.

10.41 listen, look and see. These three words are used in dialogue quite often and are capable of introducing, interrupting, and being added to a sentence, in addition to leading phrases that do the same thing. In all cases they are set apart by commas (,); however, if more drama is needed, a dash (—) may be substituted. NOTE: The word "see" can have the pronoun *you* implied before it (*see* sixth sentence), or it can be a substitute for the words *I told you* (*see* third sentence). As stand-alone words, they are dramatic and need to be followed by either an exclamation mark (!) or question mark (?).

STANDS ALONE: *Listen!* I think someone's in the house!
Look! Isn't that Fernando?
There it is! *See?*

INTRODUCES: *Listen,* you've got to get hold of yourself!
Look here, who do you think you're talking to?
See, it's just like I said it was.

INTERRUPTS: Jerry, *listen to me,* you can do it if you try.

46

> If it follows a conjunction or an adverb that would normally be set apart, the first comma can usually be waived in most instances.

CONJ: But *look,* isn't that what he said before?

ADV: Now *look here,* what are you trying saying?

ADDED ON: It won't fit, *see* what I mean?
They're coming—*listen.*

COMMAND: *See* that it's done.
Listen up!

Exception: **Referring the reader to a section of a magazine or part of a book.** The word *see* should be italicized whenever possible. However, if you cannot produce italics, do not underline the word.

See page 12 of "The Goose and the Gooseberry."

10.42 look. *See* the word "listen" in this section.

10.43 might. When this verb begins an introductory, interrupting, or add-on phrase, the comma (,) is used to set that phrase apart in the sentence. Grammatical reminder: it must never immediately precede the preposition *of.*
I would be famous today, *might* I have gone there.

10.44 minus. Below are the definitions this word can assume in a sentence. A comma (,) precedes it when it begins a phrase which introduces, interrupts, or is added to a sentence.

LACKING: I was *minus* a car and bus fare.
Phrase: *Minus a car,* I couldn't get to the interview.

LESSENED BY: Five *minus* three is two.
Phrase: It's been a good life, *minus that prison term.*

Exception: **Acts as a noun in the sentence.** Do not insert double quotation marks before and after it.

That's the only minus I can see with the program.

Exception: **Part of a grade.** Do not insert insert a hyphen before it when it is preceded by the single alphabetic letters A, B, C, or D.

I think I deserved more than a B *minus* on that test.

10.45 **namely**, which is synonymous with the phrases **that is** and **to wit.** This word and its synonymous phrases always introduce interruptive or add-on information that serves to support the statement being made, and they follow a semicolon (;). However, *namely* can be used to precede a list, and in that situation a preceding colon (:) is more desirable. *To wit* is an odd, uncomfortable hookup of two unrelated words which is used primarily in legal documents, and they too may precede a list. Elements in the list are separated by commas (,), unless phrases are added to them; in that case, separate them with semicolons (;). See the second example.

MEANS...

that is to say:	There was nothing anyone could do; *namely,* the last possible option had already been lost.
BEFORE A LIST:	Many of them had gotten involved: *namely,* the Hoot Owl Club, who provided the facilities; Captain Hornblower, who let them use his boat on the weekends; and the countless volunteers who manned the phones.
Dramatic:	It only has two ingredients—*namely,* vinegar and water.
	He wanted justice—*that is,* his kind of justice.
INTERRUPTIVE Personal comment:	She was broke (*that is,* if you didn't count the thirty cents and a stick of gum which she had in her purse) and the thought of welfare frightened her.
Identifies:	The Jeffersons—*namely,* Paul and Edgard—held a grudge against the Pattersons.
ENDS SENTENCE:	He ordered his employees to do it over: starting at the first point of assembly, *namely.*
Exception:	**The abbreviation "i.e."** It may be used as a substitute for *that is,* although not in fiction. And it should certainly not be overused. Precede it with a comma (,).
	It only has two ingredients, i.e., vinegar and water.

48

10.46 neither. The word *neither* may perform as an adjective, conjunction, or pronoun. As an adjective, it immediately precedes a noun or pronoun, and *nor* is not subsequently implied. As a conjunction, the word *nor* should appear—and without a preceding comma. (DO NOT use the conjunction *or* with *neither.*) As a pronoun, it acts as a substitute for the names of two people or two things.

ADJECTIVE:

Introductory phrase

Neither criminal taking the blame, both managed to get out of it.

Add-on phrase: It all turned out to be a bust, *neither* plan living up to its supposed potential.

But if the word *nor* subsequently follows, insert a comma (,) before that word, because *nor* begins an afterthought.

They arrogantly decided that *neither* group would be able to vote, *nor* would they even consider the possibility.

CONJUNCTION

First word: *Neither* the threat of a good spanking *nor* a horrible ghost story changes his behavior.

Midsentence: I felt that I had *neither* a firm grasp of the problem *nor* even an idea of what the problem was.

PRONOUN

Emphasized: *Neither*—and I mean it!

Follows intro: With broccoli costing so much, *neither thought it was worth buying.*

Side comment: They were poor as church mice (*neither* owned a coat *nor a pair of gloves*) and we took up a collection.

Add-on phrase: They looked at the long road still ahead of them, *neither feeling up to the trip.*

Conjunction omitted: *Neither* felt poor; *neither* felt rich.

49

Exception:	**"Neither" and "nor" are separated by one word.** No punctuation is needed before either word unless the former begins the second of two related sentences (*see* second example).
	Believe me when I tell you that *neither* I *nor* my secretary were informed about the meeting.
	They said they wanted me to be kept up to date; *neither* I *nor* my secretary, however, were told anything about the meeting.
Exception:	**"Nor" links a singular and plural noun.** The tense of the verb is dependent upon which noun is nearer to that verb. In the first example, the plural noun "Brothers" is closest; in the second, the singular noun "Fabian" is. In neither case is "nor" preceded by a comma. For your quick identification only, the verbs have been underlined.
	Neither Fabian *nor* the Jones Brothers <u>were</u> able to carry a tune worth mentioning.
	Neither the Jones Brothers *nor* Fabian <u>was</u> able to carry a tune worth mentioning.
Exception:	**"Nor" precedes "neither."** Change the latter to "either," and put a comma (,) before it when it ends a simple sentence.
	Nor do I see any goodness in his good will, *either.*

10.47 **nevertheless.** This is an adverbial conjunction, and typical punctuation situations where it may be used are virtually identical to those pertaining to the adverb "yet."

10.48 **no and yes.** The biggest difference between these two words is that *no* can lead a phrase while *yes* cannot. Otherwise, the punctuation situations affecting these two words are practically identical. They may introduce, interrupt, or be added to a complete thought, requiring one or more commas (,) to set them apart because they represent nonessential information.

REMOVABLE:	*No*, it's not something I'd want to do on a regular basis.
	But Hortense, *no*, she wouldn't hear of it.

It was the hundredth meeting we had sat through where, *yes*, the same things were discussed, and where, *yes*, nothing was proposed to do anything about them.

I didn't like it, *no*.
Please—*no!*

But omit the comma when the word is part of a short exclamatory sentence, and insert an exclamation mark (!) after the last word. For more drama, insert a dash (—) after *yes* or *no*.

Yes you can!
No—I can't!

AFTER "BUT": But as far as that goes, *yes*.

SERIES: *No, yes,* maybe—somebody make up their cotton-pickin' mind.

PHRASE: *No doubt about it,* that is the ugliest dog I've seen.
That, *no doubt about it,* is the ugliest dog I've seen.
I wanted no praise, *no* hollow pats on the back.

DRAMATIC: I felt the tug of time—*no illusion this*—and doubled my efforts that I might finish it before the deadline.

I think that you'll soon understand—*no, rather I should say it's going to be a mind-boggling revelation*—that regardless of your efforts, you're not going to change him.

COMMENT: Big Ben (*no*, I don't know what his real name was) held the job of sheriff for eight years.

CONJUNCTION
OMITTED: *Yes*, he would call her; *no*, he would not let on that he knew.

FOLLOWS...
   sir, etc: *No sir*, that's not what I said.
It was, *yes ma'am*, about that long.
That wasn't me, *no sir*.

But if it precedes "miss," insert a comma between the two words.

51

No, miss, that's not what I said.

say
saying: Who can say no to an offer like that?
I kept saying yes, and she kept saying no.

STANDS
ALONE: Did I like her? No!
Did she like me? No.
I suppose that's her on the phone. No?

Exception: **Dialogue.** When using *yes sir* in dialogue, the two words may be combined if it is essential to show that they are spoken quickly. But do not abuse this privilege.

"Did you hear what I said, sergeant?"
"Yessir!"
"And may I expect my orders to be carried out?"
"Yessir! Right away, sir!"

Exception: **Used repetitively in a series of options.** If *no* or *yes* is used repetitively in response to a series of options being considered, colons (:) should precede them, with semicolons (;) inserted after the last word of each group.

His mind juggled the possibilities. Perhaps he would buy the house on Jeeper Street: *no*, he didn't want to live there alone; maybe he would take a trip to a distant land: *no*, he didn't like foreigners; or possibly he would become a philanthropist: *no*, there was all that paperwork.

10.49 **nor.** This conjunction follows *neither, not, no, never, nothing,* or *none* in a sentence. Except when it follows the word *neither*, it is always preceded by a comma (,). Please refer to the word "neither" in this section, to see how the two are used in conjunction with one another in a sentence. Below, the brackets indicate which words are implied in the sentence.

SENTENCES: You can't make me, *nor* can anyone else [make me].

It was not the best of times, *nor* was it the worst of times.

PHRASES: I found no honor among them, *nor* any coherent principles, *nor* any understanding of human beings in general

52

10.50 north. *See* the word "east" in this section.

10.51 not. This negative word can be an integral, unremovable word in a sentence that should not be accompanied by punctuation; or it can be the leader of a full sentence or removable phrase, in which case punctuation is essential to set its group apart.

PHRASE: *Not* satisfied with the way things were going, he decided to take another approach.

They concluded that Marcia, *not* having been a member since 1981, would have to pay a fee.

Dramatic: Then the state of Texas—*not Arkansas as everyone had expected*—made a motion to redraw the boundaries.

She is perhaps the most popular person in the neighborhood—*not that I care.*

Multiple: He stood before the shouting crowd, *not feeling a bit of guilt, not asking to be heard, not making any move to defend himself.*

Correction: But then Jeanine (*not Jeanie*) Holthauzer was the only witness to the accident.

SENTENCE:
Related: They filed silently into the Great Room; *not one was wearing underwear.*

Implied
words: I do not mean that one setting there. I meant that one over there!

Not that one. That one!

Personal
comment: The city council voted unanimously to shut down the park (*not one,* I'll bet you, *has ever been there*), and next week they are going to begin cutting down the trees.

Dramatic: Today, members of city council—*not one arrived on time,* by the way—voted to shut down the park.

Exception: **"Not" is followed by "but."** No comma is necessary before "but."

He was *not* tired but rather lonely for his wife.

53

Exception: **"Not only" is followed by "but also." No** comma is necessary before "but."

They had *not only* one every game in August but also in October as well.

10.52 notwithstanding. This is an adverb, adverbial conjunction, and a preposition. As a conjunction, it stands between two contrary statements and agrees that both are true, while admitting that one cannot resist the other—a shotgun marriage, so to speak. Below, under the parts of speech headings, are the definitions this word is capable of assuming in a sentence, which can be helpful when determining when or if to use punctuation.

ADVERB
all the same	Even though she was engaged, he asked for her hand *notwithstanding*.
nevertheless	I had always hated opera; *notwithstanding*, I found myself being captivated by its theatrics.

CONJUNCTION
in spite of the fact that:	She wept for him, *notwithstanding* it was she who turned him in to the hated secret police.

PREPOSITION
in spite of:	*Notwithstanding* his chronic weight problem, Hugo Munges ordered a dozen cheeseburgers and five pounds of fries.

10.53 now. This adverb, conjunction, or noun can be a part of a common expression, act alone as a single word, or serve as leader of a full sentence. As a conjunction, the word *that* often follows it. Below are the definitions it can assume in a sentence. Knowing how you are using the word can be helpful in determining if accompanying punctuation is necessary.

ADVERB
nowadays:	*Now* you can hardly tell the boys from the girls. That's how it is *now*.
recently:	I saw it happen just *now*.
phrase	*Now* taking their toll on him, he decided to give up.
immediately	*Now* finding himself surrounded, he tried to negotiate.

54

| during the present time: | *Now* he is looked upon as a pioneer in the field. |
| | He is looked upon as a pioneer in the field *now*. |

things being as they are:	*Now*, is that any way to run a railroad?
	I suspect, *now*, they'll have to promote him.
	They're going to raise taxes—*now?*

at this point:	*Now* you have over-exercised.
	So, *now*, it's a matter of waiting him out.
	There's little else we can do *now*.

| CONJUNCTION: | *Now* that he has won the lottery, you would be surprised at how badly he manages his money. |
| | She felt no obligation to answer his letter, *now* that he was back in town. |

| COMMON EXPRESSION: | *Come now*, you're joking. |

10.54 **"O"** The single letter O is always capitalized when used as an interjection, and it indicates one of two things: (1) something or someone is being spoken to; or (2) despair or hope is being expressed. The last word of the group it leads is followed by an exclamation mark (!). Always used in poetry.

| SPOKEN TO: | O America! |
| | O my poor dears! |

| DESPAIR: | O such fraud! |
| HOPE: | O to see her again! |

10.55 **of.** Grammatical tip: do not use it in place of the verb *have*. But with regard to punctuation, do not insert a comma after it when it immediately precedes a conjunction-led phrase which cannot be removed from the sentence(refer to the third example below: the phrase *or as the primary disciplinary procedure* is unremovable). This word is a pure preposition, and explanations regarding this part of speech is adequately covered under Rules 17.2 through 1.7.5.

| INCORRECT: | I could ~~of~~ done it, had I been given more time. |
| CORRECT: | I could *have* done it, had I been given more time. |

| BEFORE A CONJUNCTION: | When using the program as part *of* or as the primary disciplinary procedure, remember that it has yet to be proven effective in all situations. |

PHRASES: The preacher spoke of love, of forgiveness, of turning the other cheek, but no one paid any attention.

10.56 **oh.** This interjection is frequently used to represent a pause in a sentence and is accompanied by a comma (,), although it may be used more dramatically and have an exclamation mark (!) follow it as well.

PAUSE Oh, I really think I should go.
Oh, yes we will!
Oh, no you don't.

EMPHASIZED: Oh! What a movie that was!
Oh! Oh! Oh! That hurts!

Exception: **Writing dialogue.** "Oh" is one of those interjections which allows its last letter to be repeated, to create a certain effect.

Ohhhhhh, no. Don't tell me that.

10.57 **once.** This highly adaptable word is an adjective if it describes a noun; an adverb if it relates "when"; a conjunction if it joins sentences; a noun if it substitutes for a name. Unless it stands alone, a comma (,) is used to separate it or its phrase apart from the other information; for more emphasis, the dash (—) may act as a substitute.

DESCRIBES: The *once* King of Terribut could not understand why he no longer had a throne.

TELLS "WHEN": *Once* I had it all.

Removable: *Once,* I was sure I would be rich.
It was Percival, *once,* who said he hated war.
That's the way it was, *once.*

Removable
as a phrase: *Once done,* I think you'll like it.

Then, *once* I get the hang of it, I won't mind skiing off mountain ledges.

But when there is no recognizable pause before its interrupting phrase, the comma before *once* may be waived. In this example, the word *that* is implied before it.

I think [that] *once* I get the hang of it, I won't mind skiing off mountain ledges.

He played the song twice—*once* for me and *once* for her—using our Player piano.

I've tried it twice, *once carefully.*

Strong pause:
Once—that's all I'm going to tell you.
Do it two more times—*once with feeling.*
Yes, I did fall—*once.*

Removable comment:
Blip Wumpkins (*once, his name was Sletch Slump*) became the caretaker of the lodge after proving conclusively that he could unclog sinks.

JOINS SENTENCES:
I'll come over to your house *once* you have decided not to watch TV while I'm there.

Related sentence:
At first he didn't like the song; *once* he started, though, he began to warm to it.

Strong pause:
She knew better than to name him as a reference: *once* she had called him a communist pig, and he had never forgotten it.

Dramatic:
I had every intention of going on a diet—*once* I reached three hundred pounds.

NAME SUBSTITUTE:
Once is not enough.

STANDS ALONE
No commas:
How many times was I there? *Once.*
Once! A likely story.

10.58   **or.** Like "and," this is a popular conjunction; however, it always offers an alternative to a preceding sentence, phrase, or word (e.g., You may have this *or* that)—even when it begins a sentence and is capitalized.

CAPITALIZED
Strong pause:
Or you could say this: Every time you come in late, you will have to do that much overtime.

New sentence:
Or how about the time you said you would never eat shellfish?

57

Phrase:	*Or* assuming the worse, she may have already married the bum.
MIDSENTENCE	
Interrupts:	He said he would, *or* at least I think he did, and I feel we owe him the benefit of the doubt.
Emphasized:	These are supposed to be good times—*or* that's what they would have you believe—and we are not supposed to worry.
Multiple alternatives:	You could tell her you're sorry; *or* you could send her a box of candy; *or* there is the possibility of a singing telegram; *or* you could just forget the whole thing and date someone else.
ADD-ON	
Phrase:	How many of them care about her, *or even ask?*
Dramatic:	How many of them care about her—*or even ask?*
OR MAY NOT	
No pause:	He may *or may not* sign the contract today.
Pause:	These activities were videotaped and have subsequently been turned over to a producer who may, *or may not,* want to use it as a basis for a movie.
Emphasized:	The videotape was turned over to a producer who may—*or may not*—see it as a potential movie.
Exception:	**Follows "either" or "whether." It is not preceded by a comma.** You will <u>either</u> eat that food *or* go hungry. I don't know <u>whether</u> they pay anything *or* not.
Exception:	**Follows an interruption which begins with "or" and ends in a preposition.** Omit the comma before and after the interruption, but keep the comma (,) before the second "or." In this example, the interruption is *or attached to.* We think it is leaning against *or attached to* the barn, *or* it is a total illusion.

But the interruption may be emphasized with a dash (—) before and after it; in that case, no comma before the second "or" will be needed.

We think it is leaning against—*or* attached to—the
barn *or* it is a total illusion.

10.59 **otherwise.** The punctuation which accompanies this word is dependent upon what definition—shown at the left, below—is being applied to it. But when it immediately precedes an adjective or verb, no comma is required (e.g., She was an *otherwise* gracious host).

IN A DIFFERENT
MANNER: Julie felt like crying for him; *otherwise*, she believed he was getting what he deserved.

IN OTHER
CIRCUMSTANCES: Daily life in prison was torture to Algernon's soul, but it was like home *otherwise*.

Daily life in prison was torture to Algernon's soul. *Otherwise* it was like home.

10.60 **ought.** Grammatical tip: Never precede *ought* with the words *had* or *hadn't*. Furthermore, use *ought not* instead of the contraction *oughtn't*.

INCORRECT: You ~~hadn't~~ *ought to* have done that.
CORRECT: You *ought to* do that, if you can.

INCORRECT: I *oughtn't* to play my music so loud.
CORRECT: I *ought not* play my music so loud.

10.61 **pardon.** *See* the word "excuse" for punctuation assistance.

10.62 **period (the word).** The word "period" causes few if any punctuation problems when it functions as a noun. But when it represents a "spelled-out" punctuation mark that indicates the definite end of something, it always follows a complete thought and is preceded by a comma (,). However, use a dash (—) if more emphasis is required.

COMMA: That's the way it's going to be, *period*.
EMPHASIZED: That's the way it's going to be—*period!*

10.63 **please.** Here are several punctuation situations which may attend this frequently used word.

BEGINNING:
No pause after: *Please* do as I say.
Pause follows: *Please*, Ginny, do as I say.
Pause emphasized: *Please*—is it too much to ask?

MIDDLE:
No pause after: Ginny, *please* do as I say.

59

Pause before/after: I ask you, please, to do as I say.

ADD-ON:
Pause precedes:	Do as I say, *please.*
Dramatic pause:	Do as I say—*please?*
Strong pause:	Do as I say. *Please!*

FOLLOWS "SAY":   Is it below you to say "please" ?

10.64 **plus.** Below are the definitions which this word may assume within a sentence. Knowing how you are using the word can be helpful in determining what punctuation, if any, should accompany it.

ADDED TO: Our bunch *plus* their members will give us a total of thirty people.

INCREASED BY: My monthly pension, *plus* stock dividends, gives me nearly a thousand dollars a month to live on.

THE OWNER OF: He had all that farmland, and he was *plus* a new house.

Exception: **As a conjunction between two sentences.** It should not be used as a conjunction; use a real conjunction instead.

Frank is a good father, ~~plus he is~~ a good sport.
Frank is a good father *and* a good sport.

Exception: **Part of a grade.** Do not insert a hyphen (-) before it when it is preceded by the single alphabetic letter A, B, C, or D.

I didn't score any higher than a C plus on that test.

Exception: **Acts as a noun.** Do not use double quotation marks (" ") before and after it.

Getting that account turned out to be a big plus.

10.65 **preferring:** When used with the preposition *to* in a phrase which presents two options, insert a comma (,) before it when it does not lead off the sentence; otherwise, insert the comma after the last word of its phrase. Note: When the two options being spoken about are not displayed, the words *rather than* and *instead of* are implied and need not be used (*see* last two examples).

ACCEPTABLE:	He wasted his time at the dinner table, *preferring to* talk rather than eat.
Better:	He wasted his time at the dinner table, *preferring* talking to eating.
"RATHER THAN" "INSTEAD OF"	Wilbur declined their invitation, *preferring to* stay at home.
	Preferring to stay at home, Wilbur declined their invitation.

10.66 provided, providing. These two words may serve as either a verb or a conjunction. As a conjunction, they must lead full sentences.

CONJ:

Sentence 1:	*Providing* all of you sneeze at once, I think we can knock this door down.
Sentence 2:	He said he would stay, *provided* no one would sneak into his bed while he was sleeping.

VERB

Introductory	*Provided* for by his great uncle, Winthrop felt financially secure.
Add-on:	She sent Winslow on his way, *providing* him with a day's ration of food and two day's supply of water.
Exception:	**Verb subsequently follows.** Never use the past tense of a verb after "provided" or "providing."

PAST:	He wanted to eat, *provided* that Bessie had baked the the cake as she promised.
PRESENT:	He wanted to eat, *provided* that Bessie would bake the the cake as she promised.

10.67 rather. The punctuation which accompanies this adverb is the same as the word "instead," which is explained elsewhere in this section.

10.68 right. See the word "left" for punctuation assistance.

10.69 say. The meaning applied to the word (shown below, to the left) is critical to understanding what type of punctuation to use, if any.

61

MEANS....

by the way:	*Say*, didn't you tell me that you hated okra? Oh, *say*, you should see Alma's new coat.
let's say:	*Say* you're riding on a train, and the train stops. What would be your first reaction? For the sake of argument, *say* his charges have merit. Now the government, *say*, is willing to be a partner in such a scheme for the sake of its economic survival.
INTERJECTION:	*Say!* That was a dandy, wasn't it! *I say!* Wasn't that fun!
LEADS PHRASE:	*Say what you will*, I still don't think he did it. Yet, *say what you will*, I don't think he did it. I don't think he did it, *say what you will*.
Exception:	**Say what?...Say again?** In dialogue, and to represent a colloquial way of speaking, either of these two word combinations may be used when a fictional character wants something repeated. They stand alone. I think Abraham Lincoln was short. *Say again?*
Exception:	**Acts as a noun.** No quotations marks are needed before and after the word. She finally had her *say*.

10.70 see. For punctuation guidance, refer to the word "listen" in this section.

10.71 should. When this verb begins an introductory, interrupting, or add-on phrase, the comma (,) must be used to set that phrase apart. If it leads off a two-word question which is attached to a sentence, insert a comma before it and a question mark (?) after the last word. However, if a question is not being asked, replace the question mark with a period (.). Note: this word must never immediately precede the preposition *of*.

PHRASE:	And this, *should it have been done*, would have us millions.
QUESTION:	It shouldn't do that, *should it?*

Confirming: It shouldn't do that, *should it.*

10.72 **since.** If this word assumes one of the three meanings shown below, it is a conjunction; otherwise, it is functioning as a preposition. As a preposition, it performs as the first word of a phrase rather than a sentence. The comma (,) is inserted before the word or after its group, except when it is a midsentence preposition.

CONJUNCTION

continuously from
the time when:

She's been that way *since* she had the baby.
Since she had the baby, she's been that way.

following upon
the fact that:

Since the bush hadn't bloomed, he cut it down.
He cut it down, *since* the bush hadn't bloomed.

inasmuch as:

I don't plan to do anything about it, *since* you don't care.

PREPOSITION

during the
time after:

Since the plague, farming hasn't been worth a plug nickel around here.

continuously
throughout the
time after:

And Mingo, *since* the government took his land, has been vowing revenge.

ADVERB

up to the
present:

Since, Betty has felt no reason to trust him.
Betty, *since,* has felt no reason to trust him.
Betty has felt no reason to trust him *since.*

WITH TIME:

Since 1948, everything has been going downhill.
Everything has been going downhill *since 1948.*

Exception:

Emphasis needed. Insert a dash (—) before the word when you wish to force a dramatic pause.

No, I haven't seen her—*since* you know when.

63

10.73 so. This popular word may act as an adverb, conjunction, or interjection, and the definitions it may assume can be found under the parts-of-speech headings below. Knowing the meaning you are attaching to the word can be helpful in deciding what punctuation to use—if any. Included below, too, are examples of (1) when, as part of *so long as* and *so you*, it helps to form phrases (2) when it is part of an oath, and (3) when it is included in a statement of surprise.

ADVERB

just as [I] said:	I think it is *so.*
thereabouts:	She said that thirty or *so* came to watch him. I'm sure there were a hundred or *so.*
therefore:	*So,* what we may conclude from this is that you cannot get measles from a weasel.
too/indeed	He did *so!* He did *so.*
very	It was all *so* boring, *so* time-consuming, *so* completely unnecessary.
very well	*So,* if that's the way you feel about it. *So*—now what?

CONJUNCTION

as:	She said she was sick to death of the way they keep raising our taxes (*so* am I) and that she was going to stop paying them.
as a consequence of which:	His habit was getting out of hand, *so* he stopped.
in such a way that:	They tied him up *so* he could never get loose.
therefore:	They have made no effort to assert themselves and become employed, *so* why should the state continue to support them in the fashion to which they have grown accustomed?
with the purpose that:	He bought her twenty long-stem roses, *so* she would have ten left if the other ten died.
	So he could drive the car, he told the attendant to fill it up with gas.

INTERJECTION is that so	So! You expect me to believe that, do you?
OATH:	*So* help me God!
	So help me God, if he sings another song I'm going to kill him with my bare hands.
	I'm going to kill him with my bare hands if he sings another song—*so* help me God!
STATEMENT OF SURPRISE:	*So* you're the Great Gildersleeve, are you!
SO AS:	Can it be changed *so as* to make it longer? *So as* to make ends meet, he tied them.
SO THAT Adjective:	It was *so* quiet *that* we began to grow scared. The cigarette—*so round, so firm, so fully packed*—was actually a stick of chalk.
Means "to such an extent":	He loved Betsy Wurmingler *so*, he wouldn't tolerate anything bad said about her.
SO LONG AS:	*So long as* you continue to act that way, I don't think she'll ever come back.
	Meanwhile he'll hang onto his cabin in the woods, *so long* as the trees remain.
SO YOU:	Your mother, *so you* would be kept warm, always gave you an extra blanket.
	That's the way it's going to be, *so you* can expect it.

10.74 **sobeit.** *See* the word "amen" for punctuation assistance.

10.75 **someday, somehow, sometime, sometimes, someway, someways,** and **somewhere.** These words may introduce or interrupt a sentence by themselves, requiring commas (,) to set them apart.

REMOVABLE:	*Someday*, you can count on it. *Someday*—you can count on it. I think, *someday*, we're all going to be rich. You'll get yours—*someday!*

NO PAUSE:	*Someday* it will.
	I think that *someday* justice will be done.
	I hope it happens *someday*.

| PAUSE: | We must make money someway, *someday*. |

| SERIES: | *Someday, somewhere, somehow* I'll get even. |

PHRASE

| Removable: | *Someday when you least expect it*, he'll come walking through that door with a big smile. |
| | I wouldn't be surprised that, *someday when we figure this thing out*, we'll discover it to be an unprofitable pursuit. |

| Emphasized: | *Someday in the spring*—that's all he said. |
| | One of these days—*someday when we least expect it*—he'll show up. |

10.76 south. *See* the word "east" for punctuation guidance.

10.77 still. This word may perform as an adjective, adverb, conjunction, or noun, but most punctuation problems surface when it functions as an adverb. The meanings it is capable of assuming as an adverb and conjunction are shown below the speech-part headings below. Matching how you want to use the word with the one of these definitions can be quite helpful in determining the correct punctuation.

| NOUN: | It happened in the *still* of the night |
| ADJECTIVE: | Like they say, *still* waters run deep |

ADVERB

yet:	*Still*, none of us had the background to challenge his argument.
not having stopped:	*Still* raining in the uplands, the people in the lowlands began to get worried.
now (as previously):	The roll was taken; *still* A.W.O.L. was Private Toots.
all the same:	I know it's not good for me, but I crave it *still*.
	Still, I'd rather be in Philadelphia.

CONJUNCTION

| nevertheless: | It's not much; *still*, it's the best I could do. |

66

VERB

INTRANSITIVE: *Stilled,* the horse finally accepted its rider.

10.78 **suppose.** When it leads off one sentence which is immediately elaborated upon by another, a colon (:) should be inserted between those two sentences. However, this often requires editing, as shown below in the first two examples. It and the pronoun "I" may interrupt or be added to a sentence, requiring the use of the comma to set them apart (*see* third and fourth examples below).

ORIGINAL: ~~Let us~~ suppose we did this. ~~For example, suppose~~ ~~we~~ turn Act Three into Act One and ~~then~~ drop Act Two altogether.

EDITED VERSION: *Suppose we did this:* turn Act Three into Act One and drop Act Two altogether.

INTERRUPTION: These things, *I suppose,* have been on your mind.
ADD-ON: She's his sister, *I suppose.*

10.79 **sure.** Punctuation problems may surface when it acts as an adverb and is synonymous with *indeed* or *of course,* or when it joins another word to form a new concept that can be an adjective or noun.

OF COURSE: *Sure,* it's easy for you to say that now.
                          The details, *sure,* will have to be worked out.
                          I like her, *sure.*

INDEED: Oh *sure,* I believe he's telling the truth.
                          I believe he's telling the truth—*sure.*

MEANS...
    really: He *sure-enough* tried, I'll say that for him.
    reliable: That's a *sure-fire* way of getting yourself killed.

STANDS ALONE: *Sure.* And I'm the Tooth Fairy.
NOUN: Jingo said it was a *sure thing.*
LEADS PHRASE: *Sure as I'm sitting here,* that's what she told me.
                          He's coming—*sure as anything!*

10.80 **that.** Capable of serving as an adjective, pronoun, adverb, or conjunction; it may even launch a stand-alone phrase. Further, it should be used instead of the pronoun "who" when the indefinite article "the" precedes the noun. (*See pronoun* below.) But most punctuation problems surface when it performs as a conjunction and links two sentences. Below the heading CONJUNCTION are the meanings it may assume when it serves as that part of speech.

ADJECTIVE
  Repetitive: I felt that I had once been in *that* town, *that* house, *that* room, *that* bed.

PRONOUN
  Related
  sentences: *That* is the source of all my troubles; *that* will prove to be my final undoing.

  Follows "the":   The Hamilton *that* I'm talking about was the Secretary of the Treasury, not the city in Ohio.

STAND-ALONE
PHRASE: *That* it would only be true!

CONJUNCTION
  seeing that: *That* none of them could be charged with anything, he decided not to prosecute.

  as a fact that: You must accept *that* it happened.

  in order that: He blew the bugle sweeter than usual, *that* everyone would pause and reflect on his friend's passing.

  so that: He moved his chair closer to hers, *that* they might talk and hear one another.

  because: The athlete sighed *that* he could not do what he once could.

  when: It seemed only yesterday *that* she was sixteen and in love with Horace Hemp.

Exception: **Repetitive conjunction.** When used as a repetitive conjunction, identical words must be implied before each entry. In the example below, the words *she became convinced* are implied before the last two insertions of the word, each of which is preceded by a comma (,).

She became convinced *that* their families would begin to squabble if they married, *that* she would be ostracized by marrying someone outside her faith, *that* they would never allow her to return.

But if phrases are added to one or more of the entries, precede "that" with a semicolon (;). In the example which follows, the extra phrases have been cast in italics for your quick identification.

She became convinced that their families would begin to squabble if they married; that she would be ostracized, *without a doubt,* by marrying someone outside her faith; that they would never allow her to return, *even if she begged them.*

10.81 **then.** Besides acting as an adverb and conjunction, it can function as an adjective (e.g., the *then* Secretary of Agriculture....) and a noun (e.g., That was *then;* now is now). Most punctuation problems occur, though, when it serves as a conjunction or adverb. Below, under those headings, are the definitions which this word is capable of assuming in a sentence—definitions which can be quite helpful in determining the correct punctuation.

ADVERB
at that time:	There were few in the room *then.*
soon afterward:	The team, *then,* tied the score.
next:	*Then,* we tried to prime the pump.

CONJUNCTION
as a consequence:	She called him a liar to his face; *then,* h e slammed the door and left.
in that case:	Vanilla costs less than chocolate? *Then,* let's get vanilla.

10.82 **thereabout.** Below are the meanings this adverb is capable of assuming in a sentence.

NEAR THAT:	It weighed sixteen tons, or *thereabout.*
APPROXIMATELY:	It cost a thousand dollars, *thereabout.*

10.83 **thereafter.** Below are the definitions which this adverb is capable of assuming in a sentence. Match how you are using the word with one of them and it will help you solve your punctuation problem.

ACCORDINGLY:	I was accused of something that I didn't do; *thereafter,* the stigma of it placed my acquittal in dark shadows.
FROM THAT TIME ON:	I was, *thereafter,* a hermit for ten years. I was a hermit *thereafter.*

10.84 **thereby.** Below are the definitions which this adverb is capable of assuming in a sentence. Match how you are using the word with one of them and it will help you solve your punctuation problem.

NEARBY:	It is in the house or *thereby.* *Thereby* was the enemy's camp.

CONNECTED
WITH THAT: The old neighborhood was declining; *thereby*, the small entrepreneurs began leaving as well.

10.85 **therefore.** This is an adverbial conjunction, and the meanings which it may assume are as follows: (1) *on that account* or *ground;* (2) *consequently;* (3) *hence;* (4) *for this* or *that reason.* Unless it enters a sentence with no preceding pause, it is usually set off by one or two commas (,).

WORD IS
REMOVABLE: *Therefore*, they had made no plans concerning what to do if disaster occurred.

He tried, *therefore*, to find some other way of getting them to pay the debt.
She was unable to do anything, *therefore*.

PHRASE IS
REMOVABLE: *Therefore believing the witch was in the well*, he tried to make an appointment at the soothsayer's office.

He forgot to pick up the salami at the store, *therefore leading them to think he was stupid*, and they sent him back to get it.

She had lied to him before, *therefore making him think she might be lying now*.

RELATED
SENTENCE: The tide was turning in their favor; *therefore, he began making plans on how to decorate his office in the capitol building.*

Exception: **No pause precedes it.** No comma is needed.

He *therefore* tried to find some other way of getting them to pay the debt.

Exception: **Conclusion or question follows it.** When it leads off, you may insert a colon (:) after it and capitalize the first word of the question; or you may insert a comma (,) and not capitalize the question.

COLON: *Therefore:* What right does management have to make us take those tests?

COMMA: Therefore, what right does management have to make us take those tests?

10.86 therein. Below are the meanings which this adverb is capable of assuming in a sentence. Match how you are using the word with one of them and it will help you solve your punctuation problem.

IN THAT
PLACE: *Therein* lies the answer; will you open it or shall I?

IN THAT
TIME: It occurred on the fifteenth; *therein* she had gotten married, won the lottery, and lost her luggage.

IN THAT
RESPECT: But Henry was not a church-goer. *Therein*, I suppose you could almost call him a heathen.

IN THAT
MATTER: Take a look at a city dump; *therein* lies all the ingredients for making a fortune.

10.87 thereupon. Below are the definitions which this adverb is capable of assuming in a sentence. Match how you are using the word with one of them and it will help you solve your punctuation problem.

AT ONCE: As soon as you hear the bell, run to the house *thereupon*.

IN CONSEQUENCE
OF THAT: The cat ate the mouse; *thereupon*, it came down with indigestion.

UPON IT or THAT   Falling *thereupon*, he fell asleep.

10.88 though. Below are the definitions which this conjunction is capable of assuming in a sentence. Match how you are using the word with one of them and it will help you solve your punctuation problem.

NEVERTHELESS: His heart, *though*, was in the right place.

                  The enemy had the city surrounded; *though*, it didn't affect the will of its citizenry.

                  But I still love pancakes, *though*.

GRANTING [THAT]: *Though* he didn't win the award, he still felt honored to be nominated.

                  The award—*though* some people laughed about its significance—held great meaning for him.

She was indeed pretty, *though* she had had more face-lifts than a kitchen floor in neat freak's house.

AND YET: I don't love her any more, *though* I confess that a bond still exists between us.

NOTWITHSTANDING
THE FACT THAT: It it a cause that is certainly just, *though* many innocent people are going to be hurt along the way.

10.89 **thus.** Below are the definitions which this adverb is capable of assuming in a sentence. Match how you are using the word with one of them and it will help you solve your punctuation problem.

IN THAT CASE: *Thus,* no bears were there.

SO: Their mood *thus* far is more conciliatory than antagonistic.

THEREFORE: The problem, *thus,* can be identified.

   Thus: The whole field of auto design shifted dramatically when that car became popular.

TO SUCH
A DEGREE: Because the market had fallen *thus,* Peter lost most of his life savings.

IN THAT or THIS
MANNER: Since things had developed *thus,* what choice did he have?

10.90 **till.** This word refers to the subject of time, and it is a conjunction if it substitutes for any of the meanings shown below. When it leads an introductory group of words, a comma (,) will be needed after the last word of that group; otherwise no accompanying punctuation is required.

UNTIL: *Till* Wilma says she wants our help, I think we had better stay out of it.

No pause: I think we had better stay out of it *till* Wilma says she wants our help.

UP TO SUCH
TIME AS: *Till* she discovered a few things, he didn't see any reason to tell what happened.

72

He didn't see any reason to tell what happened *till she discovered a few things.*

Exception:	**Strong pause is needed before the word.** Insert a dash (—).

I will never do any more work for them—*till* they pay me, that is.

10.91 too. Below are the meanings which this adverb is capable of assuming in a sentence. Match how you are using the word with one of them and it will help you solve your punctuation problem.

IN ADDITION:	*Too,* they had begun to curtail loans.
	They had begun to curtail loans, *too.*
ALSO:	Their roof, *too,* was developing a leak.
EXTREMELY:	It is *too* beautiful.
INDEED:	She is *too* married!
	I am *too!*
LIKEWISE:	And Jerry felt he deserved a cookie *too.*

10.92 unless. Acts as either a preposition or a conjunction. If it means the same as *excepting,* it is a preposition and the verb is only implied. In the second example, the verb *happens* is implied.

PREPOSITION

except: It would never have happened *unless* for that.

excepting: *Unless* an earthquake [happens], I think it's safe to say that the house will be standing tomorrow.

CONJUNCTION

except that: *Unless* we stand by our principles, they will continue to take advantage of us.

if it be not
a fact that: I think Sheila just walked into that store, *unless* I'm mistaken.

Exception:	**Strong pause needed.** Insert a dash (—) before it.

He had never hit a home run in his life—*unless,* of course, you count that time when he played PeeWee Ball.

Exception:	**Leads a complete thought which cannot be removed.** When that sentence rounds out the meaning initiated by the other sentence, no

comma should precede it. A pause will rarely be detected before it.

I won't say anything *unless* you do.

10.93 **until.** This word performs as either a preposition or a conjunction, and the rules which govern it are not unlike those which apply to the word "till," explained earlier in this section. As a conjunction it precedes a complete thought; as a preposition, it leads a phrase.

PREPOSITION

up to the
time of: *Until* the gunfire, I didn't think they were really serious about robbing the place.

up to *Until* then, I thought she would change.

> But if these prepositional phrases are placed last, there is no pause before the first one and no comma is needed; in the second one, however, it might be necessary to keep the comma to force a pause and prevent any confusion.

I didn't think they were really serious about robbing the place *until* [I heard] the gunfire.

I thought she would change, *until* then.

before: The concert doesn't start *until* nine.
(preceded by
a negative)

CONJUNCTION

to the
time when: *Until* we meet again, I hope you get saddle sores all over your body.

No one, *until* Bingo Billy rode two horses at the same time, had ever tried the dumb stunt before.

to the (place
degree) that: Deputy Pugh Puggins wanted justice to be served, *until* he finally found himself biting his knuckles in desperation.

Exception: **Strong pause before it.** Insert a dash (—).

He thought he would never fall in love—*until* he met he.

Exception:	**Leads a complete thought which cannot be removed.** When it leads a complementary sentence which rounds out the meaning initiated by the other sentence, no comma should precede it. A pause will rarely be detected before it.
	Don't fire *until* you see the whites of their eyes.

10.94 up *See* the word "down" for punctuation guidance.

10.95 used. Applicable when writing about the past.

| INCORRECT: | He *use* to do it, but no more. |
| CORRECT: | He *used* to do it, but no more. |

10.96 well. This comfortable, handy—though sometimes abused—word can serve as an adjective, adverb, interjection, noun, and verb. During conversations people often start sentences with it, for it acts as a natural pause.

INTRODUCES:	*Well,* what did you expect?
Emphasized:	*Well*—are you coming or not?
INTERRUPTS:	Yeh, *well,* that's what you say.
	The evidence—*well,* I guess you could call it that—amounted to nothing more than a one-line note.
IN A SERIES:	*Well, well, well, well, well!* What have we here?
STANDS ALONE:	*Well!* Did you ever see such a thing?
LEADS PHRASE:	*Well before noon,* Henrietta had cleaned the house.
Emphasized:	I told her he was fine—*well as could be expected.*

10.97 west. *See* the word "east" for punctuation guidance.

10.98 what. This often-used word can perform as an adjective, adverb, conjunction, or pronoun. The meanings it can assume as an adverb and conjunction are listed under those headings. Matching how you are using the word with one of them can be helpful in determining what kind of punctuation to use.

ADJECTIVE:	*What* malarky! *What* stupidity!
	In *what* manner did he speak?
ADVERB (+ with) partly as a result of	He won the election, *what with* his outrageous campaign promises and *what with* his family's reputation.

75

CONJUNCTION

as well as:	She did *what* she could.
so far as:	*What* I know about it, he could be the one.

PRONOUN

Question:	What?
	She told him what?
Surprise:	What! I don't believe it!
	What! are you kidding me?

Related	
sentence:	The prime minister resigned; *what* followed was chaos in Parliament.
Repetitive:	Tell me *what* you want, *what* you expect me to do specifically, *what* you think this company will gain by it.

EXPRESSION

Introduces:	*What the blazes*, let's go ahead and do it.
Interrupts:	But then, *what the heck*, it's not my fault.
Add-on:	Give it a try, *what the hell*.

Exception:	**Followed by, but not joined to, the word "ever."** When the word *ever* is separated from *what* , it assumes the meaning of *in the world* and no punctuation is necessary. In the sentence below, it would otherwise read *What in the world can this mean?* If it is joined to the word, it becomes a pronoun.

What ever can this mean?

10.99 **when** and **where.** Either of these often-used words may serve as an adverb, noun, or pronoun, although most punctuation questions occur when they appear as adverbs. When either leads off a sentence, they usually launch a complete thought and no punctuation need immediately follow them. There are, however, occasions when that is not true. (See "First Word" below.) Using *where* as the sample word, here are some punctuation situations:

PARTS OF SPEECH

adverb:	You said you called *where?*
noun:	Don't give me the *"where,"* tell me when.
pronoun:	Can you tell me *where* this happened?

FIRST WORD

No punctuation:	*Where* did all this take place?

Strong pause follows:	*Where:* The Blue Room of the Plaza Hotel.
Interruption follows:	*Where,* just where, did you hear that?
Emphasized:	*Where*—will you just tell me that?

INTERRUPTION

Commas:	Down in Keester, *where the ballplayers take spring training,* they're trying to get the residents to vote for a new ballpark.
Dashes:	In Dartmouth Place—*where, if legend is correct, Johnny Bobb wrote his famous letter to the mayor of Woodbridge, expressing his disdain of taxes*—there is now being taken under consideration the abolition of the vote.
Quick comment:	In Dartmouth Place (Where is that, anyway?) there is supposed to be a bronze memorial to the Stone family.

ADD-ON

One:	It took place on the lovely greens of Tabbatha Place, *where* Chico Chunk once kissed Bella Bubbles square on her choppers.
Several:	He wanted to travel where kings had walked, *where* poets had felt, *where* armies had conquered, *where* priests had prayed, and *where* they bagged those little sassy seeds.

But if phrases are added to the complete thoughts, separate the original entries with semicolons (;) and the phrases with commas (,). For quick identification, the extra phrases have been italicized below.

He wanted to travel where kings had walked, *dragging their servants behind them;* where poets had felt, *just after their morning hangovers;* and where they bagged those little sassy seeds, *which came shelled and unshelled.*

CONJUNCTION OMITTED: Traffic was held up for fourteen days; *where* the accident was, there is now a marble monument standing.

77

STRONG PAUSE: The answer was simple: *where* the cars were parked would have to be the site of the new building.

Question: I ask you one thing: *Where* was Edgar Puff when we needed him?

SERIES: Who, what, *where*, *when*, and how: these are the questions one must find the answer to, in developing a story.

LAST WORD: For heaven sakes, not when—*where!*
STANDS ALONE: Where?

Where. Did you hear that, fellas? He wants to know where.

10.100 whenever. This is an adverb and adverbial conjunction. It represents the words *at whatever time*.

ADVERB: You're welcome at my place—*whenever*.

CONJ. *Whenever* I graduate from college, I'm going to be among the first to say, "I told you so."

10.101 whensoever. Punctuation accompanying this word is similar to that found under the rule pertaining to "whenever."

10.102 where. See the word "when" for punctuation assistance.

10.103 whereas. To the left of the sample sentences below are the definitions which this conjunction is capable of assuming in a sentence, which can be quite helpful when deciding when—or if—to use punctuation.

WHEN IN TRUTH: Burt told them that he had never seen the house before, *whereas* he had often stayed there overnight.

SEEING THAT: *Whereas* the party of the first part broke the agreement, the party of the second part is just plain mad about it.

10.104 whereby. This is an adverb and adverbial conjunction. As an adverb it launches a question, representing the words *by what* or *how;* as a conjunction it can mean *through which, near,* or *by.* In the second sentence below it represents *through which.*

Whereby did you come by your fortune?

CONJ: He went to the Veteran's Bureau, *whereby* he hoped to get a work permit.

10.105 **wherefore.** This is an adverb and adverbial conjunction that is rarely if ever used in the United States any more. As an adverb it begins a question, representing the words *why, to what end,* and *for what reason.* As a conjunction, it means *for which reason.* In the first sentence example below, it the words *to what end* are implied.

ADVERB: If you did not do it for your own gratification, *wherefore* were the acts committed?
CONJ: The economy could no longer function on false pretenses, *wherefore* it fell with such a clatter that everyone's hopes were crushed beneath the rubble.

10.106 **wherein.** This is an adverb and adverbial conjunction. As an adverb it begins a question, representing the words *in what* or *in what regard.* As a conjunction, it means *inside of which.* In the first example below, it is assuming the definition *in what regard.*

ADVERB: If that is true, then *wherein* is the other false?

CONJ: There stood the Billiker Building, *wherein* John Billiker had planned for and made fortunes on the backs of others.

10.107 **whereof.** This is an adverb and adverbial conjunction, though it is rarely if ever used in the United States today. As an adverb it begins a question, representing the words *from what* or *of what.* As a conjunction, it stands for *of which* or *of whom.* Consider using these actual definitions rather than the word itself.

10.108 **whereon.** This is an adverb and adverbial conjunction, though it is rarely if ever used in the United States today. As an adverb it begins a question, representing the words *from what* or *of what.* As a conjunction, it stands for *of which* or *of whom.* Consider using these actual definitions rather than the word itself.

10.109 **whereupon.** This is an adverb and adverbial conjunction, but in the United States its role as an adverb (used to begin a question) is completely outdated. But it still shows up as a conjunction, where it represents the words *after which, in consequence of which,* and *upon which.* Below it is acting as a conjunction.

Pete flicked mashed potatoes at Ansul, *whereupon* Ansul returned the favor by squirting him with apple juice.

10.110   wherever. This is an adverbial conjunction. In the examples which follow, it is always connecting two sentences—no matter where it is inserted. If there is a pause before or after its word group, insert a comma (,).

Wherever you go, I go.
I thought I would stop *wherever* that road ended.
You can go to hell, *wherever* that may be.

10.111   whether. This conjunction helps to introduce alternative possibilities in the sentence, and it is always followed by *or*, another conjunction. A comma is not required before "or" unless "whether" is repeated.

FOLLOWED BY...

or   *Whether* he graduated from Belleview High *or* San Paulo High, I cannot say.

But if a verb follows the alternative led by *or*, no comma after the phrase is needed.

Whether he graduated from Belleview High *or* San Paulo High <u>is</u> not the point of this discussion.

or whether   I think you should tell us *whether* you believe that, or *whether* you don't.

He didn't actually say whether he did—or *whether* he didn't.

If "whether" begins the sentence and another sentence is attached by means of a comma (,), the comma before "or whether" is omitted.

Whether he attended Belleview High *or whether* it was another school, I don't think it matters.

"OR NOT" IMPLIED

Implied   I think he should know *whether* she is telling the truth. [or not]

Not implied   She wanted the room painted blue, *whether* or not.

10.112   which. A comma (,) only precedes this pronoun when it begins information which could easily be omitted from the sentence without causing confusion, or any harm to the sentence. Such information simply provides extra knowledge about the thing you are writing about and needs to be set apart, usually coming in the form of an interrupting or add-on phrase. It may also be capitalized and begin a sentence if a heavy pause needs to be indicated before it.

CAN'T REMOVE: Wasn't it the Guru Canyon *which fell in on itself?*

I like the parties *which start early and end late.*

REMOVABLE
   Interrupts: These eggs, *which are ready to hatch new chicks,* were purchased at the supermarket yesterday.

   Add-on: He crossed the state line on a three-wheel motorcycle, *which is against the law.*

HEAVY PAUSE: After that, Homer kept his mouth shut all through dinner. *Which* was akin to stopping a runaway freight train dead in its tracks.

10.113   **while.** The meanings which this conjunction may assume are shown below. By matching how you wish to use the word with one of these shown below, it is easier to determine if it needs be preceded by a comma.

AS LONG AS: How can I go *while* you have my rubber ducky?

While I was bringing home the bacon, everything was fine.

AT THE SAME
TIME AS: Then, *while* you're trying to get the car started, I'll bake some bread.

While you were playing chess, I noticed your dog was smoking your pipe.

ALTHOUGH: He may have said he performed extensive research, *while* I happen to know he didn't.

WHEREAS: He obeyed, *while* the others would not.

10.114   **who.** Precede this pronoun with a comma (,) when you are trying to differentiate one person from another. Look at the first sentence example below: Jack has more than one sister; therefore the information following *who* is added to help clarify which one is being written about. But if Jack only had ONE sister, differentiation is no longer a problem; so the information following *who* becomes unimportant to the true meaning of the sentence and needs to be set apart (see second example).

NEED TO
DIFFERENTIATE: Jack's sister *who got a divorce last week* sat down alongside me and began talking about turnips.

NO NEED TO
DIFFERENTIATE: Jack's sister, *who got a divorce last week,* sat down alongside me and began talking about turnips.

Exception: **"Who" and its information cannot be removed after a noun or pronoun.** No comma is needed before the word when its removal seriously weakens the meaning being conveyed.

I think it was his sister Betty *who got a divorce last week.*

It was they *who* got the rumor started about the world being round.

Exception: **Interruption immediately follows "who."** A comma (,) will have to be inserted before and after it when no differentiation is being made between that person and another; but only place punctuation AFTER the pronoun when a distinction must be made (*see* second sentence). The interruption has been underlined for your quick identification.

Jack's sister, *who,* <u>from what I hear,</u> got a divorce last week sat down alongside me and began talking.

Jack's sister *who,* <u>from what I hear,</u> got a divorce last week sat down alongside me and began talking.

Exception: **Followed by, but not joined to, the word "ever."** When the word *ever* is separated from *who*, it assumes the meaning of *in the world* and no punctuation is necessary. For example, the first sentence below would otherwise read *Who in the world are you talking*

82

about? But if the words are joined, both become a single pronoun.

Who ever are you talking about?

10.115 **why.** This word may serve as an adverb, interjection, or noun. As a an adverb, it usually represents the words *for what reason* (or *cause*); as an interjection, it indicates surprise. The sentence examples provide punctuation guidance.

PARTS OF SPEECH

Adverb:	I can't say *why* he went.
	I can't say *why* he went, *why* he didn't take a shorter route, *why* he didn't stay there, nor *why* he decided to come back.
Interjection:	*Why!* Will anyone answer that question for me?
Noun:	Forget about the "why"; concern yourself with the "who."

FIRST WORD

Pause follows:	*Why,* you don't know what you're talking about.
Common expression:	*Why sure,* I guess we can do that all right.
Series:	*Why, why, why,* Maria?

QUESTION

After intro:	When you really think about it, *why* would any-one want to buy something that old?

When a question asked by someone or one's self is being repeated, it is capitalized.

	And I kept asking myself, Why, why, why would he do such a thing?
After a strong pause:	It leaves one haunting question: *Why* did he leave in the middle of the night and come back?
	Not who—*why?!*
Personal comment:	It was reported that the gun was registered in her name, that she had been seen carrying it (*Why*

haven't any witnesses testified to that?), that she bore a grudge against him and had sworn she'd get even.

INTERRUPTION
Emphasized:

I had never expected the day to be so hot—*Why, it would burn a man's brains out!*—and I got to the point where I would have jumped into pond scum.

Comment:

They are convinced (*why* I shall never know) that spring follows summer.

LAST WORD
Series:

In journalism you have to get the who, what, where, when, and *why*.

10.116 **yes.** *See* the word "no" for punctuation assistance.

10.117 **yet.** This is an adverb and conjunction which can assume several different meanings, and it is interchangeable with the word *still*, which has been explained elsewhere in this section—except that *yet* may be preceded by a negative such as *not*. While it may assume several different meanings in a sentence, punctuation dilemmas usually only occur when it is acting as a conjunction. During those times, it introduces what can only be called contrary information. The meanings it may assume as a conjunction are shown at the left, below.

ALTHOUGH [IT WAS]:
BUT [HE IS]:
NEVERTHELESS:

It was funny, *yet* amateurishly done.
He is kind, *yet* quite temperamental.
I heard as much, *yet* I don't believe it.

STILL:

Yet to hear from her husband in twenty years, she nevertheless believed he would come to his senses and return to her.

Exception:

Appears in the middle rather than at the beginning of an interrupting phrase. Commas are not needed to set it apart.

There you have it—fiscally sound, simple *yet* innovative, with no chance of recession.

Exception:

Needs to be emphasized at the end of a sentence. Insert a dash (—) before it.

You haven't seen anything—*yet*.

Adjective

The adjective describes a noun. To write "The man searched the cupboard" says little about him. But by simply placing the adjective "hungry" before "man," more significance is added: "The *hungry* man searched the cupboard." Two adjectives may be used: "The *blind* and *hungry* man searched the cupboard; or more than two: "The *blind, hungry*, and *desperate* man searched the cupboard." Moreover, the adjective may come after the noun rather than before: "The man was *hungry* and *desperate*."

11.1 **Adjective is the first word.** When it can be removed without being missed, the comma (,) should be used to set it apart from the other information. But when the word is part of an opening phrase, the comma (,) follows the last word of that phrase.

REMOVABLE: *Victorious,* he vigorously raised his fist in the air while his opponents were shaking theirs back at him.

LEADS PHRASE: *Every* movement having been monitored with regard to his opponent, Weezel decided he was facing someone who knew nothing about politics.

11.2 **Midsentence adjective.** When it is an integral part of the sentence and can be read without any noticeable pause before it, no punctuation is needed to set it apart; but if it is removable, use commas (,) to isolate it. Insert a comma before it when it leads off a removable phrase, and put another one after the last word of that phrase.

INTERRUPTS: The politician, *victorious,* realized he would soon be expected to govern.

PART OF PHRASE
   Interrupts: It was Tom's weakness, *every* time he went there, to try to convince the old man he had been right.

   Added to: She wanted it, *every* last acre of it.
   Dramatic: She wanted it—*every* last acre of it.

   Can't remove: It was Tom's weakness *every* time he went there.

SERIES
   After verb: The politician was *victorious, vindicated,* and also *vexed* over his unexpected popularity.

            To defend this land I want *every* man, woman, and child; *every* dog, chicken, and cow; *every* gun and slingshot; every car and wagon; *every* last thing that can move or be moved, to be at my disposal.

Added to: She wanted it—*every* acre, *every* tree, *every* stone, *every* drop of water.

11.3 **Adjective ends the sentence.** If the adjective cannot be removed from the end of a sentence without being missed, no punctuation is needed before it. However, if it acts as an add-on word—that is, an afterthought—a preceding comma will be necessary. Use a colon (:) when a strong pause can be detected before it and it acts as a one-word summarization, etc. Employ the dash (—) if more drama is desired.

COMMA: He stood before the shouting crowd, *victorious.*

DASH: And here, today, he was standing before the shouting crowd—*victorious.*

COLON: If you follow these guidelines we have developed for your campaign, you will find that you can only be one thing: *victorious.*

11.4 **Two-word adjective.** When two words combine to help describe a noun or pronoun, a separating hyphen (-) is usually required. If the second word ends in *ing, ed, en,* or *d,* a hyphen is usually required before it.

2 WORDS: This *see-saw* attitude of yours is cutting me the wrong way.

"ING" The *innocent-acting* prisoner proved to be as guilty as they said he was.

11.5 **Three-word adjective.** Two hyphens (-) are needed when a three-word adjective is created.

They were a pair of *rough-and-ready* guys.

Exception: **Two of the words are frequently seen together** (e.g., *Revolutionary War, Boston Massacre,* etc.). Hyphens are not used at all; instead a dash (—) is required, and its placement depends upon the nature of the adjective itself. In the first example below, *World War One* is the three-word adjective that modifies "era," and the dash comes after the prefix "Pre." In the second example, however, *Kansas City* and *Miami* are the adjectives, and the dash is placed between them.

In the *Pre*—World War One era, we thought there would be no more wars.

He booked a ticket on the *Kansas City*—Miami flight.

11.6 **Two pairs of adjectives.** This is not a situation which often arises, but that it exists at all is worth noting here. A perfect example is *good cop bad cop* or *nice cop tough cop*, which, as combinations, are used as either multiple-word adjectives or adverbs. As an adverb, they follow a verb and do not need separating commas. But if inserted before another noun, you will want to divide them with a virgule (/).

ADVERB: They were playing *nice cop tough cop*.
ADJECTIVE: Stop giving me that *good cop/bad cop* routine.

11.7 **City and state act as an adjective.** When a city and state precede a noun and help to describe it, no hyphens are used. Also, make sure a comma (,) follows the name of the state. But if only the city or state is used, no comma is used.

BOTH USED: The *Miami, Florida,* building contractors were up in arms about the proposed new taxes.

ONE USED: The *Miami* building developers were up in arms about the proposed new taxes.

Adverb

The adverb often causes punctuation problems. Its primary objective is to give the verb in the sentence more meaning. For example, to merely write, "She is" would make the reader ask, "She is *what?*" The adverb adds information to the verb, which in this case is the verb *is*. By inserting an adverb, the reader's question is answered: "She is *here*." Two adverbs in a row may be used: "She is *here, somewhere*." Or it may be an adverbial phrase: "She is *by my side*."

The adverb (words which end with the letters "ly" are almost always adverbs) tells the reader where, or when, or why, or how, or to what degree something was, is, or will be done. And it may appear before or after the verb, though not immediately. In this sentence, for example, the *degree* is provided: "*Frequently*, what I like is biscuits and gravy on Sunday." But in this sentence, the adverb tells *when:* "If he doesn't *soon* arrive, we will have to leave without him."

12.1 **Adverb begins the sentence.** If it can be removed without being missed, a comma (,) should follow it. The same rule applies when it is part of a phrase, although the punctuation follows the last word of that phrase.

REMOVABLE: *Again,* we simply cannot afford these mistakes.

PART OF PHRASE: *Again on the defensive,* he picked up a stick and threw it at the goose.

12.2   **Midsentence adverb.** When it, or a phrase which it may lead, is an integral part of the sentence and can be read without any noticeable pause before it, no punctuation is needed to set it apart; but if the word or phrase is removable, use commas (,) to isolate it. Use a dash (—) when the adverb or adverbial phrase needs to be emphasized.

WORD

No pause: We will *again* try to do what we have yet failed to do.

Pause: The old mill, *again,* had withstood the ravages of mankind.

Comment: They lost by two points (again) and drowned their sorrows in a barrel of chocolate milkshakes (again).

Related sentence: You probably think I'm cooking for your benefit only; *again,* you're wrong.

PHRASE:

Interrupts: Jim Fedders, *again accepting the challenge from Boris,* soon wished he'd kept his mouth shut.

Added to: He accepted the role in the play, *again playing a tough guy with no heart.*

12.3   **Adverb ends the sentence** If it can be removed from the end of a sentence without being missed, punctuation should precede it; but when it helps to complete the thought already established in the sentence, do not separate it. Use a dash (—) if the word needs to be emphasized.

CAN'T REMOVE: Will you say that *again?*
REMOVABLE: He looked at her and laughed, *again.*
DRAMATIC: He really said it—*again!*
SERIES: They tried again, and again, and *again.*

12.4   **Adverb stands alone.** Adverbs which are capable of standing alone because of what precedes or follows them may be followed by a period (.), question mark (?), or exclamation mark (!).

PERIOD: Yes, he won the race. *Again.*
QUESTION MARK: You mean she went there? *Again?*
EXCLAMATION MARK: *Again!* It's happened again!

12.5   Adverb ends in "ly." Many adverbs which end in the letters "ly" can be punctuated in the same manner. Using the adverb *simply* as an example, here are a few ways in which such a verb might be punctuated.

BEGINNING

Removable: *Simply,* it managed to reach a wider audience at half the cost.

Sets up sentence: *Simply:* no player will be allowed practice until he or she has passed the test.

> NOTE: Only a few adverbs which end in "ly" can be followed by a colon (:) when they are first words.

Phrase: *Simply one of the best to play the game,* Gee Whilikers still offers advice to the young players.

Series: *Simply, painstakingly, and with reverence,* the minister wrote his last sermon.

MIDSENTENCE

Conjunction
missing: Edmund Whillikers spoke *simply,* movingly, almost as if he had actually been among those giants in our history.

Phrase: The garden, *simply lovely in the spring,* looked like a weed patch in late summer.

Add-on: She outdid everyone that year, *simply making her garden the showplace of the entire neighborhood.*

END

Add-on: He did it quickly, *simply.*

Exception: **Word is "respectively"** (definition: *in the order designated).* It is not set apart from the other information in the sentence when it appears as the last word.

It was divided among Bill, Sue, Harry, and Wilma *respectively.*

12.6   Two- and three-word adverbs. Words which combine with other words to form a new adverb do not usually need hyphens (-) to separate them, although there are many exceptions to this rule. Your best source is a recently published, comprehensive dictionary. Your librarian can also be of significant help.

He went *hat in hand* to the boss's office.

Conjunction

The conjunction is traditionally used to link two or more sentences together; it also separates words and phrases. As a joiner of sentences, it can act as the first word; but when linking words and phrases, it is found within the sentence. Sometimes it may even end a sentence (e.g., when you are using *though*), but in that particular instance it is not marrying sentences, words, or phrases.

13.1 **Conjunction begins a sentence.** When a conjunction is a capitalized first word, it is usually acting as a joiner of complete thoughts, which needs a comma (,) to separate them. In the first example below, *although* and its group could easily follow the word "go." whether another sentence follows its group or not. But when a sentence is not attached to its group by means of a comma, the conjunction relates to the sentence which immediately precedes it

FIRST WORD: *Although* I didn't feel like it, I decided to go.

Switched: I decided to go, *although* I didn't feel like it.

Follows up: She said absolutely no. *And* she calls herself a friend.

13.2 **Between sentences.** This is where the conjunction can usually be found. As a joiner of sentences, a comma (,) precedes it; as a joiner of phrases and words, however, it is only preceded by a comma when they are in a series and the conjunction is used to marry the last two (*see* Rule 13.3).

SENTENCES: Jonus felt absolutely no compassion for him, *and* he continued reading his paper without saying anything.

PHRASES: Jonus, feeling no compassion for him *and* quite bored with it all, continued reading his paper without saying anything.

WORDS: Jonus, uncompassionate *and* bored, continued reading his paper without saying anything.

Exception: **Two sentences of four words or less.** No comma is needed before the conjunction.

90

I felt vindicated *and* I think she did, too.

13.3 **Conjunction in a series or phrases.** Inserted before the last word or phrase in a series. Many say that it is not necessary to insert a comma (,) before the conjunction,, but not to do so is a sloppy punctuation habit that has distinct disadvantages when it is essential that the reader view the last two elements in a series as being separate. Take a look at the first example below: the store sells chicken and dumplings separately; however, if the comma is removed, it indicates that they are sold together—even though another conjunction does not precede *chicken*. Finally, when the conjunction is repeated several times, no comma is needed before it (*see* second and third sentence examples).

WORDS: At that store you could buy *sausage, wieners, turkey, hamburger, dressing, chicken,* and *dumplings.*

Conjunctions
repeated: At that store you could buy sausage *and* wieners *and* turkey *and* hamburger.

At that store you could buy sausage *or* weiners *or* turkey *or* hamburger.

PHRASES: Jim, having passed the test, having given a pint of blood, *and* even having bought that polka-dot tie, was still not permitted to join the stupid club.

13.4 **Conjunction ends the sentence.** Very few pure conjunctions are able to function as the last word, although several adverbial conjunctions can (e.g., *however*). A preceding comma (,) is the required punctuation mark.

He knew she would be there, *though.*

Indefinite Article

This part of speech is only represented by three words: *a, an,* and *the.* They cause no punctuation problems by themselves, for they cannot introduce, interrupt, or be added at the end of a sentence. Phrases which begin with any of these three are set apart by punctuation, with the comma (,) coming before them or after the last word of the phrase they introduce.

14.1 **Indefinite article begins a sentence.** Punctuation is not necessary unless it begins the second of two related sentences; in that case, insert a semicolon (;). But if it follows a strong pause and begins a sen-

91

tence that elaborates, explains, summarizes, etc., precede it with a colon
(:).

NO PUNCTUATION: *The* train sped through the depot at eighty miles
                  per hour.

SEMICOLON: Wall Street collapsed like a house of cards; *the*
                  stockbrokers couldn't even cash in their chips.

COLON: She wanted only one thing: *a* chance to get even
                  with him.

14.2   **Indefinite article begins a phrase.** Use the comma (,) to separate introductory, interruptive, and add-on phrases that begin with an indefinite article. However, use the parentheses to encase comments; and
precede it with a colon (:) when it begins an explanation, summarization, conclusion, etc.

INTRODUCTORY: *A* trustworthy soul, he believed everyone.

INTERRUPTION: The mountain climber, *an* incomparable athlete,
                  slid all the way down the little hill.

  Dramatic: He handed her the gift—*the* one which was wrapped
                  in pink paper—thinking that she would decline it.

  Comment: If you find the answer to that (*a* formidable task,
                  indeed), you can find the answer to anything.

ADD-ON   None of the players were hurt, *the* linebacker being
                  an exception.

  Dramatic: Truly, it was an injustice—an outrage that shud-
                  dered their bones.

EXPLAINS: It was called the "Watusi": *a* tribal dance that was
                  exported from Africa and modernized in America.

SERIES: It's that easy—*a* cup of vegetable soup, bread, *a*
                  glass of ice tea, and the meal is complete.

Exception: **Interruption is short, begins with "the,"
                  and no pause can be detected before it.** No
                  punctuation is needed before the indefinite article.

                  We *the people* have a great investment in this na-
                  tion.

Interjection

The interjection is inherently dramatic and usually stands alone, demanding that an exclamation mark (!) follow it; in fact, when writing fiction the exclamation mark may even come at midsentence. The author Lewis Carrol used this technique to great effect when writing *Alice in Wonderland* (*see* Rule 15.2). Some interjections, however, may simply be used as pauses at all points within a sentence. As such, they only need to be separated by commas (,).

15.1 **Interjection stands alone.** Follow it with an exclamation mark (!). Some interjections are longer than one word. The question mark (?) may sometimes follow the exclamation mark when more emphasis is needed, but it is punctuation technique that should be sparingly.

ONE WORD:	Whoopee! Wow!
MORE THAN ONE:	*All right already!* Stop complaining! Okay!?

Exception: **Showing sarcasm.** Follow the interjection with a period (.).

Your mother-in-law is coming to visit us? And she's going to stay for the summer? Whoopee.

15.2 **Midsentence interjection.** When used as a pause, the comma (,) should accompany the interjection rather than the exclamation mark. But on those occasions when you would like to dramatize the word at midsentence, the exclamation mark (!) may be inserted immediately after the word, even though it does not end the sentence—a technique, however, which should be employed only sparingly.

PAUSE   *Golly,* I don't know whether I will or not.
When you put it like that—*gee,* I guess so
So that's the way you feel about it, *huh?*

DRAMATIZED: Then I heard a *bang!* on the door.

Exception: **Interjection serves as a verb.** Do not follow it with an exclamation mark. Among the interjections which serve as verbs include, for example, *behold, cease, charge, crash, desist, fire, hark, hold, hush, imagine, listen, look, say, shoot,* and *stop.* But in some fiction writing, this rule may sometimes be broken.

Will you please *stop* doing that?

Exception: **Interjection acts as a noun.** No punctuation should follow it. Among those which are capable of doing that include *attention, bingo, crash, dear, fire, fore, gangway, good* (also an adjective), *goodness, hold, hush, look, nuts, rats, rubbish, well,* and *woe.*

And a *hush* fell over the crowd.

Noun

A noun provides the name of a person, group, place, thing, philosophy, action, etc. While they share many similar punctuation situations, not all can be treated absolutely alike.

Note: Unless a noun is a one-word title, it should ever be italicized. They have only been italicized in the sentence examples for your convenience, so you may quickly identify them.

16.1 **Noun stands alone.** For a noun to stand alone, the information which precedes or follows it must be highly supportive. Such a noun may be followed by a period (.), exclamation mark (!), or question mark (?).

PERIOD: *Greed.* It will be the characteristic trait of the 1980s.
QUES. MK. What do you want? *Money? Fame? Honor?*
EXCL. MK. *Wilfred!* Come here this instant!

16.2 **Noun begins the sentence.** Punctuation follows and separates it from the other information in these instances: (1) a strong pause follows it, in which case a colon should represent that pause; (2) it is part of a series, requiring a comma after it; or (3) someone is being addressed, in which case a comma is needed.

STRONG PAUSE: *Responsibility:* it is the meeting of one's obligations without any guidance.

SERIES: *Responsibility,* caring, and intelligence were the hallmarks of his life.

ADDRESSING
SOMEONE: *Jerry,* please open the door for me.

Exception: **Strong pause needs more drama.** Use a dash (—) instead of a colon. A series of words may likewise be set apart in the same manner.

94

Responsibility—that's something you wouldn't know anything about.

Responsibility, caring, and intelligence—that's what I said and that's what I meant!

16.3 **Noun interrupts the sentence.** It will need a comma (,) before and after it, unless it is being dramatically inserted into the sentence; in that case, use the dash (—). The dash is often employed to set off an interrupting noun when other commas precede it in the sentence (*see* second example). If there are two nouns side by side, with the second one interrupting the sentence and identifying the other noun, separate them with a comma (*see* third example).

COMMA: And then, *Thursday,* we will implement our plans.

DASH: That singular, horrendous word—*cancer*—raised the hair on my neck when I heard the doctor say it.

IDENTIFIES: Their leader, *Doug Peterson,* gave a six-hour speech and put everyone to sleep.

Exception: **Noun is a quick explanation or identi-fica-tion.** Place it inside a parentheses.

                 It is my opinion that the caretaker (Willy Laxlow) entered the hall and blew his nose at the most inopportune time.

Exception: **"The" is omitted before a job title.** Do not separate the nouns with a comma, which in this case is "Chief Accountant" and "Fred Flux."

                 You could always see Chief Accountant *Fred Flux* at the doughnut shop.

16.4 **Noun is the last word of a sentence.** A sentence-ending noun is separated by punctuation in these instances:

1. *Acts as a one-word repeat of the information which precedes it.* Precede it with a comma (,) when the pause before it is slight.

    That's what I like most of all, *lollipops.*

2. *Strong pause precedes it.* Precede the noun with a colon (:). However, use the dash (—) instead if you want to dramatize the word.

95

It is the one thing he never had: *courage.*
It is the one thing he never had—*courage.*
What will it cost you? Four hundred dollars—*tops.*

3. *The conjunction "and" is missing before it.* Insert a comma (,).

She wanted to create competition, *jealousy.*

16.5 **One-word hyphened nouns.** There are some nouns that, even though they are not combined with another word, have hyphens of their own. Check your dictionary, or call your librarian, if you have a noun that you think may need hyphens.

Hamilton was George Washington's *aide-de-camp.*

16.6 **Two- and three-word nouns.** One or more hyphens (-) are needed to separate the words, although there are many exceptions to this rule. In the first sentence which follows, neither word is a noun by itself; in the second example, only the last one is. However, in the last two examples both words are nouns, and in one instance they are written as separate words; in the other, they are combined. Rather than guess, it is better to find your word combination in a comprehensive dictionary.

1 HYPHEN:	Billy Bumpkin was an *also-ran* during the election.
2 HYPHENS:	She was my *great-great-grandmother.*
SEPARATED:	What's the company's *box number?*
JOINED:	His *bankbook* showed no balance.

Exception: **Preposition or conjunction separates the nouns.** No hyphens are needed.

PREP:	Did you get a *bill of sale?*
CONJ:	I'll go if my *ball and chain* will let me.

Exception: **Two-word noun acts as a description.** Do not hyphenate. In this example, *civil defense* is a two-word noun that is performing the duties of an adjective; *technique* is the noun it is describing.

Critics argue that this *civil defense* technique is virtually worthless.

16.7 **Noun shows ownership.** An apostrophe (') is used after the word, followed by the letter S.

PROPER NAME:	That's not *Jim's* boat, it's *Tom's.*
GROUP:	I guess you could that it is their *party's* motto.
	It is the *men's* prerogative to ask.

PLACE:	It is the State of Ohio's constitutional right.
	Mt. McKinley's apex can't be reached by automobile.
THING:	The heart's arteries can become clogged.
Exception:	**Noun ends with the letter S.** There are two options: (1) an apostrophe S ('s) may still be inserted after the letter, or (2) just the apostrophe may be placed after the noun's S.

EXTRA "S":	I thought it was *Phyllis's* job.
NO ADDED "S":	I thought it was *Phyllis'* job.

16.8 **Noun is joined to a verb.** Joining a noun to the verb "is" is acceptable. The "i" is omitted from the verb and replaced with an apostrophe ('). For example:

INSTEAD OF THIS....	*Jerry* is going to the Mardi Gras.
THIS....	*Jerry's* going to the Mardi Gras.

But when joining a noun to verb such as "will," extraordinary care must be taken to prevent any awkwardness. If it sounds strange, it will read strangely. In this instance, it is a technique that is restricted almost exclusively to the writing of dialogue. For example:

Burt'll be mad if he finds out. Wait and see.

16.9 **Nouns in a series.** Insert a comma (,) between each.

INTRODUCES:	*Jim, Harry, Tom,* and *Bill* will be here soon.
MIDSENTENCE:	At the table sat the *president, vice-president, secretary,* and *accountant* reading comic books.
ENDS SENTENCE:	What I like best of all is *gambling, drinking, sleeping,* and *eating.*
Exception:	**Conjunction is omitted.** The comma is still used to separate them, unless each needs more emphasis; in that case, follow them with exclamation marks (!) or question marks (?).

Jim, Harry, Tom—get in here at once!
Jim! Harry! Tom! Gosh, it's good to see you!

Preposition

The preposition shows the relationship between two nouns or pronouns—or a noun/pronoun and a word which is capable of acting as other parts of speech Regarding the latter, for example, the word *dare* can be a noun or a verb: as a verb, one might write, "I *dare* you to cross this line"; but as a noun one might write, "I accept your *dare.*"

A preposition precedes a noun or pronoun, which is why strict grammarians often insist that you should not end a sentence with a preposition (e.g., "Who are you going *with?* " should be changed to "*With* whom are you going?"), but the practice is in such wide use that most of the die-hards have long since thrown up their hands in surrender. Anyway, married to the noun or pronoun, the preposition can help form a phrase that acts as multiple-word adjective or adverb. For example, here is a prepositional phrase acting as multiple-word adverb: He found himself growing sleepy *during the last act of the play.*

17.1 **Pure prepositions.** There are many parts of speech which, as a result of where they are placed in a sentence, may function as prepositions. In fact, some are used as prepositions so frequently that one tends to forget that they pull duty as other parts of speech as well: among the most common of which include the words *after, for, in,* and *minus.*

However, the following words perform as PREPOSITIONS ONLY: *against, amid, amidst, among, at, barring, concerning, during, excepting, from, into, of, onto, per, regarding, respecting, toward,* and *with.* Therefore, you may refer to Rule 17.2 for a broad explanation regarding how to punctuate the phrases they lead.

17.2 **Guidelines for punctuating prepositional phrases.** The prepositional phrase causes more punctuation headaches than any other kind of phrase when it does not introduce a sentence. This is basically because the pause before it is practically negligible and its overall importance is not immediately recognizable. When separating punctuation is needed, the comma (,) is usually the mark of choice—unless more drama is needed, in which case the dash (—) is employed.

Generally, if you can answer yes to any of the following four questions, then accompanying punctuation will be needed to set your prepositional phrase apart from the other information in the sentence.

1. Can a definite pause be detected before or after the phrase is read?
2. Is the phrase especially long?
3. Will confusion result if the phrase is not set apart?
4. Can the phrase be easily moved to another location without causing harm to the sentence?

Below, the prepositional phrase has been crossed out to show you how the meaning of the sentence can be severely damaged without it, because they are dependent upon one another and neither can be removed.

LINK IS...

Strong:
We should drive by ~~to see if they're home.~~
We should drive by to see if they're home.

~~To fix the washer~~ we had to use hairpins.
To fix the washer we had to use hairpins.

BUT if the information after the phrase is lengthy, insert a comma (,). To test it, read the sentence as if the phrase were at the end without a preceding comma.

To fix the washer, we had to use hairpins that we borrowed from that sweet-looking chick who lives on the third floor.

Weak:
It was the greatest fight I have ever seen, *to my way of thinking.*

Two strong links

Strong/weak:
I had to tell her to tell Bill to tell my uncle, *to get my mother some perfume.*
Weak link

To get my mother some perfume, I had to tell her to tell Bill to tell my uncle.

17.3 **Preposition leads an introductory phrase.** When the phrase can be removed without being missed, set it apart by using a comma (,)

REMOVABLE: *At the beginning,* all of us believed him.
CAN'T REMOVE: *At the beginning* I want you to start.
Tested: I want you to start *at the beginning.*
PAUSE FOLLOWS: *At the very least,* you could have called.
STOP CONFUSION: *At that,* it was cheap.

Exception:
Needs emphasis. Follow it with a dash (—).

At the beginning—that's exactly where I want you to start.

Exception:
No pause follows it. When the pause after the phrase is virtually nonexistent and confusion will not result without punctuation, the comma may be omitted.

At the beginning I didn't actually believe that only Adam and Eve had that big garden all to themseleves.

17.4 **Prepositional phrase interrupts the sentence.** Except when no pause can be detected before the first word of the interruption, the prepositional phrase needs to be set apart, using the comma (,).

REMOVABLE: Terry, *at his very best,* was never the great architect that he thought he was.

NO PAUSE: They had found *at the very start* that it wouldn't do any good to complain.

Exception: **Phrase acts as interrupting personal comment.** Encase it in parentheses. No capitalization of the preposition is needed. An exclamation mark (!) or question mark (?) may be added to the phrase for emphasis or to show doubt.

They sold a hundred thousand copies of that picture (at least) to the unsuspecting tourists.

They sold (at Lorenzo's?) a hundred thousand copies of that picture to the unsuspecting tourists .

Exception: **Phrase needs to be emphasized.** Insert a dash (—) before and after it.

That room—*at the top of the stairs and to the left—* was where I optimistically planned my future.

17.5 **Prepositional phrase is added to the sentence.** It needs to be set apart by a comma (,). But if the phrase has a strong link to the other information and cannot be removed without causing confusion, the comma is omitted.

REMOVABLE: It's the kind of thing you expected to happen, *at the very least.*

CAN'T REMOVE: It was explained carefully to him yesterday that it was essential that he show up here *at my house.*

Exception: **Phrase acts as a personal comment.** Encase it within a parentheses, and put the period (.) after the last parenthesis. However, an exclamation mark (!) or question mark (?) may also be inserted before the last parenthesis if the phrase demands it. No capitalization of the preposition is needed.

I gave him the five hundred dollars (against my better judgment).

I gave him the five hundred dollars (against my better judgment!).

Exception: **Phrase needs emphasis.** Insert a dash (—) before it.

We must make sure that Festus becomes the next president—*at all costs.*

Exception: **Two prepositions are in close proximity.** It may sometimes cause confusion if the add-on prepositional phrase is not separated. Without the adverbial phrase "at ten" in the example which follows, no comma would have been needed before the second "at."

The Baxters left the party at ten, *at the host's request.*

17.6 **Prepositional phrase leads a related sentence.** When two related sentences are being joined and a prepositional phrase leads off the second one, the conjunction may be omitted and replaced by a semicolon (;). If the phrase is unremovable, no comma need follow it.

At the circus you will find clowns; *at* the Pentagon you will also discover them.

17.7 **Prepositional phrase follows a strong pause.** In this instance, it is usually leading off information which explains, summarizes, concludes, or elaborates on the information which precedes it; therefore, a colon (:) should be placed before it. A dash (—) may be used when it is necessary to dramatize that pause for special effect. If removal of the prepositional phrase would seriously damage the meaning of the sentence it introduces, as it would happen in the following two examples, do not place a comma after it.

ELABORATES: Then he added his final touch to the house: *at the south gable he included a stained glass portrait of his horse.*

CONCLUDES: The deduction is obvious: *at eleven o'clock there will be three knocks on the door, as prophesied.*

Pronoun

A pronoun is a word which acts as a substitute for a noun.

18.1 **Pronoun stands alone.** A stand-alone pronoun may be followed by a period (.), question mark (?), or exclamation mark (!). But it should relate fairly strongly to the information which precedes or follows it.

FOLLOWS: Call her tonight. Call her tomorrow. Don't call her at all. *Whatever.*

I didn't say these. *Those!*

TWO: Who? Him?

Exception: **Who** and **me.** When these two pronouns are used, they are joined by either a comma (,) or a dash (—), and me is followed by a question mark (?).

Who, me?
Who—me?

18.2 **Pronoun is immediately identified.** When the pronoun is immediately followed by information which specifies who you are writing about, or at least provides information that makes it less general in nature, the identification is is treated like any other interrupting phrase. If the pause after the pronoun is slight, use commas (,) to set off the identification; if heavy, insert a dash (—). But when it acts as a quick reminder, place the identification in parentheses.

PAUSE
    Slight: *He*, the sheriff, felt that Percival Potgut rather than Hank Hunk was the one who robbed Ezra's store.

    Heavy: *They*—the people who live up on Harrow Hill—have never tried to be friendly with us.

IDENTIFIES:
    Singular
    pronoun: But it was *she* (Martha Munch) who wrote it, not Alma Winslow.
    Plural
    pronoun: She said she wouldn't pay *them* (the repair people) a dime.

They (Millie, Monte, and Moe) asked no quarter and received none, much to their chagrin.

> But if the identification is short, begins with the indefinite article *the*, and no pause can be detected before it, no punctuation is needed after the pronoun. In this example, the interruption *the people* provides a quick identification of the pronoun *we*.

We the people have a great investment in this nation.

18.3 **Pronoun begins a phrase.** Whether the phrase introduces, interrupts, or is added to a sentence, set it off by using the comma (,).

INTRODUCTORY: *Her* mind apparently miles away from the task at hand, Sally's daydreams almost caused her to put coffee grounds in the soup.

INTERRUPTIVE: But the Anglidanians, *each* looking to fulfill some ideal which was literally impossible, managed to gridlock the conference.

ADD-ON: He walked across the desert like he said he would, *his* tongue swelling up and almost choking him.

Exception: **Interruption needs more emphasis.** A dash (—) should be inserted before and after it.

Most—*one* especially— did not want her to become a member, so they turned down her request.

Then Osgood—*another of his wild-haired projects having gone awry*—blamed everyone but himself for the way things had turned out.

18.4 **Pronoun leads an interrupting sentence.** When a pronoun-led sentence interrupts another, it will need to be set apart by dashes (—) or encased in parentheses.

PARENTHESES: They said the door was locked (I still find that hard to believe) with two latches that took six keys apiece to open.

DASH: They said the door was locked—she claimed that it wasn't—with two latches that took six keys apiece to open.

18.5 **Pronoun interrupts a sentence by itself.** Punctuation depends upon the nature of the interruption. When preceded by the normal pause,a comma (,) is required before and after the pronoun. But should

103

a heavy pause precede and follow it, a dash (—) should represent those pauses.

PAUSE

Normal: There they stood, *everyone*, looking into the shop window like forlorn waifs.

Strong: Anyone can do this—*anyone*—and I can't understand why you can't get the hang of it.

Anyone can do this—*anyone!*—and I can't understand why you can't get the hang of it!

Plan "A," Plan "B"—*whichever*—but get the job done.

But notice that in this next example only one dash is used before the pronoun; this is because, through the insertion of a comma (,) AFTER it, a brief pause is introduced rather than a sharp break. In this way, the pronoun is married to that information.

Plan "A" or Plan "B"—*whichever*, it was certain that he couldn't lose.

Exception: **Pronouns which do not have to be set off with commas.** *Himself, herself, myself, itself, themselves,* and *ourselves* do not have to be set off with commas when they follow a noun or another pronoun.

FOLLOWS

Pronoun: It is we *ourselves* who will have to pay.
You know *yourself* that I was first in line.

Noun: It was Jim *himself* who called the producer.

18.6   **Pronoun begins an add-on phrase or sentence.** Punctuation depends upon the nature of what is being added: if undramatic, a comma (,) is all that is necessary before it; if dramatic, use a dash (—).

SENTENCE: It was a way of getting even, *she figured*.

PHRASE

Undramatic: Give me the blue or red one, *either* will do.
Dramatic: I love the houses on this street—*mine most of all*.

104

18.7 **A series of pronouns.** Separate them with commas (,).

MIDSENTENCE:	I cannot say if it was *him, her,* or *Jerry* who fired the first shot.
END OF SENTENCE:	All right—I want *you, you,* and *you.*

18.8 **Pronoun ends the sentence.** A comma (,) should be inserted before it when it follows an interjection or a common expression; but when a strong pause precedes it, use a colon (:). Another option would be the dash (—), when more drama is desired. Finally, when a last-word pronoun repeats a previous pronoun—even though they are not the same, precede it with a comma.

AFTER...
Interjection	Hey, *you!*
Common exp:	Come on, *you.*
Strong pause:	There's only one likely suspect: *him.*
(dramatic)	There's only one likely suspect—*him.*

REPEATS FIRST
PRONOUN: It's a hard way to make a living, *that.*

EMPHASIZED   Yes, it affected her and me—*everybody.*
               That's right—*one.*

18.9 **Pronoun is used repetitively and shares the same lead-in words.** After the first pronoun, precede each of the others with a comma (,). In the two examples below, the information implied before each pronoun has been underlined. Notice, too, that *and waved a tearful good-by* is part of the opening statement and must be preceded by a comma to prevent it from possibly being confused with the preceding repetitive phrases.

And so General Horatio turned around and looked back at *his* mansion, *his* wife of some twenty years, *his* gardener who had seen him through hard times, and waved a tearful good-by.

He gave *his* heart and soul, his evenings off, *his* everything.

Exception: "Who" or "which" is used repetitively. Precede them with semicolons (;). *This is the same man* is implied before each pronoun in the following example.

This is the same man *who* said he would never consider political office; *who* told his friends that he would retire after the war; *who* even refused to attend the convention; *who* insisted that they take a recount when it was obvious he had won by a landslide.

18.10 Pronoun appears twice in a row. No separating comma is needed when no pause exists. The first sentence which follows is a classic example of when not to use a comma, for both pronouns are vital and cannot be removed. Furthermore, there is no pause between them. But when a definite pause does exist, as in the second example, the comma (,) is essential in order to make the reader make a split-second stop before continuing.

I told *you you* would wind up in this mess.
Of *these, these* are the best.

18.11 Pronoun indicates ownership. To show that a pronoun, has something—whether that "something" is tangible or intangible—insert an apostrophe S ('s) after its last letter. But if the pronoun is plural and already ends in S, add the apostrophe only.

SINGULAR PRONOUN: It's probably *anybody's* ball game now.
PLURAL PRONOUN: They thought it was the *others'* turn.

Exception: **Possessive pronoun.** Possessive pronouns such as *his*, *hers*, and *theirs* already imply ownership and do not need the help of an apostrophe.

It's either *theirs* or *ours*.

Exception: **It.** To indicate ownership, this pronoun must only receive the letter S without any apostrophe.

I thought *its* tail was on fire.

18.12 Pronoun joins a shortened verb. Few of us talk as precisely as this:

You had better make sure your *addition is* right or
there will be hell to pay, I will tell you that.

Instead, we might lop off the head of one word and the legs of another, and then jam the wounded things together. Remarkably, these large scale literary and verbal amputations which all of us perform on words every day will produce something which sounds far less awkward to the ear. That's why we do it. That's language. It's a shorthand that everyone understands and accepts. And, on paper, what we subtract from single words is represented by an apostrophe ('). Therefore, the sentence shown above becomes this:

You'd better make sure your *addition's* right or
there'll be hell to pay, I'll tell you that.

Using the apostrophe to join a shortened verb to a pronoun is greatly encouraged when writing dialogue. But how we TALK and how we READ are two entirely different matters. Too many contracted words on paper slows the reader down. So, keep one thing in mind: *When you are writing something other than that which contains the language of fictional characters or quotes from people living or dead, too many pronoun and verb marriages is not a good practice.* Instead, be judicious when including it. For example:

> ...and *there's* nothing I can do about it. I cannot complain to my boss nor can I tell my co-workers. I am caught between my conscience and my desire to get ahead. *They'll* pay for it, let me tell you.

18.13 **The pronoun "you" as part of a curse word.** If it and the other word stands alone, only ending punctuation is required, which may be a period (.) or an exclamation mark (!), depending upon the intensity you wish to attach to the curse word. But when it precedes, interrupts, or is added to the sentence, set off its complementary word—or words—by using the comma (,) Also, the addition of the word *why* to the curse word does not change anything, unless a question is being asked; in that case, a question mark (?) will be essential.

STANDS ALONE:	You bastard. You bastard! Why *you bastard.* Why *you so-and-so!* Damn you!
QUESTION:	Why, *you bastard?* Just tell me why.
INTRODUCES:	*You bastard,* you. *You bastard,* I saw what you did!
INTERRUPTS:	But then, *you bastard,* you had to have more.
ADD-ON:	You, *you bastard!* Oh, *you bastard.*
Exception:	**More emphasis is needed.** Use the dash (—) to divide them. This is especially true when the curse word is comprised of several words (*see* last example). *You bastard—you'll do anything, won't you!* Well, well—*you bastard.* That's right—*you rotten, stinking, no good bastard!*

107

Verb

No sentence can exist without it, for it tells the reader what the noun or pronoun is doing or has done (e.g., He *jumped* on the the politician's bandwagon), no matter if it is mental or physical action—or simply relates that the noun or pronoun IS (e.g., Bruce *is* the best). A complex sentence, which contains phrases, will almost always have more than one verb.

19.1 **Verb begins the sentence.** It needs a comma (,) after it when it can be removed without damaging the sentence. An introductory verb adds spice, not important information.

Winning, he became excited and wanted to bet even more.

19.2 **Verb begins an introductory phrase.** Such a phrase is set apart by a comma (,).

Directing her in the play, Nick realized she had untapped talent.

Exception: **Strong pause follows the phrase.** Represent the pause with a colon (:), for what follows it is providing some type of elaborating information (summarization, conclusion, etc.) Employ the dash (—) if more emphasis is needed.

Directing her in a play: the thought of it ran shudders down Nick's spine.

Directing her in a play—no, it can't be done.

19.3 **Verb interrupts the sentence by itself.** Unlike other parts of speech which may interrupt a sentence, the verb in the same situation usually adds important information and might seriously damage the meaning of the sentence if removed. But like an interrupting adjective, adverb, etc., it too must be set apart by commas (,). In this example, there are two verbs: *began*, which is absolutely crucial to the sentence, and *swimming*, which tells the reader what Ozzie was doing when he lost his fear of the water. Interrupting verbs frequently end in "ing."

Then Ozzie, *swimming*, began to lose his fear of the water.

Exception: **Two interrupting verbs side by side.** Separate them with a comma (,). Then, insert a dash (—) before the first one and another after the last one.

On two wheels—*screeching, careening*—his car came flying around the bend and almost hit Mr. Jones' cow.

108

19.4 **Verb leads an interrupting phrase.** An interrupting phrase led by a verb is set off in a sentence, using a comma (,) before and after it. A verb-led phrase often provides crucial information; but although its elimination would cause harm to the overall meaning being conveyed, it is still separated.

INTERRUPTING
PHRASES

One: Then Ozzie, *swimming* as fast as he could, saved her before she went under for the third time.

Two: Then Ozzie, *swimming* as fast as he could and *yelling* for her to hang on, saved her before she went under for the third time.

Exception: **Conjunction between two interrupting phrases is removed.** Insert a dash (—) before the first phrase and another after the second, and separate the two phrases with a comma (,).

Hortense—*losing* her reputation, *finding* sympathy in spider's thimble—didn't let things bother her voracious appetite.

19.5 **Verb begins an add-on phrase.** An add-on phrase led by a verb needs a comma (,) inserted before it, even though removal of the phrase might well leave a serious hole in the meaning being conveyed.

There went Ozzie, *swimming* as fast as he could.

Exception: **Strong pause precedes the phrase.** Represent the pause with a colon (:), for the verb and its group is providing some type of elaborating information. Employ the dash (—) if more emphasis is needed.

That's one thing I don't like about politicians: *complaining about the other fellow instead of doing what we put them in there for.*

Old man Higgins sat on his porch and hummed—*smiling like a snake that was ready to strike.*

19.6 **Verb ends a sentence.** A comma (,) will be needed before the verb when it is attached to the sentence as a one-word add-on.

By the barn door stood Hector Hank, *smiling.*

Exception: **Strong pause before it.** Insert a colon (:) to represent that pause. A verb in this situation acts as an one-
word elaboration on that which precedes it. For more
drama, use a dash (—).

Hector Hank stood by the door and found himself doing
what he always did at that time of day: *smiling.*

Hector Hank stood by the door and found himself doing
what he always did at that time of day—*smiling.*

19.7   **Verb is part of a series.** Commas (,) are used to separate verbs in
a series. Also, while it is usually customary that the last word in a
series follow a conjunction—i.e., *and* or *or*—in some cases the conjunction may be omitted when the series is preceded or followed by a
strong pause, a punctuation circumstance which requires a colon (:)
when either the series or the other information acts in some elaborative
manner. The dash (—) may be used if more emphasis is desired.

BEGINNING: *Dining, dancing,* and *dusting* were Maria's favorite
pastimes.

Strong
pause: *Dining, dancing, dusting:* these were Maria's favorite
pastimes.

Dining, dancing, dusting—what else is there?

MIDDLE: I saw him *skip, jump,* and *hop* with all the grace of
someone running with their pants down around their
ankles.

And so Elmira Swinehorn and Alice Hunkster—*hitting,
slapping, scratching*—managed to break loose and call
the police.

END: The gentlemen *ate, drank,* and *paid.*

Strong
pause: I'll stick with the Three D's: *dining, dancing,* and *dusting.*
It was the same old stuff—*dining, dancing,* and *dusting.*

19.8   **Verb begins a second related sentence.** When two heavily related sentences are being joined without a conjunction, replace that conjunction with a semicolon (;). In this example, the conjunction *but*
has been omitted.

110

Loaning him the money is all well and good; *getting* him to pay you back will be an experience you will never forget.

19.9   **Contracting "not" and some verbs.** Except when writing dialogue or quoting someone word for word, this punctuation privilege should not be greatly used—especially when writing something which is more formal, such as a report. The letter "o" is omitted from the word *not* by replacing it with an apostrophe ('). Then, by adding it to a form of the verb "to be" (e.g., *was, is, can*, etc.), a negative verb is formed and one word does the job of two. But when contracting the verb itself, the letters which are removed and replaced with an apostrophe vary.

ORIGINAL
SENTENCE: I *cannot* do it and I *will not* do it, and I *do not* think you should try to make me.

"NOT"
CONTRACTED: I *can't* do it and I *won't* do it, and I *don't* think you should to try to make me.

ORIGINAL
SENTENCES: Tom *is* going to be elected, mark my words.
                This *will* be the time we *will* all remember.

VERBS
CONTRACTED: *Tom's* going to be elected, mark my words.
                This'll be the time *we'll* all remember.

Exception: **Will not.** The contraction which represents these two words is *won't*, which means the second letter "i" has been replaced with the letter "o."

                I *won't* do it. Will you?

19.10   **Two-word verbs.** Words which combine with other words to form a new verb—a verb which shows action taken by someone or something—frequently need hyphens (-) to separate them, although there are many exceptions to this rule. Your best source is a recently published, comprehensive dictionary.

He *back-numbered* the invoice, so everything would come out right.

Introductory Phrase or Dependent Adverbial Clause

20.1 **When does it need a comma?** A dependent adverbial clause which precedes the main thought almost always needs a comma (,) after it. The phrase, however, is more flexible and is attended by various shades of grey.

TELLING THEM APART. Mentally remove the words before the noun or pronoun of the so-called phrase. If the rest of the information can stand alone as a sentence, it is a dependent clause and needs to be separated. In this example, the word "she" is the pronoun.

> ~~Before~~ *she did anything* she called her mother.
> *She did anything* can stand alone; therefore, it is a dependent clause.
> *Before she did anything,* she called her mother.

But the phrase, on the other hand, absolutely prohibits any removal of its words in this manner. For example, here the word "time" is the noun:

> ~~Before that~~ *time* she had always called her mother.
> *Time* cannot stand alone as a sentence; therefore, it is a phrase.
> *Before that time,* she had always called her mother.

SHORT ADVERBIAL CLAUSE. When the dependent adverbial clause is short and there is no discernible pause following it, nor any chance that confusion may result without punctuation, the comma may be omitted after it. For example:

> *Before she died* I couldn't imagine living without her.

PHRASE LEADS OFF A SHORT SENTENCE. If the absence of the phrase would seriously disturb the meaning of a short sentence, no punctuation should follow it. You can often test its importance by reading the phrase as if it were last in the sentence rather than first, or by simply imagining that it is omitted altogether. Using either approach, you can see that the opening phrase in the first example is vitally important to understanding the meaning.

ORIGINAL: *Without apples* you can't make an apple pie.
REMOVED: You can't make an apple pie.
SWITCHED: You can't make an apple pie *without apples*.

PHRASE LEADS OFF A SENTENCE OF REGULAR LENGTH. When an important introductory phrase precedes a sentence of regular length, there exists a difference of opinion about whether or not it should be followed by a comma (,). One side insists it is almost always necessary because of the natural pause which exists between it and the information which follows—even though its removal would cause harm to the sentence. It tells the reader to take a split-second rest before continuing. Those who hold strongly to this opinion insist that if a phrase reads awkwardly with or without a preceding comma when it *ends* a sentence, it is a sure sign that punctuation is needed when it *begins* the same sentence. For example:

INTRODUCES: *To some degree,* you have to know something about apples before you can make and bake an apple pie.

Awkward: You have to know something about apples before you can make and bake an apple pie, *to some degree.*

But those who oppose this view have logic on their side as well. They point out that simply because a phrase, with or without punctuation, reads awkwardly at the *end* of a sentence has no bearing whatsoever when the phrase *begins* the same sentence. Different situations demand different rules, they argue. In fact looking at the same sentence again, it is hard to discern a pause between the phrase and the information which follows it; therefore, omission of the comma is not a tragic loss. For example:

NO PAUSE: *To some degree* you have to know something about apples before you can make and bake an apple pie.

What should you do? Besides the obvious—that is, using a comma (,) after an opening phrase to ensure that confusion will not occur in some grammatical situations—here are some guidelines which may be helpful:

USE A COMMA WHEN
THE PHRASE BEGINS
WITH...

A verb: *Finding* his wife not at home, he crawled through the window and then opened the door to let himself in.

An adjective: *Outraged* by the insinuation, Jasper gave a flying kick at the anvil and broke his foot.

A preposition, and
phrase is lengthy: *Without a dream in his head or a dime in his pocket,* Orville Thatch rode off toward fame and fortune.

113

The prepositional
phrase is short and
there is no pause: *At least* you could have called.

On that basis I admit the plan seems to have considerable merit and is worth considering.

20.2   **Reads better at the end of the sentence.** Even though it need not be set apart when in that position, it may well need a comma after it when it *begins* a sentence—unless a short sentence follows it and its contribution is crucial. Also, review Rule 20.1.

END: You should have sent her flowers *as well.*
BEGINNING: *As well,* you should have sent her flowers.

Note: The phrase *as well* happens to represent one of the many punctuation paradoxes that exist in the English language. While it means the same as *too*, which itself would be set apart if placed at the end of a sentence, it does not enjoy the same punctuation treatment.

20.3   **Two equally important phrases precede the main thought.** When either could be used effectively as an introductory phrase, only insert a comma (,) after the first one.

In the sixth century, in cases of flu and other common maladies diseased victims were wrapped in hot towels.

Exception: **Linked by a conjunction.** A comma (,) should be inserted after the last word of the second phrase.

After baking six pies and *making the beds upstairs,* she did the washing and ironing.

But if both phrases begin with the same word, insert a comma between the phrases as well.

After baking six pies, and *after* making the beds upstairs, she did the washing and ironing.

20.4   **Phrase is longer than the sentence which follows it.** A comma (,) should follow it. In the example below, the word *try* is actually a shortened version of *you should try to do the best you can.*

In the name of all that's right and honorable, try.

114

20.5 **Phrase or dependent clause relates to time or place.** Here are three punctuation guidelines:

1. If the sentence is brief and the phrase is essential, no comma is necessary— particularly when there is no pause. In this example, a dependent clause leads off.

   After she left him in October he began dating.

2. If the phrase adds interesting information but could be removed without being missed, place a comma (,) after it, even though it might not need one if read last. But please review Rule 20.1.

   In St. Louis, they got married.
   Back then, I wanted more from her than she was willing to give.

3. If the information following the phrase is lengthy, insert a comma (,) after the phrase.

   Over there, you can buy cheese and candy at prices which nearly everyone considers to be ridiculously low.

20.6 **Common expression.** A common expression is a "throwaway" phrase which can launch, interrupt, or end a sentence. It is never important and is almost always set apart. Some common expressions can actually be highly abbreviated sentences where missing parts of speech are implied rather than stated.

You know, I think you've got something there.
For the life of me, I can't understand why he did it.

Exception: **No pause after the expression.** No comma is needed to set it apart. This usually occurs when the information which follows the expression is quite short and the whole statement is emphatic.

Of course you can!

Exception: **Strong pause after the expression.** Insert a dash (—), instead. Use of the exclamation mark (!) is another option, but only when high drama is desired and no pause is desired after it.

Good heavens—what were you thinking about?
My God! is that all you think about?

20.7 **Three-word phrase is missing a conjunction.** In addition to a comma (,) following the phrase, another must act as a substitute for the missing conjunction. In the first example, the conjunction *and* is missing; in the second, *or* has been omitted.

Bound, *gagged,* he knew it was useless to continue resisting.
This, that, it didn't seem to make much difference.

20.8 **Multiple introductory phrases.** They demand commas (,) between them.

With that in mind, with the weight of evidence being overwhelming, and *disregarding the swirling rumors,* how can you possibly stand there and tell all of us that there is no there Santa Claus?

20.9 **Contains implied words.** An introductory phrase containing implied words still demands a comma (,) after it.

ORIGINAL: *~~As for~~ me,* I wouldn't have gone that far.
IMPLIED: *Me,* I wouldn't have gone that far.

ORIGINAL: *~~After finding~~ no room at the inn,* Mary and Joseph went on.
IMPLIED: *No room at the inn,* Mary and Joseph went on.

20.10 **Precedes sentences that have the same subject and verb.** There are two options: (1) insert a comma after the phrase rather than before the conjunction; (2) insert a comma before the conjunction rather than after the phrase. The words displayed between brackets are those which are implied.

COMMA AFTER...
Phrase: *As a plumber,* you have no doubt run into this problem and [you have] found that the customer cannot understand what he has done wrong.

Conjunction: *As a plumber* you have no doubt run into this problem, and found that the customer cannot understand what he has done wrong.

20.11 **Precedes two closely related sentences which do not have the same subject and verb.** There are two options: (1) insert a comma before the conjunction rather than after the phrase; or (2) keep the comma after the phrase and substitute a semicolon for the conjunction.

116

COMMA

Before conj. *As a plumber* you have no doubt run into this situation, and it is likely that you will continue to encounter it.

After phrase: *As a plumber*, you have no doubt run into this situation far more often than you care to admit to anyone; it is likely that you will continue to encounter it.

20.12 Followed by a natural pause. Except in the case of some short sentences, the phrase needs a comma (,) after it. As you can see from the following example, the pause appears even when the phrase is switched to the end of the sentence.

FIRST: *Despite loving her,* Billy declined the offer.
LAST: Billy declined the offer, *despite loving her.*

Exception: **Begins with a preposition.** The pause between it and the sentence often disappears when the phrase is shifted to the end of the sentence. Therefore, it is difficult to test the importance of such a phrase by reading it last instead of first.

PAUSE: *After baking pies* , she did the washing.
NO PAUSE: She did the washing *after baking pies.*

20.13 Strong pause follows Quite likely the phrase is being defined, explained, or elaborated upon; therefore, a colon (:) should follow it. The first word after a colon need not be capitalized unless the information can easily stand alone, leaving no doubt in the mind of the reader with respect to its meaning.

EXPLAINS: *Leaping into the thick of things:* it was a trait for which he was well-known.

SUMMARIZES: *Comedy or drama:* it's obvious he can handle neither.

CAPITALIZED: *Leaping into the thick of things:* That trait of doing something before considering the negative factors has been characteristic of him.

Exception: **Needs special emphasis.** Insert a dash (—) after it, providing a stronger pause. The first example contains one opening phrase; the second, two; but in the third, the conjunction is omitted.

Bellying up to the bar—that's what every one of those guys will be doing when they hit town.

117

Bellying up to the bar and *throwing their weight around*—that's what they'll be doing tomorrow.

New York, Hollywood—what difference does it make?

Exception: **Even more emphasis is needed.** Use the exclamation mark (!) rather than the dash, and then continue the sentence without capitalizing the next word. This unusual technique can be a quite effective, but it should only be used once in a great while.

Such a life! and so little time to live it.

20.14 Question follows an opening phrase. Insert a comma (,) after the phrase and do not capitalize the first word of the question. In the second example, the word *what* represents a full sentence, for the words *did she do* are implied after it.

Based on that, are you saying that toilet paper is recyclable?
After baking six pies, what?

Exception: **Strong pause precedes the question.** If the question elaborates on the introductory phrase, insert a colon (:) before it and capitalize its first word. Otherwise, a dash (—) is more appropriate and no capitalization is necessary.

A sight for sore eyes: Does that mean you are, or are not, happy to see him?

At the risk of sounding foolish—is that what you're saying?

20.15 Interruption soon follows the phrase. The comma (,) after the phrase is usually waived, because the interruption demands priority. Moreover, two many commas in the sentence can create confusion. In the example which follows, the opening phrase is "for example."

For example how many of them, the ones with the glad hands and big smiles, will be there when you really need them?

Exception: **Interruption needs emphasis.** Insert a dash (—) before and after it, and returned the comma (,) to its position after the introductory phrase.
For example, how many of them—I'm talking now about the ones with the glad hands and big smiles—will be there when you really need them?

118

20.16 **Introductory phrase, followed later by a series.** Whether the series contains phrases or single words, no punctuation is needed after the opening phrase. In the first example below, the follow-up series consists of single words; in the second, it is comprised of phrases.

SERIES OF...

Words: *With that in mind* we bought bacon, potatoes, lettuce, and cooking oil.

Phrases: *All in all* we had a terrible time, what with losing our luggage, missing our train, and getting there a day late.

Exception: **Series is set apart with dashes (—).** Return the comma (,) after the opening phrase.

All in all, we had a swell time—what with losing our luggage, missing our train, and getting there a day late.

20.17 **Add-on phrase is preceded by an introductory phrase.** One of three things may determine whether or not an opening phrase will need to be followed by punctuation: (1) the add-on follows a relatively short sentence, so the introductory phrase needs no comma after it; (2) the sentence between the phrase and add-on is lengthy and contains no commas, so a comma is placed after the introductory phrase because it will cause no confusion; or (3) the add-on is emphasized with a dash (—), so a comma is placed after the introductory phrase. Below, the add-on phrases are underlined.

SENTENCE

Short: *In that case* I think you should, <u>if you want my opinion</u>.

Lengthy: *At the very least*, he just wanted to be treated like any relative who might stop by for a Sunday afternoon chat, <u>nothing more</u>.

Dash: *In great haste*, I went to Jake's house to borrow a cup of nuts and bolts—<u>that's all</u>.

Exception: **Confusion is possible.** Some opening phrases regularly demand that the pause which naturally follows them be represented by punctuation, regardless of whatever word or phrase is added to the sentence. In that situation, the pause is forced into the sentence through the insertion of a comma (,). Below are two examples: the first one shows you the introductory phrase without a

119

comma, and you can see how it could confuse the reader; the second example has the comma inserted.

COMMA
Needed: *Considering that* I made a pact with him, knowing full well that he might not live up to his part of the bargain.

Forced: *Considering that,* I made a pact with him, knowing full well that he might not live up to his part of the bargain.

Midsentence Phrase

21.1 **Phrase interrupts the flow of a sentence.** A comma is needed before and after the phrase. Two examples:

ADDS INFO: Gretchen, *often mistaken for Greta Garbo,* never gave acting a second thought until she went to her first movie.

IDENTIFIES: The director of the play, *Osgood Throckmorton,* had never been in a theater before they hired him.

EXPRESSION: His money, *you know,* was inherited.

TIME/PLACE: Meanwhile, *back home,* the anger within the Congressman's district turned into disgust.

But, *in December,* he had a change of heart and began planning the wedding.

No pause: Although *in December* we expect to see more snow than usual.

INSTEAD
RATHER: The home building technique that features a steel frame *rather than a wooden one* is making its debut in Union Township.

Exception: **No pause before or after the phrase.** The comma is omitted. This usually includes phrases which begin with prepositions, or short two-word phrases like *if any* and *if ever,* including common expressions. However, if the pause is more noticeable than usual, use the commas. Here are examples:

120

It seems that *in the final analysis* it certainly was.
Although broke, he did not *at the same time* feel poor.
And there were few *if any* who that liked the music.
I will not *directly or indirectly* challenge you.

Exception: **Often-heard phrase** (likely a cliché). When it follows an introductory word or phrase that is set apart, insert one comma (,) before it, thereby joining the often-heard phrase to the rest of the sentence.

Today, *all of a sudden* the lawyer is saying that his client is indeed guilty.

Regarding the Weejee Fly, *on average* how long is its life span?

Exception: **More emphasis needed.** Insert a dash (—) before and after the phrase. A phrase set apart in this manner is usually of the throwaway type and would not really be missed if removed. The second example is a common expression; the last one is a series of words and phrases.

Gretchen—*a dead ringer for Greta Garbo if there ever was one*—never gave acting a second thought until she went to her first movie.

Her face—*thank God*—wasn't touched.

Finally, Reginald—*recognized by most reasonable-thinking men as a discredit to his profession*—stood up to have his say.

Exception: **Side-by-side identical words.** Separate them with a comma (,), and set the phrase part with commas.

The lives of comics, *for many, many of them,* hang in the balance with each audience.

Exception: **Conjunction is omitted from the phrase.** A comma (,) must be inserted to represent the conjunction—unless to do so would upset the logic of the phrase itself.

Nevertheless his efforts, *desperate, feverish though they might have been,* were not enough to permit him to achieve his goal.

121

SERIES: Finally there was Reginald, *ugly, smelly,* and *a discredit to his profession,* who stood up to have his say.

21.2 **Interrupts another interrupting phrase or dependent clause.** The required punctuation depends upon the strength of the second interruption—that is, can a definite pause be detected before the phrase? The pronouns *which* and *who* are rarely preceded by a dash (—), which frequently requires sentence restructuring. In the following examples, the interruptions-within-the-interruptions are underlined.

That particular belief of the Romans *which holds,* with perhaps some exceptions, *that whatever goes up must come down,* is gaining wide acceptance today.

That particular belief of the Romans—*whatever goes up,* excluding balloons, *must come down*—is gaining wide acceptance today.

Exception: **Second interruption needs emphasis.** Use the dash (—) to set the phrase apart.

That particular belief of the Romans, *whatever goes up— excluding balloons—must come down,* is gaining wide acceptance today.

21.3 **Acts as an opinion, identification, or explanation.** The phrase is normally encased in parentheses. However, you may place a dash (—) before and after it when more drama is desired.

OPINION: She married Tom Swanson (a big mistake) before she ever became famous.

IDENTIFIES: Ezra Phutt (brother-in-law to Amanda Mull) lived to be a hundred years old.

Exception: **Identification within a parentheses.** When a noun is in parentheses and some type of identifying information is needed directly after it, it must be placed between brackets, for a parentheses inside a parentheses is not appropriate. In this example, identifying information is being supplied about Julius Caeser.

This philosophy *(a holdover from the realm of Julius Caeser* [in power after 12 A.D.] *which states that whatever goes up must come down)* is gaining wide acceptance today.

21.4 **Acts as a contrast to what precedes it.** The phrase needs to be set off in the sentence with commas (,), and it usually begins with conjunctions like *but, not,* and *though,* which introduce such a constrast.

She was a cheerful lass, *though discontented with her marriage,* and she had made plenty of friends in the village.

> Exception: **No pause before it.** The contrasting phrase needs no separating commas. Frequently, the word before the phrase will seem as if it were actually a part of phrase itself. Notice, for example, that no pause seems to exist between *loyal* and *but* in the following sentence.
>
> Isn't it odd how many loyal *but totally unwitting* bureaucrats there are when something goes wrong in their departments?

> Exception: **Contrast + additional comment.** Set the comment apart by placing it in parentheses. A comment can be called a throwaway phrase, for though it adds literary spice, it is not really important.
>
> He was a good ballplayer, *not a great one (nor would he ever be),* and he was worth the money he was asking for next season.

21.5 **Interrupts as a common expression.** Common expressions are usually isolated in the sentence, because they add no essential information.

And then, *of all things,* he asked me if I'd go out with him!

> Exception: **Ample punctuation already exists.** The commas which are used to set the expression apart are often omitted.
>
> Since the project had failed, thanks to bad planning, he couldn't *of course* consider any new ventures at that time.

> Exception: **Follows an introductory phrase.** When it soon follows an introductory phrase which is set off, the commas which normally surround the expression are often omitted.
>
> Excuse me, but *you see* sometimes you can use the wrong disciplinary approach.

21.6 **Provides identifying information about a person or group.** Insert a comma (,) before and after the phrase.

LOCATION:	Standing there was Daniel Boone, *of Kentucky,* with a beanie under his coonskin hat.
	Jasper Jenkins, *of Denver, Colorado,* said he used the soap for thirty days and suffered no ill effects.
ASSOCIATION:	Sneak Snelly, *of the FBI,* was given a pension.
JOB TITLE: Title interrupts:	Hank Pilfer, *General Manager of the Tinker Toy Company,* can't give a speech worth two hoots.
Name after title:	The General Manager of the Tinker Toy Company, *Hank Pilfer,* recently suggested that lunch hours be reduced to fifteen minutes.

> But if the indefinite article *the* is removed before the job title, commas are not needed after the person's name.

	General Manager of the Tinker Toy Company *Hank Pilfer* recently suggested that lunch hours be reduced to fifteen minutes.
NAME:	His father-in-law, *Pedro Gonzales,* has been the driving force behind his success.
More info:	His father-in-law, *(Pedro Gonzales, the Hall of Fame pitcher)* has been the driving force behind his success.
Exception:	**Phrase is indelibly linked to the name.** The tip-off is often the appearance of the preposition *of* as the first word of phrase No commas are necessary.
	Then the celebrated DooWah Diddy Boys *of Dallas* began to sing their cotton-pickin' hearts out.

21.7 **Interrupting phrase needs to be emphasized.** Insert a dash (—) before and after the phrase. However, reserve this particular punctuation mark for those times when it is quite important to dramatically set something apart in this manner. Overuse completely destroys the effectiveness of the dash.

Both teams—*avowed enemies ever since that controversial call in 1981*—are scheduled to play each other on the day before Thanksgiving.

Exception: **Needs even more drama.** Insert an exclamation mark (!) after it. But reserve this technique for those phrases which are themselves dramatic and are capable of standing alone. It is certainly not a technique that allows for extensive use, for two dramatic punctuation marks are not normally seen together.

That—thank goodness!—is the end of it.

Exception: **Side-by-side interruptions.** There are two ways of handling the punctuation: a dash (—) may precede the first one and follow the second one, with a comma (,) separating both; or the dash may be used in place of the comma as well. Between the two, strict grammarians doubtlessly prefer the first option.

None of them—*workers or managers, rich or poor*—wanted to make the necessary sacrifice.

None of them—*workers or managers—rich or poor*—wanted to make the necessary sacrifice.

21.8   **Multiple interruptions.** When there are several interruptions, insert a dash (—) before the first phrase, or dependent clause, and another after the last one in that group, and separate them from one another by using the semicolons (;). If some have missing words, replace those with commas (,)

In the case histories which follow—*the first three of which show stress being verbalized; the fourth, an attempt to glorify; the fifth, a result of overconfidence*—notice how all of the patients came to the same conclusion.

21.9   **Interruption begins with "who" or "which."** Consider the following questions when preparing to punctuate:

1.   **Preceded by a series of words or groups of words.** If the interrupting information relates to ALL of them, insert a comma (,) before "which" or "who" and after the last word of the interruption. But if the interruption only applies to the word or group of words which immediately precedes it, omit the comma before "who" or "which." It certainly helps when that word or phrase is preceded by *a, an,* or *the.*

RELATES TO...
All: The display of guns, planes, and tanks, *which were stolen from the army,* did not improve the peasants' opinions of the rebel leader.

125

Last word or group:	The display of guns, planes, and <u>the</u> tanks *which were stolen from the army* did not improve the peasants' opinions of the rebel leader.

2. **Preceded by a proper name.** Insert a comma (,) before and after the "who" phrase when it is removable. But if *who* is not a part of the phrase, insert the comma after it.

PHRASE IS...

Removable:	Then Doody Brooks, *who was the class leader,* surprised his teachers by flunking every course.
Unremovable:	It was Doody Brooks who, *as class leader,* surprised everyone by quitting school.

21.10 Interruption begins with the conjunction "or" and introduces another option. Use commas (,) to set the phrase apart. This does not change when another interrupting phrase which also begins with "or" is added.

1 PHRASE:	Automobiles which are painted red, *or used and reconditioned cars,* will be sold at auction this Tuesday.
2 PHRASES:	Automobiles which are painted red, *or used and reconditioned cars, or trucks with more than a hundred thousand miles,* will be sold at auction this Tuesday.
Exception:	**"Nor" follows "no" and joins two words.** No comma is needed to set off the interruption.
	I wanted no money *nor correspondence* from them.

21.11 Begins with "by" and follows the verb "said." No commas are needed to isolate the phrase.

Johnson is said *by prosecutors* to have committed the bank robbery before the clerks had their coffee break.

21.12 Interrupting phrase immediately follows a conjunction which is linking two sentences. Here are four ways of handling it: (1) include the conjunction as part of the phrase; (2) isolate the phrase with commas; (3) add the conjunction and phrase to the second sentence; (4) isolate the conjunction with commas.

Make conjunction part of interruption:	Tom Turkey was in love with her, but *on the other hand,* he couldn't give up his Friday night poker game.

126

Isolate the phrase:	Tom Turkey was in love with her but, *on the other hand,* he couldn't give up his Friday night poker game.
Add conjunction & interruption to 2nd sentence:	Tom Turkey was in love with her, but *on the other hand* he couldn't give up his Friday night poker game.
Isolate conjunction:	Tom Turkey was in love with her, but, *on the other hand* he couldn't give up his Friday night poker game.

21.13 Precedes a series, or a word or phrase added to the sentence. A midsentence phrase which would normally be set apart in a sentence will frequently not need accompanying punctuation—unless, of course, that interruption is especially strong and demands it. The add-on phrase and the series in the examples below have been underlined.

ADD-ON:	I think you could say that *above everything* he felt that loyalty was demanded, <u>if not naturally expected</u>.
SERIES:	To the great dismay of the board members, the company *under Johnson* was <u>stopping research and development, firing employees, reducing production, and losing large shares of the market</u>.
Exception:	**Emphasizing the phrase.** Use the dash (—) to set the phrase apart.
	I think you could say that—*above everything*—he felt that loyalty was demanded, if not naturally expected.

Add-On Phrase

22.1 Phrase is added to a sentence. In this instance it often acts as an afterthought; that is, it introduces information which is extra but not essential, and it needs to be set apart by a preceding comma (,). With the exception of the interjection, all parts of speech can be used to launch an add-on phrase.

ADJECTIVE:	It is a comforting notion, *this idea that our technology is the world's salvation.*
ADVERB:	The machine has been very easy to use, *actually making my job much easier.*

127

CONJ.	You are going to have to find your way out of this mess, *or perish.*
IND. ART.	Their success is owed to the patacuchi nut, *a tree product that can be grown year-round.*
NOUN:	There are many things which remain mysterious, *spring being one of them.*
PREPOSITION:	It was less than we expected, *to be sure.*
PRONOUN:	I don't want to see a movie, *his especially.*
VERB:	She dwelled in a sea of mediocrity, *advancing up the mainmast in her own dull, lackluster way.*
Exception:	**Add-on has its own internal punctuation.** It must still be set apart from the sentence. In the example below, the conjunction has been omitted in the phrase and is represented by a comma.

The issue is whether John Throckmorton should be trusted, *given his murky, questionable past.*

22.2   Common expression. As an add-on phrase, it is almost always set apart by a comma (,), for it adds no essential information.   If more drama is desired, use a dash (—) instead.

There was nothing I could do, *of course.*
Then I missed the last train from Berlin—*wouldn't you just know it.*

22.3   Acts as a contrast. If it begins with words like *but, not, though,* etc. and introduces information contrary to what precedes it, set it apart by using a comma (,).

She was angry, *but patient.*
He was hurt, *not angry.*

22.4   Phrase repeats the meaning of the previous sentence. Even though not it is not word for word, it demands a comma (,) before it. But when the relationship is so close that no pause can be detected, the comma may be omitted.

REPEATS:	It consumed his mind daily, *blocking out common reason.*
NO PAUSE:	They kept coming *again and again.*

22.5   Phrase is preceded by a traditional add-on word. When an add-on phrase follows a word which is usually set apart at the end of a sentence (e.g., *either, too*, etc.), a comma should precede the phrase only—not the word.

ADD-ON WORD: Not much was done about it, either.

+ ADD-ON
PHRASE: Not much was done about it either, *despite all of the evidence which had been gathered over the years.*

Exception: **Phrase needs emphasis.** Insert a dash (—) before it and return the comma before the add-on word which precedes it.

                Not much was done about it, either—*despite all of the evidence which had been gathered over the years.*

22.6   **Phrase needs to be emphasized.** Whether the add-on phrase is short or long, insert a dash (—) before it.

SHORT: She decided that she wouldn't do that again—*not ever.*
            I'll try—*very hard.*

LONG: I found the general to be far more gracious than rumor had led me to believe he might be—*hospitable to a fault and possessing a keen sense of humor about every facet of his army life over the past thirty years.*

22.7   **Multiple add-on phrases.** When more than one add-on phrase follows a sentence, separate them with commas (,). In the following example, there are three add-on phrases.

You won't be able to get there from here, *try as you may, no matter what map you have,* and *despite the hour of the day.*

Exception: **Add-on phrases need emphasis.** Insert a dash (—) before the first one.

                That's the exact moment when it should have occurred—*when their hospitalization was threatened, the day all of their benefits were placed under severe review.*

But this next example shows the unusual punctuation technique where both add-on phrases receive dashes before them. Suppose you attach add-on phrases to this sentence: *Emotions run hotter when ideas, events, and arguments are polarized and personified* and they do not apply specifically to the words "polarized" and "personified." Here is what to do: (1) insert a dash after *polarized;* (2) include your add-on

129

phrase(s); (3) insert a semicolon; (4) insert a dash after *personified;* (5) include your add-on phrase(s).

Emotions run hotter when ideas, events, and arguments are polarized—*cast in terms of right or wrong, rich or poor;* and personified—*cast in terms of factions and their leaders.*

22.8   **Phrase cannot be removed.** If its removal would leave a significant gap in what is being conveyed, no preceding punctuation need set it apart.

I think she'll go crazy *if given a summons.*

22.9   **Artificial pause needed.** Some add-on phrases are not obvious, primarily because the writer hears no pause before them—and, indeed, none may not exist. But to the reader it can prove to be confusing in some instances. Therefore a comma should be inserted to force an artificial pause in order to make the reader pause before continuing. In all three of the following examples, a comma is needed to force a pause before a preposition.

CONFUSING: She came in in her red snowsuit.
FORCED: She came in, in her red snowsuit.

In the next example, it is essential to insert a comma after *degrees;* otherwise the reader may think the temperature rose eighty-one degrees, even though the word "from" is not in the sentence.

CONFUSING: The temperature then rose ten degrees to ninety-one.
FORCED: The temperature then rose ten degrees, *to ninety-one.*

In the next example, a pause must be forced before the word *with.*

CONFUSING: He watched Flossie Flannagan accept the Golden Rule Award with misgivings.

FORCED: He watched Flossie Flannagan accept the Golden Rule Award, with misgivings.

22.10 **Strong pause precedes it.** When this occurs, the add-on phrase is acting as an explanation, summary, confirmation, elaboration, definition, conclusion, etc. In that case, insert a colon (:) before it. For even more emphasis, however, a dash (—) may be employed.

What I'm talking about is that often-used phrase which one hears about two people who are about to be married: *head over heels in love.*

Hope—*something which you should not give up.*

22.11 Pronoun, followed by identification. When a pronoun is followed by a phrase which identifies it, a comma (,) must separate them.

It was she, *the lady in red.*

Exception: **Two pronouns with identifying phrases.** If only identifying information follows and separates them, the comma (,) should be placed before the second pronoun.

We made a good team: I *the one with experience,* he *the embodiment of logical thought.*

Phrases in a Series

23.1 Series of phrases begins sentence. Besides using commas (,) to separate them from one another, insert a comma after the last one as well—unless a verb immediately follows it (*see* second example).

Finding himself without friends, his reputation stained, and *his resiliency not as bouncy,* Jim sat down and ate a bowl of oats.

Cursing his captors, imagining freedom, and *playing mental games* was the only thing which kept his spirit up.

Exception: **Strong pause follows.** This usually indicates that the series is preceding an explanation, conclusion, confirmation, question, etc. A colon (:) is therefore needed. Use a dash (—) for more drama.

QUESTION: *Above par, below par, double bogey,* and *a hole-in-one:* What golfer worth his salt doesn't know what they mean?

EXPLAINS: *Cotton for the shirts, polyester for the pants,* and *wool for the socks:* these are the materials we will use to create a new fashion.

Cotton for the shirts, polyester for the pants, and *wool for the socks*—these are the materials we will use to create a new fashion.

Exception: **Introductory series needs more emphasis.** Follow it with a dash (—).

Ready on the right, ready on the left, ready on the firing line—let's eat!

Come on, come on, come on—let's get it over with.

23.2 **Series of phrases interrupts sentence.** Besides using commas (,) to separate them from one another, insert a comma before the first one and after the last one. In the first example, the last phrase is preceded by the conjunction "and"; in the second, the conjunction is omitted.

CONJUNCTION...
Included before
last phrase:

But Reginald, *not having eaten in two days, his heart full of revenge,* and *tired of all this talk about sacrifice,* said he wasn't going to take it anymore.

Omitted before
last phrase:

She went to their house, *her mind not on her job, fully expecting it to be routine, the thought of danger quite remote,* and there she saw Chester with a gun.

Exception:

Series needs to be emphasized. Insert a dash (—) before the first and last phrase in the series, in addition to separating each with commas.

It tells how men—*proud of their heritage, bound to their beliefs, forever doomed to convince others of their cause*—endured and stood together against their ancient enemy.

But if other word groups are added to the elements in a series, separate the original phrases from each other by using semicolons (;); then, insert commas (,) between the original phrases and any new group which has been added to them. In the sample sentence which follows, the darkened words represent the original phrases; those in italics represent the new additions.

It tells how men—**proud of their heritage,** *loyal or calculating;* **bound to their beliefs,** *yet cautious;* **forever doomed to convince others of their cause,** *though hopeless*—endured, struggled, lost hope, regained fervor, and

132

charged; then as a body came and stood together against their ancient enemy.

23.3 **Series of phrases or dependent clauses are added to a sentence.** The first one requires a comma (,) before it, and each succeeding phrase is preceded by a comma too. For emphasis, insert a dash (—) before the first or last phrase.

3 PHRASES: It had not been a red-letter day for ol' Billy, *taking everything into account, including the tip he got on a horse in the fifth race which didn't pay off*, and *assuming things were only going to get worse from here out.*

EMPHASIZED: It had not been a red-letter day for ol' Billy—*taking everything into account, including the tip he got on a horse in the fifth race which didn't pay off*, and *assuming things were only going to get worse from here out.*

Last phrase only: It had not been a red-letter day for ol' Billy, *taking everything into account, including the bad tip he got on a horse in the fifth race which didn't pay off*—and *especially his misplacing the week's payroll.*

SAME WORD: It could've been worse, *considering our luck, considering our financial straits*, and *considering our innocence in such matters.*

Edited: It could've been worse, *considering our luck, our financial straits*, and *our innocence in such matters.*

Exception: **Phrases are long and share the same lead-in word(s).** They should be separated by semicolons (;), with the conjunction omitted before the last one. In this example, the word *assuming* is implied before each phrase in the series.

He knew the bank could weather the firestorm of public opinion, *assuming* the newspapers would stop publishing those unfavorable editorials and inflammatory letters-to-the editor; that he could regain the depositor's confidence through a well-planned advertising campaign; that no one would find out that he had embezzled a couple hundred grand.

Exception: **Series follows a strong pause.** It usually means that it is acting as a summary, explanation, conclusion, confirmation, elaboration, etc; a colon (:) is therefore needed before it. Separate the phrases with semicolons

(;) when they are longer, say, than three words. For more drama, a dash (—) may be used rather than a colon (*see* second and third examples).

Colon: Elements combined to produce an exhausting life-style: *caring for an aged mother; instructing her two young children in mathematics; tilling the cornfield;* and, of course, *constantly fighting the banks and land developers to save her property.*

Dash: There is no unbridled joy in Mudville—*Casey having struck out; hot dog sales having fallen off by 50%; the lawsuit by the third baseman now having come to trial.*

There it is—*fiscally sound, innovatively designed,* and *easy to produce.*

But if only the last entry of the series needs to be emphasized, insert a dash between it and the others. In the following example, the last phrase also has a common expression attached to it.

He had once again crumbled under pressure, *this time pathetically, this time for all to see—whimpering as he did, of all things!*

23.4   **Phrases and words in the same series.** They are treated the same as if they were were all words or all phrases: they are separated from one another by commas (,). The conjunction before the last entry may or may not be omitted; in this example it is.

I found the journey to be *enlightening, an educational bonanza, inexpensive, a tonic to my lowly spirits.*

23.5   **Numbering each phrase.** Place the numbers in parentheses and insert a conjunction before the last number. If no conjunction is used, or if phrases are added to phrases (requiring commas between) use semicolons (;) instead of commas.

COMMAS: The Quick Company is a well-respected company, being (1) one of the best innovators, (2) a benefactor for the arts, and (3) the apple of an environmentalist's eye.

SEMICOLONS: The Quick Company is a well-respected company, being (1) one of the best innovators; (2) a benefactor for the arts; (3) the apple of an emvironmentalist's eye.

Added phrases: The Quick Company is a well-respected company,
being (1) one of the best innovators, according to
the API Survey; (2) a benefactor for the arts, going
back some ten year;s ; (3) the apple of an eviron-
mentalist's eye.

23.6   Quoting a well-known phrase. A well-known phrase is likely to
be a cliché. Insert double quotation marks (") before and after it. When
using more than one in a series, however, place a comma (,) *after* the
closing quotation mark of each phrase.

"A sight for sore eyes", "a chip off the ol' block", and "fit as a fid-
dle" are just a few of the clichés I heard that night.

Stand-Alone Phrase

24.1   Explanation. The majority of phrases can be made to stand alone.
They are followed with a period (.), exclamation mark (!), or a question
mark (?). A stand-alone phrase acts as a literary shorthand, sometimes
implying full sentences without all of the words being present to make
it so.

SETS THE MOOD FOR
THE NEXT SENTENCE: *What a joke.* For example, they didn't know
where my file was and my name wasn't even
registered.

All right already! You don't have to keep repeating it!

RELATES TO
PREVIOUS SENTENCE: Great things were expected of me; but I,
thinking that I had all the time in the world,
let the years roll by until I suddenly realized
that I was too old to take advantage of my talents. *So much for that!*

Highlighting a Phrase

25.1   Multi-word noun. May be italicized or placed between double quotation marks (" ").

The expression "for gosh sakes" originated under Emperor Gosh.

135

25.2 **"was the by-word" follows.** May be italicized or placed between double quotation marks (" ").

Helping ourselves was the by-word on Wall Street before those trading scandals broke.

25.3 **Technical term.** May be italicized or placed between double quotation marks (" ").

"Homing in," the radar identified the unidentified flying object and sent a split second message to the operator.

Common Phrase Abbreviations

Compared to words, few phrases are abbreviated; and when one is, it usually looks very little like the phrase it is supposed to be representing. This is often understandable, for many of them are Latin abbreviations. They come in handy when developing footnotes or when implying that more information is available than you are willing to provide, but they should never be employed at the beginning of a sentence. A comprehensive list of abbreviations can be found near the end of a good dictionary. Also, refer to the index of this book. Below are four of the more commonly used.

26.1 **e.g.** Represents *for example*, and a period (.) follows each letter. A comma (,) must also follow this abbreviation, which means it must never be used at the end of a sentence. It is normally preceded by a semicolon (;); however, if placed inside a parentheses, no semicolon is needed. If it is attached to an interrupting phrase which needs to be dramatically isolated, use the dash (—).

SEMICOLON: Cold weather does not play a role; *e.g.*, the farmers have adopted new techniques that allow vegetables to grow in subzero temperatures.

PARENTHESES: Innovativeness on the part of the farmer has greatly lessened the impact of bad weather on crops (*e.g.*, they have adopted new techniques that allow vegetables to grow in subzero temperatures) and this has greatly enhanced the country's ability to maintain agricultural parity.

DASH: Cold weather is another factor which no longer bothers the farmers—*e.g.*, soil treated with H-20 has solved that ancient dilemma—but insects remain another matter.

26.2   **et al.** Represents *and others.* A period (.) does not follow either component of this abbreviation, but a comma is necessary before it when it does not follow a series of words or phrases. Never put a conjunction before it.

IN A SERIES:	In the room was Agnes Tutweiler, Charles Dark, T.J. Arnold, Dominic Hunk, *et al.*
NO SERIES:	In the room was Agnes Tutweiler *et al*, trying to make sense of it all.

26.3   **etc.** Represents *and so forth* or *and so on*, and a period (.) is used at the end. Inserted after a series of words or phrases, and is always preceded by a comma (,). Never put a conjunction before it or the word, or phrase, which precedes it.

MIDSENTENCE:	The buildings, roads, railroad tracks, *etc.* were all severely damaged.
END OF SENTENCE:	Severely damaged were the buildings, roads, railroad tracks, *etc.*

26.4   **i.e.** Represents *that is.* It is preceded and followed by a comma (,), and a period (.) is placed after each letter; but if placed inside a parentheses, the comma which normally precedes it is dropped.. For more emphasis, use a dash (—) to isolate it and the phrase it introduces.

INTRODUCES INTERRUPTION:	There was a great rush to buy the property, *i.e.,* those who could afford it, and the owners were besieged with bribes before the actual day of the sale.
Parentheses:	I signed up for several courses at the local university (*i.e.,* the few made available to me) without really knowing if I would even be able to attend.
INTRODUCES SERIES:	The cars being advertised, *i.e.,* the Buicks, Cadillacs, Fords, and Dodges, turned out to be a hoax on the part of the used car dealer.
Emphasized:	The cars being advertised—*i.e.,* the Buicks, Cadillacs, Fords, and Dodges—turned out to be a hoax on the part of the used car dealer.
INTRODUCES ADD-ON:	I signed up for several courses at the local university, *i.e.,* the few made available to me.

Common Expression

27.1   **Explanation.** A common expression is usually comprised of two or three words, although sometimes more, and rarely does it add anything of significant value to a sentence; as a result, it must be set apart by punctuation because it is so easily removed. A common expression is, of course, commonly used—bordering on, and sometimes attaining the status of, a dog-eared cliché.

Most are inherently dramatic and require a following exclamation mark (!). Such an expression may well be a drastically shortened sentence which has a key part of speech omitted, although that missing component is implied and taken for granted by almost anyone who hears or reads the expression. These same common expressions, however, may also be subdued and followed by a period (.); it all depends on the context in which they are placed.

There are literally thousands of common expressions, some used by almost everyone; others are restricted to geographic regions. Some expressions have an enormous longevity, going back hundreds of years; others enjoy only a brief popularity, based upon the nature of things in a certain time period, then die natural deaths, existing only in some dictionaries and other books regarding language.

27.2   **Stand-alone expression.** Most common expressions are quite capable of being capitalized and standing alone, requiring a period (.), exclamation mark (!), or question mark (?) after them. But to do so, they need to be preceded or followed by information which will justify their existence.

ORIGINAL:	You had better back off!
Edited:	~~You had better~~ back off!
Final:	Back off!
Name follows:	Back off, Jerry!

DRAMATIC:	*Who cares!* I sure don't!
UNDRAMATIC:	Yeh. Sure. *Tell me about it.*

27.3   **A toast.** Common expressions used to toast an occasion are followed by an exclamation mark (!) to indicate the exuberance of the person doing the toasting. But if a somber mood is necessary, use the period (.) instead. Sometimes two toasts in a row may appear, as shown in the second sentence.

CHEERFUL:	Well, it's midnight. *Bottoms up!* *Here's to you and yours! Good luck!*
SAD:	Yeh, she left me. *Here's mud in your eye.*

138

27.4   **Showing friendship.** Common expressions which are used to show friendship are often full sentences in disguise, their missing words implied rather than stated. Used dramatically, they are followed by an exclamation mark (!); otherwise use a period (.).

ORIGINAL: I want God to bless you.
Edited: ~~I want~~ God ~~to~~ bless you.
Final: God bless you.
Dramatic: God bless you!

27.5   **Expressing a negative.** Common expressions which convey a negative thought can be heavily shortened sentences whose missing key parts of speech are implied instead of spelled out. Such expressions may be followed by either an exclamation mark (!) or a period (.), depending on the nature of what is being conveyed.

ORIGINAL: By no means will I do it!
Edited: By no means ~~will I do it~~!
Final: By no means!
Undramatic: And was it his fault? *By no means.* In fact, it was mine.

27.6   **Expression begins sentence.** A common expression which introduces a sentence is almost always followed by a pause, and that pause should be represented by a comma (,). Common expressions, which are themselves dramatic in nature, may be followed by a dash (—) for more emphasis. In the second example below, notice that the question is intensified by following the question mark with an exclamation mark.

You know, I think it's about time we went to Florida.
Holy cow—what was that?!

Exception: **No pause after the expression.** This situation usually occurs when the information which follows the expression is quite short and the whole statement is emphatic. But it may also occur when the other information is lengthy (*see* second example below). No comma is needed to set the expression apart.

Of course I will!

In fact I can't remember a time when Aunt Martha wasn't baking or cooking something.

27.7   **Strong pause follows introductory common expression.** This usually indicates that a colon (:) should be used rather than a conjunction, because the sentence which follows is providing some type of elaborative information, possibly in the form of a summarization, conclusion, confirmation, explanation, definition, etc.—any of which are capitalized when their meaning is not weakened when the introduction is removed. For more drama, however, the dash (—) may sometimes be substituted for the colon.

An explanation: They spent more time on tactical maneuvers than they did on the strategic type.

Bottom line—there will be no peace conference in South America this year.

27.8 **Expression interrupts the sentence.** Commas (,) should be used to set it apart. But if no pause can be detected before it, the punctuation is omitted.

PAUSE: Please, *I beg you,* give me another chance.

NO PAUSE: And he joined in *right along* with them.
What *in God's name* are you doing?
But *heaven forbid* that I come in late.

Exception: **Strong pause before the expression.** That pause will need to be represented by something more dramatic than a comma. Therefore, insert a dash (—) before it and retain the comma which normally follows it.

Maybe it isn't perfect for someone making a thousand bucks a week—*but hey,* it'll do for me.

Exception: **Sentence has other punctuation.** The commas used to set off an expression should in most cases be omitted, to prevent overpunctuation. If the expression appears awkward without commas, then keep them.

Then it was Jerry who said *of all things* that, barring unforeseen circumstances, he would marry the first woman he meets on the first of next month.

27.9 **Expression is added to the end of a sentence.** It demands to be set apart by a comma (,), because it is comprised of "throw away" words. But when the expression needs to be emphasized to create a special effect, a dash (—) should be inserted before it. For even more emphasis, place an exclamation mark (!) after it, too.

No one believed him, *of course.*
No one believed him—*of course!*

27.10 **Expression is used repetitively.** The repeated common expression needs to be separated by commas (,), question marks (?), or exclamation marks (!). If the latter two are used, the first word of the expression must be capitalized each time.

UNCAPITALIZED: Come on, come on, come on!
CAPITALIZED: Thank you! Thank you! Thank you!

27.11 Precedes a question mark. Some common expressions are added to the end of a sentence and demand a following question mark (?), because an answer is expected in return. In fact if the pause before them is exceptionally heavy or ample punctuation already exists, a dash (—) may precede them; but this, however, is not a punctuation technique that lends itself to extensive use.

I was scared to death. *Know what I mean?*
I didn't want to hurt his feelings—*you dig?*

27.12 Double punctuation marks. Some common expressions are inherently dramatic and demand an exclamation mark (!) after them. Moreover, to show surprise, a question mark (?) may precede the exclamation mark. Even an ellipsis (...) may be inserted to indicate to the reader that the voice is trailing off. Keep in mind, though, that this technique should not be abused.

What the Sam Hill?!...

27.13 How ever...what ever...and who ever. These pairs of words are normally seen combined into single words. But when they are divided, the word *ever* takes on the meaning "in the world." These colloquial words do not lend themselves well to being written, except perhaps when creating dialogue for dramatic scripts, for seeing them spelled this way can be confusing to the reader.

How [in the world] are we going to get out of this mess?
What ever are we going to do with him?

27.14 Common expression begins with the pronoun "I", "it", or "you." Such an expression is actually a mini-sentence and is often comprised of just a noun and pronoun, nothing more. When it is joined to a sentence, a comma (,) is normally sufficient to set it apart; however, if the expression is an important, unremovable introduction, no separating punctuation should be used. Insert an exclamation point (!) after the expression when emphasis is needed; a dash (—) before or after it when a stronger pause is required.

STANDS ALONE:
    Dramatic: I give up!
    Undramatic: *You're right.* I should've turned left.

BEGINNING
　Unremovable:　*You must admit* he's good looking.
　Removable:　*I told you before*, I'm not going.
　Dramatic:　*I swear*—can't you kids do anything right?

INTERRUPTS:
　Unremovable:　And yet *it seems to me* you're happy.
　Removable:　All of these things, *I'm sure*, can be worked out.

ADD-ON:　Buford is the meanest man in Hefford County, *I swear*.

　Dramatic:　I had every disease in the book—*you name it*.

Exception:　**Strong pause follows introduction.** Usually, a dash (—) can represent the pause; but when the information which follows elaborates on the common expression, the formal colon (:) is needed.

You guessed it: she's not coming.

List of Full and Partial Phrases

While most phrases are punctuated as explained under Rules 20.1 through 23.6, listed here in alphabetical order are familiar full and partial phrases which sometimes break the chains of punctuation logic. No effort has been made to show all possible punctuation situations of these phrases; rather, attention is primarily focused upon their unique characteristics, showing when punctuation is omitted when expected and vice versa.

28.1　**above all.** As an interrupting phrase commas are not usually needed to set it apart, because no pause can be detected before it.

　INTERRUPTION:　Harry wanted *above all* to be liked.

28.2　**above everything.** In the capacity of a midsentence interruption, commas are not needed to set it apart when the words *that* or *this* precedes it.

　INTERRUPTION:　Harriet knew that *above everything* he wanted his business to survive.

28.3　**after a while.** Does not need to be set apart by punctuation when it introduces or interrupts a sentence.

INTRODUCES:	*After a while* it became rather obvious what he was trying to do.
INTERRUPTS:	All of these problems *after a while* began to take their toll.

28.4   **all along.** Does not need to be set apart by punctuation when it introduces or interrupts a sentence.

INTRODUCES:	*All along* she had been a party to his wheeling and dealing.
INTERRUPTS:	The group *all along* had tried to make inroads into the party's hierarchy.

28.5   **all of a sudden.** Needs a comma (,) before it when it follows an introductory word or phrase which is normally set apart.

INTERRUPTS:	Then, *all of a sudden* she said she didn't love him.

28.6   **all the better.** This phrase, which has the words "it is" or "that was" implied immediately before it, is added to a sentence and preceded by a comma (,).

ADD-ON:	That his archrival Wilbur Huggis was getting nervous, *all the better.*

28.7   **all together now.** The pause which follows this introductory phrase is represented by a dash (—), an ellipsis (...), or an exclamation mark (!). Except when writing dialogue, this represents one of the few times when an ellipsis may be used to represent a pause.

THREE EXAMPLES:	*All together now*—jump! *All together now*...Jingle bells! Jingle bells! *All together now!* Who do we love? We love Pinky!

28.8   **and doubtless will.** As an interruptive phrase, it is rarely if ever set apart by punctuation; but in the role of an add-on phrase, insert a comma (,) before it or employ a dash (—) for more emphasis.

ADD-ON:	I think you can—*and doubtless will.*

28.9   **and finally...and naturally...and so...and with that.** These are introductory phrases which are followed by a comma (,). The conjunction "and" is not separated from the other word through punctuation unless a very heavy pause exists; in that case a comma (,) would precede and follow *finally, naturally, so,* or *with that.*

TWO EXAMPLES: *And naturally,* we all thought it was a sign of things to come.

And, naturally, Ted had his way again.

28.10 **and first to go out of.** Soley an interruptive phrase which needs no attending punctuation. The word "first" should not precede it in the sentence.

INTERRUPTION: Elmira was the last one to go in *and first to go out of* the building.

28.11 **angry at** and **angry with.** You can be angry AT a *thing,* but you can only be angry WITH a *person.*

EXAMPLE: *Angry at the way things were going and with the people in the department who were causing it,* Bruce yelled curse words.

28.12 **any more.** This two word phrase can mean *more* or *from now on,* but add the word *than* to it and it represents the word combination *with more probability that.*

TWO EXAMPLES: She said that her apartment, *any more,* is going to be off-limits.

I couldn't jump from this ledge *any more* than you can run a hundred miles an hour.

28.13 **as compared with.** As an interruptive phrase, it does not need to be set apart in the sentence.
INTERRUPTION: All of her deeds *as compared with* her complaints were ridiculous to the extreme.

28.14 **as likely as not.** As a midsentence phrase, it does not need to be set apart by punctuation.

INTERRUPTION: I think you will find that these things *as likely as not* will do more harm than good.

28.15 **as well.** Will not need a comma before it when it ends a sentence.

ADD-ON: He was of the opinion that he had a right to the crown *as well.*

28.16 **at a glance.** As a midsentence phrase, it does not need to be set apart by punctuation.

144

INTERRUPTION: I could tell *at a glance* that there were more debits than credits.

28.17 at all costs. As a midsentence or add-on phrase, it does not need to be set apart by punctuation.

INTERRUPTION: Our principles *at all costs* must be maintained.

28.18 at every turn. As a midsentence or add-on phrase, it does not need to be set apart by punctuation, for pauses are not detectable.

MIDSENTENCE: And yet *at every turn* he tried to block our efforts to do just that.

28.19 bag and baggage. An add-on phrase which may be preceded by either a comma (,) or dash (—).

ADD-ON: She finally kicked him out—*bag and baggage.*

28.20 barely had...hardly had...and scarcely had. When the word "when" follows, a phrase launched by *barely*, *hardly*, or *scarcely* does not need a comma to set it apart.

BEFORE "WHEN":   *Barely had she gotten well* when she was in the field plowing again.

28.21 bearing the name of...going by the name of...known by the name of...and under the name of. The name which follows the word "of" in one of these phrases should be placed between double quotation marks (" ").

NAME FOLLOWS: *Going under the name of* "Spiffy Skunk," he managed to elude the police until he got a run in his stockings.

28.22 begging the question. This phrase, which is immediately followed by a capitalized question, may interrupt or be added to a sentence. If it interrupts, a comma (,) is inserted before it and another is placed after the question; as an add-on, however, a comma merely precedes it.

ADD-ON: Congress adjourned today and left the nation's burning issues to continue burning, *begging the question* Who's minding the store?

28.23 being as...being as how...being as though...and being that. Using these words to form phrases is incorrect. Instead, employ the words *since* or *because.*

INTRODUCES: *Since you're rich,* how about lending me a couple thousand bucks.

28.24 **by [their] very nature.** This phrase interrupts a sentence without a preceding pause and does not need to be set apart by punctuation.

INTERRUPTION: I have found that these things *by their very nature* soon work themselves out.

28.25 **chapter and verse.** As an introductory phrase, some type of elaborative information will follow. A strong pause can be detected, and it should be represented by a colon (:). As an add-on phrase, a dash (—) before it is usually appropriate.

INTRODUCES: *Chapter and verse:* Everyone in town thinks she's the prime suspect, because she had made threats before.

28.26 **compared to...compared with...and contrasted with.** If you are pointing out *similarities,* a phrase beginning with the words "compared to" is appropriate; to indicate *differences,* "contrasted with" is a better choice of words; however, "compared with" can be used to point out both similarities and differences.

TWO EXAMPLES: *Compared to a regular maple tree,* a bonzi maple has just as much foliage.

Contrasted with a regular maple tree, a bonzi maple is a great deal smaller.

28.27 **different from** and **different than.** These word combinations are not interchangeable. *Different than* should only be used when the words after a phrase or sentence are implied; if not implied, *different from* is the appropriate word combination. The words "were in the 1950's" are implied after *we* in the first example which follows.

TWO EXAMPLES: *Different than we,* today's young people live for the moment instead of tomorrow.

Different from the way we were in the 1950's, today's young people live for the moment instead of tomorrow.

28.28 **due to.** *Due* is not a preposition and should not be used to launch a phrase. Instead, use *on account of, because of,* or something comparable.

EXAMPLE: She failed *because of* her lack of commitment.

146

28.29 **dying by, dying from,** and **dying of.** The word combination *dying by* is used when the method of death follows; *dying from* is the appropriate choice of words when you wish to name that which caused the death; *dying of* relates to causes occurring within the body.

Three examples: *Dying by electrocution,* Pete hoped it bring a lesson home to other would-be criminals.

Charlie, *dying from loss of blood,* was too unconscious to consider the social implications of a bullet hole.

Dying of hunger in a supermarket, Bob wished he had not forgotten his shopping list.

28.30 **every now and then...every now and again...every once in a while...and every so often.** These phrases are neither preceded nor followed by a pause, and they do not need punctuation to set them apart.

INTERRUPTION: But the Thompsons will *every now and then* cut their lawn to keep up appearances.

28.31 **for a fact.** If this phrase follows a verb, no comma is needed before or after it. As a phrase added to the sentence, a dash (—) may be used to emphasize it.

TWO EXAMPLES: I know *for a fact* that she's the one who said it.
She's the one who said it—for a fact.

28.32 **for that matter.** If it is added to another phrase, or follows a conjunction like *but* or *nor*, it is not preceded by a comma.

EXAMPLE: There were no beans in the cupboard, nor even a pot in which to cook them *for that matter,* and they started to worry.

28.33 **for the most part.** As an interrupting phrase, it does not need to separated by punctuation when no pause can be detected.

INTERRUPTION: The Association's rules are *for the most part* mere trifles.

28.34 **for example** and **for instance.** If either interrupts and immediately follows a verb—or no noticeable pause precedes it— the comma can usually be omitted.

INTERRUPTION: I know *for example* that he went into the house and didn't come out.

28.35 **for short.** This is an interruptive or add-on phrase which follows and is separated from a noun. A dash (—) precedes the noun and follows this phrase.

> EXAMPLE: Algernon—Algie, *for short*—dropped out of college because he didn't have busfare.

28.36 **for this reason.** When added to a sentence a colon (:) is inserted after it, because a strong pause and explanatory-type information follows.

> ADD-ON: Shareholders wanted to buy shares *for this reason:* the company had developed a 50-year lightbulb.

28.37 **hands down.** This is an add-on phrase which demands either a comma (,) or dash (—) before it.

> ADD-ON: We won it, *hands down.*

28.38 **having laid.** Grammatical tip: When you want to show that someone or something has *already been placed,* even if neither can be seen, heard, nor touched (e.g., emphasis, blame, a trap, etc. can be laid), this word combination may be used.

> EXAMPLE: *Having laid* the hammer where he could find it, he couldn't understand why he had lost it.

28.39 **having lain.** Grammatical tip: When you want to show the past tense of someone or something *at rest,* this is an appropriate word combination to use.

> EXAMPLE: Martha finally got out of bed, *having lain between the covers for almost twenty-four hours.*

28.40 **identical to** and **identical with.** When you wish to show that two things are exactly alike, begin the phrase with *identical to.* But to show uniformity, *identical with* is the appropriate choice.

> EXAMPLE: *Identical to Oscar's in every way,* Harry's uniform was nevertheless a bit more ragged; his philosophy, *identical with that which had been sold as gospel to all of those in the '60s,* was hopelessly outdated.

28.41 **if any...if ever...and if not all.** No punctuation is required when they serve in an interruptive capacity, because no pause precedes them. The phrase *if any* is normally preceded by the word "few"; *if ever* usually follows "rarely"; and the word "most" precedes *if not all.* For special emphasis, however, they may be set apart in the sentence by preceding and following them with a dash (—).

148

TWO EXAMPLES: There were few *if any* Spaniards in the city.

                        Rarely—*if ever*—does he venture out of the house.

28.42 if not better than. This interrupting phrase is not separated by punctuation.

INTERRUPTION: At investing his money, Henry is as good *if not better than* his brother.

28.43 in a word. A dash (—) may precede it when it is added to a sentence and a strong pause is desired; otherwise, insert a comma before it.

ADD-ON: *In a word*—no.

28.44 in alphabetical order. Meaningful pauses cannot usually be detected before and after this phrase when it interrupts a sentence; therefore, punctuation is omitted.

INTERRUPTION: Here *in alphabetical order* is a list of those who contributed last year.

28.45 in behalf of and on behalf of. The word combinations *in behalf of* and *on behalf of* are not synonymous. For example: if you do something for someone—say, pick up a book at the library for a friend or simply do anything that is for his or her benefit, you are doing something *in behalf of* that person; but let's suppose you accept an award and you want the audience to know that you are representing other people who helped you get it—or you are possibly acting as a someone's representative (a lawyer is a perfect example)—then you are doing something *on behalf of* that person. Either one, however, initiates a prepositional phrase which will require the use of the comma (,) to help set it apart. Neither initiates an add-on phrase.

TWO EXAMPLES: *In behalf of all those who do not have any hospitalization,* allow me to give you this check for ten million dollars.

                        He accepted the award *on behalf of his mother,* who couldn't be there at the ceremony because they wouldn't let her out of jail.

28.46 in fact. Without a noticeable preceding pause, it does not have to be set apart when it interrupts a sentence.

INTERRUPTION: She had *in fact* done more than all the others put together.

28.47 in no way. As a midsentence phrase, it appears without punctuation. As an add-on, however, insert a dash (—) before it.

INTERRUPTION: The senator felt that *in no way* could he support such an amendment.

ADD-ON: I will not do it—*in no way.*

28.48 **in order.** Although the punctuation of prepositional phrases has been adequately covered in this book, particular attention must be paid to the combination *in order*, simply because of its widespread use. When it leads an introductory or interruptive phrase, that phrase is set apart from the other information through the use of a comma (,); it is when it follows a verb or leads an add-on phrase that punctuation dilemmas usually occur. The general rule is this: when the phrase can be eliminated without being missed, the comma (,) is used to set it apart. On other occasions the comma is essential to simply prevent confusion.

NONESSENTIAL: They finally gave Paine Inhass what he wanted and voted him into office, *in order to get some peace of mind.*

FOLLOWS VERB: She felt that in order to do make amends, she would have to pay for his hospitalization.

SHOWS REASON: Bill Bunyan said his brother Paul ate lots of spinach and did a lot of weightlifting *in order to be big and strong.*

FOLLOWS "IN": They won't be allowed in, *in order to gain favor.*

28.49 **inside of** and **in less than.** *Inside of* should not be used as a substitute for *in less than*, for these word combinations are not synonymous; and neither phrase should be isolated by punctuation when they add critical information.

EXAMPLE: *In less than* ten minutes he was there.

28.50 **in terms of.** Strict grammarians abhor the wide use of the word combination *in terms of*—and with good reason, for the preposition "of" makes it grammatically incorrect. *Concerning, of, about, in the matter of* or *with regard* (or *respect*) *to* are acceptable substitutes for this word combination. It is of course acceptable to begin a phrase with "in terms," as long as they are not followed by "of."

TWO EXAMPLES: *In terms that baffled me,* the scientist tried to explain to me why solar power wouldn't work.

Concerning wholesale prices, the nation's economy can be viewed as an out-of-control roller coaster.

28.51 **in that case** or **in this case.** When either of these phrases interrupt a sentence and follow the pronouns *which* or *who*, punctuation is rarely needed to set them apart.

INTERRUPTION: They may be heavily armed, which *in that case* I think it would be prudent of us to at least carry sling-shots.

28.52 **it so happens.** Punctuation is waived when it appears at midsentence without a preceding pause.

MIDSENTENCE: And yet *it so happens* that the Wooly Bear's basic nature is peaceful.

28.53 **just so.** This word combination assumes different meanings, and knowing the definition you are applying to the combination is instrumental in determining what punctuation is needed, if any.

MEANS...
in that position: Falling *just so*, Jeeter found that he could not get his leg out of the hole.

Just so, it was hard to maneuver it and make it stand straight.

exactly right: Wilma Nosinair used her best chinaware, placing each dish on the table *just so*.

like [someone] said: He didn't want to believe it, though nevertheless finding it *just so*.

to make sure: *Just so* he wouldn't do it again, I put tape across his toes.

28.54 **like hell.** Able to stand alone, followed by an exclamation mark (!). As an introduction, no comma follows it, but when added to a sentence, insert a comma before it.

TWO EXAMPLES: *Like hell* you will!
You'll do it, *like hell!*

28.55 **lock, stock, and barrel.** Because it carries its own punctuation, and because a heavier pause can be detected before it, a dash (—) is traditionally inserted before this add-on phrase. This is especially true when it is preceded by a pronoun.

ADD-ON: The farm was his—*lock, stock,* and *barrel.*

28.56 **more or less.** If this phrase follows a noun, pronoun, or verb a pause is rarely noticeable and punctuation is omitted. As an add-on phrase, however, it is always set apart.

THREE EXAMPLES: She *more or less* felt that justice was lacking.

Running *more or less* true to form, the horse won.

That's how they felt about it, *more or less.*

28.57 **no sooner had.** When followed by the word "than," a phrase launched by these words does not need a comma to set it apart.

"THAN" FOLLOWS: *No sooner had he called* than I remembered I was supposed to call him.

28.58 **not once but twice.** No comma need separate *not once* from *but twice* when this phrase introduces or interrupts a sentence; only when they are placed at the end of a sentence should they be divided.

INTRODUCES: *Not once but twice* I went there.
INTERRUPTS: I went there *not once but twice,* and enjoyed myself.
ADD-ON: I voted for him *not once,* but twice.

28.59 **on account of.** This word combination begins a prepositional phrase and should not represent the conjunction *because.* Therefore, if a sentence immediately follows this combination, then you are employing it incorrectly.

INCORRECT: He didn't call as he said he would, *on account of he saw her dance with Spanky.*

CORRECT: They felt that *on account of her divorce,* no one would know what to say to her.

28.60 **on average.** As a midsentence interruption, this phrase requires no offsetting punctuation.

INTERRUPTION: How many people *on average* do you think fly from Houston to Dallas?

28.61 **or adjacent to.** Usually follows *across from,* and a comma (,) is inserted before and after it.

EXAMPLE: The Parker house was across from, *or adjacent to,* the Weatherspoon place.

152

28.62 or else. This phrase is almost always preceded by a strong pause, and that pause should be represented by a dash (—). However, if additional words are added to it, creating a full sentence, drop the word *else*.

TWO EXAMPLES: Get back here—*or else!* ; (2) You'd better get back here, *or* you'll wished you had.

28.63 owing to. *Owe* is not a preposition and should not be used to launch a phrase. Instead, use *on account of, because of,* or something comparable.

EXAMPLE: *On account of the rain,* we couldn't get out.

28.64 past, present, and future. This phrase, which is comprised of a series of words, doesn't need preceding punctuation when it follows a verb or possessive pronoun (e.g., *her, his,* etc.). In other instances, however, it is usually dramatically set apart through the use of a dash (—).

EXAMPLE: That's about the size of it—*past, present, and future.*

28.65 poor fellow. Follows a person's name or a pronoun (usually *him* or *he)*, and no punctuation is required when it acts as the subject of the sentence. In the first example, it follows the pronoun *him;* in the second, it follows the noun *John.*

TWO EXAMPLES: That's all you can say for him, *poor fellow.*
That was John's fate—*poor fellow!*

28.66 poor but honest. No comma need separate *poor* from *but honest.*

EXAMPLE: Then *poor but honest* Cecil made his greatest sacrifice.

28.67 rather than and **instead of.** As the first part of phrase added to a sentence, no comma need precede it.

EXAMPLE: I prefer lemonade on a hot day *rather than* beer.

28.68 such as. A phrase beginning with these two words is either interrupting the sentence or is being added to it, and a comma (,) will be needed to set it apart. Capitalize the first word of a question when it follows this word combination, and never follow these words with a preposition (e.g., *such as in).*

TWO EXAMPLES: There isn't as much weed growth here, *such as one can find in Harlan County.*

The reporter had loose ends that needed to be tied, *such as Where was she when the lights went out?*

28.69 **the first...the former...the last...and the latter** When employed as the beginning of an add-on phrase, the phrases *the first* and *the last* should only be used when there are three or more nouns in a series and you wish to add explanatory information about the first or last one. The phrases *the former* and *the latter* are employed when there are two nouns joined by a conjunction.

THE FIRST: They have homes in Galveston, Houston, and Dallas, *the first* of which is now on the market.

THE LAST: They have homes in Galveston, Houston, and Dallas, *the last of which is now on the market.*

THE FORMER: They have homes in Galveston and Houston, *the former being the site where Cherry Blossom was born.*

THE LATTER: They have homes in Galveston and Houston, *the latter of which cost $200,000.*

28.70 **then again.** These words are not separated from one another by punctuation.

EXAMPLE: *Then again,* he had done nothing to deserve the wrath of the people on Ross Avenue.

28.71 **to be brief...to explain...to illustrate...and to prove my point.** As an introductory phrase, follow it with a colon (:) instead of a comma when the pause after it is strong. If it it interrupts and follows a verb, the comma preceding it is omitted.

INTRODUCES: *To be brief:* Everyone in the western part of town will talk your leg off; people in the eastern part keep their mouths shut.

INTERRUPTION: But *to be brief,* it's a question of money not revenge.

28.72 **to have been, to have done,** and **to have had.** They must never follow *had, has,* or *have.* These word combinations need a preceding comma (,) when interrupting a sentence.

INTERRUPTION: But Reginald, *to have had such enormous success,* must have had inside connections.

28.73 **until now** and **until then.** As introductory phrases, the customary comma which follows them may be waived when the information which follows is short. Use the dash (—) for drama.

TWO EXAMPLES: *Until now* I hadn't.

154

Until then—no.

28.74 what then. Acts like a phrase, but isn't. They must be separated from one another by a comma (,), except when they end a sentence.

INTRODUCTION: *What, then,* will they do when they learn he's been lying?

INTERRUPTION: Assuming the worse happens, *what, then,* will you do about it?

ADD-ON: When they figure out he hasn't been telling them the truth, *what then?*

28.75 why now and **why then.** These two word pairs may introduce or interrupt a sentence, but they do not constitute a phrase; they simply act like one because no pause can readily be detected between them. A comma (,) should separate them, and another placed after the word *then* or *now*, except when the pairs refer to time at the end of a sentence.

FIRST WORDS: *Why, then,* did Roger act as if he knew nothing about it?

MIDSENTENCE: If that's true, *why, then,* did Roger act as if he knew nothing about it?

END: When you wouldn't accept a gift from him then, *why now?*

28.76 year in year out. Do not place a comma between *year in* and *year out*.

INTRODUCTION: *Year in year out*, the crops got worse.
INTERRUPTION: And then, *year in year out*, the crops got worse.

Opening Word of a Phrase

Included in this section is a list of words which fall into two categories: (1) those which are quite popular as phrase-beginners, and (2) those which are used incorrectly, often confused with other words. Except for indefinite articles, most of the words in the examples shown end in "ing" or "ed."

29.1 a, an, or the. Indefinite articles help to form phrases which may introduce, interrupt, or be added to a sentence, requiring commas (,) to set them apart.

155

A:	Then Petersburg, *a city of less than a million,* had no other choice but to cry depression.
AN:	Fiducio Flamp called off his scheduled fight with Puzz Plunky, *an archenemy of his since 1948.*
THE:	*The circumstances being what what were,* I didn't see they could honestly bring that boy to trial.

29.2 **accept** and **except.** Excluding something? Leaving something out? Then use *except*, which leads an introductory, interruptive, or add-on phrase that needs a comma (,) to offset it. But to convey that something or someone is believed, received, or tolerated, use *accept*.

ACCEPT:	*Accepting their philosophy without question,* Ansel Andiron gave them his life savings.
EXCEPT:	The company's products, *except those of two years ago,* were good.

29.3 **adapt** and **adopt.** Modifying something which already exists to form something new? Use *adapt*. But if borrowing, choosing, or selecting something as one's own, *adopt* is the appropriate synonym. Either may begin a phrase which introduces, interrupts, or is added to a sentence, requiring a comma (,) to offset it.

ADAPTING:	The rebels, *adapting parts of the U.S. Constitution to shape a new nation,* soon found that it was incompatible with their own laws which they wanted to keep.
ADOPTING:	*Adopting America's form of government,* the nation's new leaders soon found that democracy was harder than they expected.

29.4 **affect** and **effect.** If a living thing (human and otherwise) is in any way influenced, emotionally or physically, the correct word to use is affected. It may begin a phrase which introduces, interrupts, or is added to a sentence, requiring a comma (,) to offset it. Often confused with "effected" which is synonymous with *caused* and *achieved*

AFFECTED:	*Affected deeply by his war experience,* he spent many years trying to discover why the disease *affected* corporals and not sergeants.
EFFECTED:	They abolished the rights of all individuals, *effecting great change and upheaval in the country.*

29.5 **affirm** and **allege.** If someone is saying that something is positively true, the truth of statement is being *affirmed* by that person. It is sometimes confused with *alleged*, which means that something is being said without absolute proof.

AFFIRMING: Colonel Slash, *affirming the documents to have been stolen*, reported it to the police.

ALLEGING: *Alleging* that Hansel Hill was the thief through sensational reporting, the television station destroyed the reputation of an innocent man.

29.6   **aggravate** and **irritate**. Not at all synonymous. A person can never be aggravated, only irritated; if things or matters worsen, they however can be aggravated. Either word is capable of beginning a phrase which introduces, interrupts, or is added to a sentence, requiring a comma (,) to offset it.

AGGRAVATED: *Aggravated by the drought*, drained of important nutrients through poor conservation, the land turned to dust.

CORRECT: *Irritating me until I could no longer stand it*, I screamed.

29.7   **as.** Phrases which begin with this word can introduce, interrupt, or be added to a sentence, requiring commas (,) to set them apart. But phrases led by "as" can be used in other ways, too. For example:

SERIES: I ask you as a man, *as a citizen, as a scholar, as your friend for more than ten years.*
NO PAUSE
  Midsentence: But you didn't *as a matter of fact* try it, did you.

               If *as an anecdote* it has bad side effects, should it be used?

  End: Bruno jumped on the wagon *as well.*
               Nothing has fallen *as yet.*

STRONG PAUSE: Nothing has fallen—*as yet.*

29.8   **assume** and **presume.** If an individual—on his or her own—chooses to adopt, take over, take for granted, or undertake, he or she is *assuming*. Phrases which begin with this word can introduce, interrupt, or be added to a sentence, requiring commas (,) to set them apart. Sometimes confused with *presuming*, which follows pronouns, is used in a legal sense, and has other meanings (*see* below).

ASSUME: Then Hector, *assuming another identity*, escaped to another country.

157

PRESUME

After pronoun: I *presume*, sir, you are talking about me.

Legal: *Presumed innocent before proven guilty*, he nevertheless knew the cards were stacked against him.

Means "seems
to prove":   That I sent you flowers *presumes* that I care.

Means "depends
too much":   *Presuming upon my good nature*, he forgot that I had a limit.

29.9   **being.** If the first word of an interrupting phrase begins with this word and it (1) follows a noun or pronoun and (2) precedes a verb, a comma (,) is rarely needed before it; but it is essential to retain the comma after the last word of the phrase. However, if the phrase follows a pronoun, a verb after the phrase will usually make the sentence read awkwardly.

FOLLOWS

Noun: Felix *being the first one there*, was not in a mood to wait any longer.

Pronoun: She *being the first one there*, I found myself being uncomfortable and barely able to make spit.

29.10   **but.** Here in alphabetical order are some of the most common phrases used which begin with this word. The sample sentence(s) provided alongside will indicate the type of punctuation, if any, which normally accompanies each phrase.

*but even
at that*   *But even at that*, we still couldn't afford the payments.
I failed the course; *but even at that* I learned something.

*but even
here*   *But even here* I'm not happy.
But even here, where food is plentiful, I'm still hungry.
I thought it was Utopia, *but even here* I have found sadness.

but even so   *But even so*, he couldn't bear the thought of losing.
Strawberries made her sick; *but even so*, she ate them.
Strawberries made her sick—*but even so*, she ate them.

but for that   *But for that*, I think we would've made it.
I think we would've made it, *but for that*.

158

but hey	But hey, don't let me stop you. But hey—am I understanding or what?
but not *exactly of*	I was in, *but not exactly of*, that group.
but of course	But of course, that was before I studied at Yale and Harvard.
	The judge let him off with a tut-tut and a fine. *But of course.*
but one thing *for sure*	But one thing for sure: you can always count on Max when the going gets tough.

29.11 **by.** When a phrase led by this word interrupts a sentence without a preceding pause, there is no need to set it apart. This always occurs when it follows the verb *said* (observe the first sentence example). Below are meanings which this word can assume in a sentence. Knowing the definition you wish to apply to it can be quite helpful in determining whether or not the phrase should be set apart by punctuation.

NO PAUSE:	He is said *by his detractors* to have had taken one coffee break too many.
MEANINGS	
according to:	By all accounts, he was there. He was there *by all accounts.*
along the course of:	Then *by the old road* the army came.
aside:	Sir Galahad put his sword *by.*
during:	The king, *by day*, was a pleasant sort. The king was a pleasant sort *by day.*
in consequence of:	By heredity his fate was sealed. His fate, *by what he said*, was sealed.
in the name of:	By all that's decent, don't take the man's land. Don't take the man's land, *by all that's decent.*
near:	The house *by the tracks* shook when the train passed.
not later than:	Hector, *by four o'clock*, was a nervous wreck. Hector was a nervous wreck *by four o'clock.*

on the basis of:	You can't draw that conclusion *by thinking that seeing is believing.*
past/beyond:	My whole life flashed *by* me.
to the extent of:	There were bees *by the thousands.*
to visit:	*Stopping by,* I was surprised they were gone. I don't mind your stopping *by.*
via:	We came *by* bus. *By bus* the trip is longer.
with reference to:	She did well *by him.* And yet, *by him,* she was more than fair.

29.12 consistently...constantly...continually...and continuously. If the same thing happens regularly, use the word *consistently;* but if it keeps repeating, employ the word *constantly.* The word *continually* means that pauses occur; *continuously* is without any pauses.

CONSISTENTLY:	*Consistently milking the cow from the left-hand side,* he decided to try the left.
CONSTANTLY:	He heard the water dripping, *constantly making plipping noises in the sink.*
CONTINUALLY:	*Continually making advances,* he finally got his face slapped.
CONTINUOUSLY:	The hours and minutes fly by, *continuously making us older.*

29.13 convince and persuade. A phrase which begins with either of these words can introduce, interrupt, or be added to a sentence, requiring commas (,) to set it apart. To *convince* is to change someone's mind by presenting evidence; to *persuade* is to make that person take action, based on whatever evidence is provided.

CONVINCE:	Reginald refused to read the trial transcript, *convinced that his friend had been accused unjustly.*
PERSUADED:	*Persuaded to take the law into his own hands,* Hector—fool that he was—torched his own house.

29.14 despite. A phrase beginning with this word can introduce, interrupt, or be added to a sentence, but it rarely if ever requires a preceding comma (,) when it leads an add-on phrase.

Hank intended to make the trip *despite what they said.*

29.15 **elicit** and **illicit.** They sound alike, but they are worlds apart in their meanings. *Elicit* means to draw forth; *illicit* is synonymous with "unlawful." *Elicit* allows "ing" or "ed" to be added to it; *illicit* permits no such additions.

Reporter Ralph Rosy, *eliciting information from the rather surprisingly talkative gangster,* filed his report and won a Pulitzer Prize.

29.16 **emerge...immerge...immerse...**and **submerge.** *Emerge* is in stark contrast with the others, for it means that something, or someone, is rising or coming forward OUT of something; the other three words imply a DOWNWARD motion—usually into a liquid. There are, however, subtle differences worth noting: *immerge* and *immerse* are synonymous and mean that whatever is being thrust into the liquid is totally covered by it. The same is true of *submerge,* only retrieval is far more difficult. All may begin a phrase which introduces, interrupts, or can be added to a sentence, requiring a comma (,) to offset it.

EMERGE:	Edgar stopped drinking, smoking, and playing the horses, *emerging as a better man in the eyes of the congregation.*
IMMERSED:	*Immersing Edgar into the church's baptismal waters,* the minister didn't like it when Edgar wanted to do the backstroke.
SUBMERGED:	The old ship, submerged forever among the coral reefs, collected barnacles and seaweed.

29.17 **exist** and **subsist.** When someone writes "He *existed* on one slice of bread and a spoonful of rice per day," the appropriate choice of words should have instead been *subsisted,* which means to stay alive by a meager supply of food and water. It always followed by the preposition "on." Both words are capable of beginning phrases which introduce, interrupt, and end sentences.

EXIST:	*Existing for two years on a desert island with no other human contact,* she was in surprisingly good spirits when they found her.
SUBSIST:	*Subsisting on white bread and navy beans,* he didn't suffer any serious health repercussions.

29.18 **hanged** and **hung.** Either word may begin a phrase which introduces, interrupts, or is added to a sentence, requiring a comma (,) to offset it. However, *hung* must never be used in relation to people.

HANGED: *Hanged by the rioting crowd,* imagine their surprise when they later discovered it was their own leader.

HUNG: Her portrait, *hung in the hallway,* ran shudders down the spine of all those who saw it.

29.19 having. If the first word of an interrupting phrase is *having,* and it (1) follows a noun or pronoun and (2) precedes a verb, a comma is rarely needed before it; however, keep the comma after the phrase's last word.

The pitcher *having thrown two fast balls,* decided to throw a curve.

29.20 hint...imply...indicate...infer...insinuate...and suggest. When these words refer to what human beings say or think, here are the guidelines for using them: To *hint* is to make a suggestion, though not directly; to *imply* is to export one's opinion, though in a roundabout way; to *indicate* is to express a preference; to *infer* is to imply, but it is based on the reasoning process; to *insinuate* is also to imply, but it has a highly negative characteristic; and to *suggest* is to offer advice. As the leaders of phrases, they can introduce, interrupt, or end a sentence; in all three cases the comma (,) is used to set them apart.

HINT: Sheila said she was tired, *hinting to the manager that she deserved a day off.*

IMPLY: *Implying that Sheila wasn't carrying her load,* Agnes stirred up trouble and the manager soon had a mess on his hands.

INDICATE: Sheila, *indicating to the manager that it might be better for all concerned if she and Agnes did not work alongside,* stirred up a hornet's nest.

INFER: The manager, *inferring that the matter was getting out of hand when he talked to the waitresses separately,* asked them to take a day off and clear their minds.

INSINUATE: Sheila blew her stack, *insinuating that Agnes started all the backbiting so she could have a day off too.*

SUGGESTING: *Suggesting that they both return to the jobs and forget the whole thing,* the manager then took the next day off and sighed with relief.

29.21 laid...laying...and lying. The information which follows provides guidance on how these words should be used and the punctuation which may accompany them.

162

laid. Use it to show that someone or something *has been* placed, or *could be* placed—even if the subject matter cannot be seen, heard, or touched (e.g., emphasis, blame, a trap, etc. can be laid). A comma sets its phrase apart, unless no pause precedes it. As an interrupting phrase, no comma is needed if no pause can be detected.

SPEAKING OF...

The past: *Laid on a stack of straw,* Wally remained there for two hours before anyone attended his wounds.

The future: All of his dreams *laid end to end* wouldn't make a good yardstick.

laying. As the first word of a phrase, LAYING can be used in the past or present tense and is capable of assuming many different meanings. For example, *laying the blame, laying taxes,* and *laying the foundation* are all proper but nothing at all alike. A comprehensive dictionary will provide many of the word combination possibilities. Generally used to show that someone or something is, or has been, placed. It may also be employed to indicate that someone is resting, but in that instance it is only applicable in the PAST TENSE. A comma (,) sets its phrase apart in all instances.

SOMETHING...

Intangible: *Laying the rumor to rest when he spoke up at the meeting,* no one ever dared to question his honesty again.

Tangible: Then Esmeralda took off her coat, *laying it carefully across the back of the chair as she watched Charles seethe.*

Resting: *Laying spread out on the mantle.,* the cat cocked his left ear and opened his right eye when he heard the can being opened in the kitchen.

lying. This word can only be used in the PRESENT TENSE when writing about someone resting. But to show that a falsehood is being conveyed, the word may be used in either the past or present tense. When it is part of a phrase, a comma (,) separates the phrase.

RESTING: *Lying* here on the sofa and watching TV, I can just see the news anchorman's eyes over the edge of my toes.

FALSEHOOD: It's terrible, *lying* like he did about his sister.

29.22   **lend** and **loan.** If it has to do with money, use the word *loan;* otherwise use *lend.* It may begin a phrase which introduces, interrupts, or is added to a sentence, requiring a comma (,) to offset it.

163

LEND:	Then Jerry, *lending Horace his blue suede shoes*, reminded him not to think of himself as Elvis Presley.
LOAN:	Bob felt sorry for him and took him aside, *loaning him five dollars and an all-day lollipop*.

29.23 most and majority. Used as an adjective, *most* means all but a few, and should not be confused with *majority*, which means more than half and always follows the indefinite article *the*.

INTRODUCES

Removable:	*Most definitely*, I demand reimbursement.
Unremovable:	*Most likely* they will want us to stay the night.

INTERRUPTS:	But it was chocolate, *most of all*, that she craved.
No pause:	You will *most likely* think I'm crazy when I tell you.

ADD-ON:	She tried to find her dog, *most certainly*.
	I felt a breeze—*most assuredly!*
	Do I want to go? *Most probably*.
Unremovable:	He loved her *most of all*.

MOST OF WHICH:	It is hard to fault the British Motor Cars, *most of which are battery-operated*, when you talk about environmentally safe vehicles.

MOST OF WHOM:	It is something you could expect from the Shoobaroohs, *most of whom have never set foot inside a classroom and are therefore illiterate*.
Emphasized:	Two hundred prisoners were paroled last week— most of whom were convicted murderers.

29.24 nor. An interrupting phrase led by this conjunction demands a comma before and after it. But it is usually used in connection with the worth *neither*, in which case it does not receive a comma before it.

It was not created for, *nor in connection with*, any of the proprietors on Seventh Street.

I found it neither funny *nor* sad.

164

29.25 **not.** Interrupting phrases which begin with this negative word are usually set apart in the sentence. But when followed by *from* and *but*, no punctuation is necessary—even though a pause may be detected.

He fell *not from but* into her arms.

29.26 **of.** Phrases which begin with this preposition can introduce, interrupt, or be added to a sentence, requiring commas to set them apart. But phrases led by "of" can be used in other ways, too. For example:

STANDS ALONE: Did I love her? *Of course!* Did she love me? *Of course not.*

SERIES: He was of that time, *of that land, of those people and the way they thought.*

NO PAUSE: Since the project had failed, thanks to bad planning, he couldn't *of course* consider any new ventures at that time.

STRONG PAUSE: Which left me nothing to do but to quit—*of course.*

29.27 **or.** An interrupting phrase launched by this conjunction requires a comma (,) before and after it.
One of the side effects, *or perhaps more precisely,* fringe benefits, of working here is that one does so little that nap time becomes an extended social pleasure.

Exception: **Or never.** This two-word phrase usually follows the word *seldom* and does not need to be set apart with commas.

The Jones family seldom *or never* ventures beyond their property line.

29.28 **proved** and **proven.** *Proved* is a verb and not interchangeable with *proven,* which is an adjective and used to show that something or someone is established in some area. To launch a phrase, *proven* needs an indefinite article (*a, an, the*) before it.

Proved to be seaworthy, the ship was taken out of dry dock and put into the *proven* hands of courage—namely, those belonging to Captain Spud.

165

The Simple Sentence

The simple sentence is comprised of one independent, unpunctuated clause which represents a complete thought. It does not normally require any punctuation to separate any of its parts. For example:

Ansul Fishback won a million dollars in the lottery.

But sometimes, because of its structure, the reader must be told to pause slightly between two words; otherwise confusion may result. That forced pause is represented by a comma (,). Rules 30.1 through 30.6 address that situation. Statements which end with a question mark are not covered in this section.

30.1   **With words omitted.** We speak in a kind of shorthand, implying words rather than using them, and this practice carries over into the way we write too. However, in most cases the absence of an implied word on paper must be noted by replacing it with punctuation—usually a comma (,). Below, the italicized words in the original sentences are those which are implied in the sentences following them. If a two-word question (or one which sounds like a question but isn't) follows the last word, it must be set apart by a comma as well.

ORIGINAL: The trouble is *that* none of us knew the regulations.

Word removed: The trouble is, none of us knew the regulations.
Two removed: Trouble is, none of us knew the regulations.

ORIGINAL: Your thinking is not orderly *and* logical.
Word removed: Your thinking is not orderly, logical.

MORE THAN
ONE WORD: Those who can *do the job* fall into one of two groups.
Those who can, fall into one of two groups.

ADDING A TWO-
WORD QUESTION: Those who can, fall into one of two groups, *don't they?*
No question: Those who can, fall into one of two groups, *don't they.*

30.2   **Side-by-side duplicate words.** This is perhaps the most obvious instance when a comma (,) is required to force a pause and separate elements in a simple sentence. But duplicate and successive verbs like *had had* which have no natural pause between them do not receive the comma.

NEEDS COMMA:	It's when you do *that, that* I get angry.
	I'll be *in, in* a minute.
	What it really *is, is* an attempt to stop the vote.

| NO COMMA: | I *had had* enough. |

30.3 **"Had" appears twice.** When "had" is used twice in a simple sentence, quite often a pause is detectable (or one must be forced) before the second one to prevent confusion. If the interrupting phrase *until we had counted our dead* were removed from the sentence which follows, no comma would be necessary; but its insertion—and one which is important, by the way, because it clarifies the meaning of the opening words—forces a pause before the second "had." That pause is represented by a comma (,).

Reports that we didn't count our votes *until we had counted* our dead, had a factual foundation.

30.4 **Second verb ends in "ing."** When a second verb ending in "ing" follows a simple sentence, the pause between the sentence and that verb may be so negligible that it would be easy to assume none existed whatsoever, that it is in fact part of the simple sentence which precedes it. However, it is probably a subtle add-on phrase; and even though it might add crucial information to the simple sentence, it still needs to be set apart.

It's quite an achievement, *jumping* a hundred feet.
I find it tiresome, *saving* fuel for the winter.

30.5 **Two of the following words appear: *who, what, where, when,* or *how*.** The second one will almost always require a comma (,) before it. The pause is usually more noticeable if the sentence elements are switched (*see* second example below).

| ORIGINAL: | *Why* did Marsha decide to go to Paris, *when* she had just come back from there? |

| SWITCHED: | *When* she had just come back from there, *why* did Marsha decide to go to Paris? |

30.6 **Contains contrasting elements.** When a simple sentence contains elements which contrast with one another, they are separated by a comma (,). This is frequently the case when the indefinite article "the" leads each. For example:

The more success he gained, *the* less he liked it.

| Exception: | **"The" is followed by an adverb which ends in "er."** The sentences can often be reduced to two words |

apiece and the comma between them omitted. Of course, the information which precedes the unpunctuated contrast must set the stage for it; otherwise it will confuse the reader.

ORIGINAL: The hotter ~~it gets,~~ the better ~~I like it.~~

NO COMMA: It's supposed to reach ninety degrees today. *The hotter the better.*

Here are some sentence elements which apply to this situation:

the better	the higher	the lower	the sooner
the colder	the hotter	the madder	the sweeter
the deeper	the less	the quicker	the wider
the greater	the longer	the shorter	the worse

30.7   **Quoting a familiar sentence.** An often-quoted simple sentence which stands alone does not require any extra punctuation; it is only when it is placed inside another sentence that double quotation marks (" ") are needed before and after it.

It ain't over till the fat lady sings. Or least that's what people tell me.

The old saying *"it ain't over till the fat lady sings"* refers to the opera, where you don't reach for your hat and prepare to leave until the fat lady sings.

Joining Two Sentences

When two simple sentences are joined they become a COMPOUND SENTENCE, and they are usually separated by a conjunction (italicized in the example below).

Ansul Fishback won a million dollars in the lottery *and* he was more surprised than anyone.

But if a clause is added to one of the simple sentences, their marriage becomes a COMPLEX SENTENCE. The clause is italicized in the example which follows:

Although the odds were heavy against him, Ansul Fishback won a million dollars in the lottery and he was more surprised than anyone.

168

31.1 **"And", "but", or "or" joins two simple sentences.** When one of these three conjunctions joins two simple sentences, a natural pause precedes it and a comma (,) should represent the pause.

It just wasn't good enough, *but* he had tried his best.

Exception: **Sentences are brief.** The comma may be omitted.

He is *and* she isn't.
Her voice is gone *and* we're poorer for it.

Exception: **Second sentence completes original idea.** No comma is needed when the second sentence rounds out an idea established by the other. Below, *I'm a poor judge of people* can stand on its own; but for it to make sense, it depends heavily on the information which precedes it.

He's as dumb as they get *or* I'm a poor judge of people.
It follows naturally *that* one of them had to be guilty.

Exception: **Conjunction is omitted** This usually makes the pause between the two sentences stronger; therefore, a semicolon (;) takes the place of the missing conjunction. In the examples below, observe how the original two sentences are edited to the point where they are quite brief and need only a semicolon to separate them.

ORIGINAL: John is listed among the missing, *but* Sally's name is not to the found there.

Edited: John is ~~listed~~ among ~~the~~ missing, but Sally~~'s name~~ is not ~~to the found there~~.

New: John is among the missing, but Sally is not.

Shorter: John is; Sally isn't.

But if the second sentence begins with a pronoun, in most cases the conjunction can be replaced with a comma (,).

He's a liar, *they* all know it.
We look at them, *we* say they're crazy.

31.2 **Two sentences joined by the conjunction "as."** When a simple sentence led by this conjunction adds crucial information, e.g., such as where, when, or why something happened, and completes the idea established by the other sentence, it should not be set apart by a

169

comma. But in the second example, the comma (,) is needed because the follow-up sentence led by "as" is unimportant and could be eliminated without being missed.

COMPLETES: The conflicting viewpoints of Edgar Putts and Melvin Mire flared last week *as* they testified before the Finance Committee.

REMOVABLE: The conflicting viewpoints of Edgar Putts and Melvin Mire flared last week, *as* I told you they would.

Exception: **"As" is capitalized and leads off the sentence.** A comma (,) will almost always be needed between the two sentences.

As they testified before the Finance Committee, the conflicting viewpoints of Edgar Putts and Melvin Mire flared last week

31.3 **Two joined sentences share the same subject.** No comma is needed before the conjunction. This rule applies, too, when the subject appears in two different forms; for instance, it may first show up as a noun in the first sentence and as a pronoun in the second one, although in some situations the pronoun in the second sentence may be omitted but implied (*see* bracketed pronoun in the second example below). In the second sentence of the first two examples below, the subject *he* is implied rather than stated; in the third example, the subject "I" is repeated and the second sentence completes an idea begun by the first one.

NOUN &
PRONOUN: *Mixus* sent a message to the Governor and *he* waited for a reply.

Pronoun
implied: *Mixus* sent a message to the Governor and [he] waited for a reply.

2 PRONOUNS: *I* was lucky and *I* kept reminding myself that luck changes.

Pronoun
implied: I was lucky and *kept reminding myself that luck changes.*

Exception: **Second sentence is longer than usual.** The insertion of a comma (,) is quite acceptable, forcing the reader to take a split-second pause before continuing.

170

Mixus sent a message to the Governor, and *began to wonder how long it would take before it would finally wind its way through the bureaucracy.*

Exception: **Conjunction and subject are omitted.** Replace the missing conjunction with a semicolon (;). The pronoun *they* is implied after the semicolon below.

They didn't try to fix it; *said it would take too long.*

Exception: **Sentences have same verb and subject.** The second sentence can often do without both, with a comma (,) representing their omission. Use a semicolon when you want the break between the two sentences to be more noticeable, especially when one of them contains a phrase which needs to be set apart by punctuation.

COMMA: *She felt* that they had not dealt fairly with her, [she felt] that they had taken advantage of her lack of knowledge.

SEMICOLON: *She felt* that they had not dealt fairly with her; that they had taken advantage of her lack of knowledge, basically because she was a foreigner.

Exception: **Second sentence needs more emphasis.** A dash (—) should be inserted before it, but be sure the second sentence is heavily related to the first sentence

She came from Cordova—and *nobody can say when.*

31.4 **Two long, heavily related sentences are joined.** Conjunction may or may not be implied between them. If it is, and a stronger pause is desired, a semicolon (;) should be inserted between the sentences; otherwise use a comma (,). Do not use the semicolon between two simple, highly-related sentences when the conjunction is retained.

SEMICOLON: There's no doubt that Edgar had a motive; I want you to know that from the very start.

COMMA: A lie is a lie, who tells it is really immaterial.

31.5 **Conjunction is the first word of two joined sentences.** This does not change the punctuation status of two simple sentences being joined, for the comma (,) still separates them. However, conjunctions such as *although* and *that* are the most frequently used in this

171

case. Sometimes—especially when using the conjunction *that*—doubt about whether or not to use a comma may arise. If the first sentence reads better if it were second, that is a sure sign it needs a comma after it when it is first.

LEADS OFF: *That* Ted Williams was one of the greatest hitters in the history of the game, no one would ever question.

SWITCHED: No one would ever question *that* Ted Williams was one of the greatest hitters in the history of the game.

Exception: **Two conjunctions.** On those occasions when the first and second sentence are preceded by a conjunction, punctuation depends on the nature of the pause before the second one. If it is slight, the comma is more appropriate. But if the pause is strong, place a period (.) after the first sentence and capitalize the second conjunction. Note: The conjunctions in these instances are usually *or*, *and*, or *but*.

COMMA: *And* he had tried his best, *but* it just wasn't good enough.

PERIOD: *And* he had tried his best. *But* the team really wanted someone who had experience playing second base.

31.6   **One sentence interrupts the other.** Punctuation depends upon the nature of the interruption. If the interrupting sentence needs a dramatic entrance, dashes (—) are used before and after it. But when the interruption acts more like a side comment, where an opinion, identifying information, or explanation is quickly provided, encasing it within parentheses is more acceptable.

DRAMATIC: None of them—you can quote me on this—have ever taken the trouble to find out why.

IDENTIFIES: None of them (I'm talking about the people who are called "managers") have ever tried to find out why.

OPINION: The sheriff (no can believe what that crook says) reported that all of them will be indicted for the crime.

EXPLAINS: The KKK (they wear white hoods over their faces to prevent anyone from knowing who they are) had a seamstress design the standard pattern for the eye holes.

Exception: **No pause before the interrupting sentence.** Sometimes a short sentence (especially those which begin with the pronouns *I, he, she, they, we*) may interrupt without a discernible pause preceding it; in that situation, punctuation will probably not be needed. But if you feel more comfortable by isolating it, do so. For example:

The real estate market *I hasten to add* is quite soft.
The real estate market, *I hasten to add,* is quite soft.
But the economy *she pointed out* was in good shape.

31.7 **Second sentence contrasts with the first one.** This usually occurs when the second sentence begins with a conjunction like *but, though, yet,* etc., and sometimes an indefinite article (*the, a*). The sentences in this situation are separated by a comma (,).

BUT: Some want stiffer penalties, *but* who will say what those penalties should be?

THOUGH: They did everything to please me, *though* it was evident that nothing would work.

YET I studied practically all night, *yet* I failed the test badly.

Exception: **Contrasting sentence needs more emphasis.** Employ the dash (—) instead of the comma. In the example which follows there are three contrasting sentences, and the dash is used to dramatically separate them from their predecessors.

Some want stiffer penalties—*but* who will say what those penalties should be? Others call for severe economic sanctions—*but* where are their ideas? And some jealously guard their political turf—*but* can we survive such protectionism?

31.8 **Joining two related sentences without a conjunction.** A semicolon (;) may be inserted between them if they are highly related and dependent upon one another. However, if the second sentence elaborates on the first one in some way (provides a conclusion, summarization, etc.) and a strong pause is evident, replace the semicolon with a colon (:). If more drama is desired, insert a dash (—) to show their relationship.

SEMICOLON: You desire money; I desire peace.

COLON: Only one thing kept him from entering the house to save his sister: he wasn't absolutely sure she was in there.

SEPARATED: Enough has been said! I believe you!
Dash used: Enough said—I believe you!

31.9 Conjunction joins a simple sentence with a complex or compound sentence. To emphasize the pause between them, use a semicolon (;); otherwise a separating comma will be sufficient. Except for the last example shown, the simple sentence precedes the compound sentence. The words in brackets have been inserted to indicate that those particular words, or something like them, are implied.

CONJUNCTION WITH
COMPLEX SENTENCE

Ample punctuation: He had considerable talent; *and he had a winning attitude,* which his record amply proves, what with six championships, ten division titles, and hundreds of trophies.

Interrupting word
follows: He was not exactly an unemployed painter, but, *absurdly,* [he was] a role model for unemployed plumbers.

Interrupting phrase
follows: It wasn't easy for you to say that, and, *assuming you were only doing it to protect me,* I think perhaps I should weigh your advice carefully.

Joined to a phrase: It wasn't easy for you to say that, *and assuming you were only doing it to protect me,* I think perhaps I should weigh your advice carefully.

CONJUNCTION WITH
SIMPLE SENTENCE: They called him an eccentric, *this gnarled old man who had whiskers down to his belly button,* and they also called him a saint.

31.10 Simple sentence interrupts compound sentence. Insert a dash (—) before and after the simple sentence. However, if it serves to provide a quick explanation, identification, or comment of some sort, then encase the sentence within a parentheses.

DASH: Many say that he's a liar, and—*this will come as a great shock to a few*—others claim that he is an incorrigibly nice guy.

PARENTHESES: Many say that he's a liar, and others (I am speaking of the extreme right-wing of the party) claim that he is an incorrigibly nice guy.

31.11 Strong pause separates a simple and complex sentence. When this occurs, the first sentence—whether it is simple or complex—is "setting up" the second sentence, which provides information which elaborates, summarizes, explains, or concludes. As a result, a colon (:) is needed to represent that pause. The simple sentence has been italicized in these examples; and here, too, is one of the few times when a colon can justifiably follow a verb—which in this case is *was*.

SIMPLE SENTENCE
IS FIRST:
I'll tell you what Jack's idea of great vacation was: even though he was invited to visit royal families all over the world, the thing he liked to do most was go for a long drive in the country.

COMPOUND SENTENCE
IS FIRST:
Of all that which he disliked, taking all of his many prejudices into account, his reserved his greatest hatred for Bachu B'Nu: *it was he who had caused him his present misfortune.*

31.12 Joining two complex sentences with "and," "but", or "or." Separate them with a semicolon (;). The second complex sentences shown below is in italics.

The nature of his subjects, the depth of his characters, and the excitement of his plots are proof of his artistry; and *it's clear that he, above all others, has won the hearts of movie fans everywhere.*

31.13 One of two complex sentences interrupts the other. Insert a dash (—) before and after it; but if it acts more like a side comment—that is, an opinion, identifying information, or explanation is quickly provided—encasing it within parentheses is more acceptable. Yet, even in this instance the dash may be employed when more drama is desired.

DRAMATIC:
Then the Hopi Tribe—*it had already been ravaged by disease, its own warring factions,* the hunger which comes from drought—became the target of other tribes which, contrary to folklore, resented Chief Running Bear's mystical insight.

IDENTIFIES:
Then the Hopi Tribe (*you may recall that they were led by Chief Running Bear, the so-called mystic*) became ravaged by disease, internal strife, and soon found found themselves the target of other tribe's revenge.

OPINION:
His suit (*it was customed-tailored, I think*) shrunk to a pathetic sight as he stood there in the rain, much to the amusement of the others who were waiting for the bus.

His suit—*mind you, I'm not making fun of the guy*—shrunk to a pathetic sight as he stood in the rain, waiting for the 10:20 bus.

Joining Three Sentences

For information regarding the meaning of simple, compound, and complex sentences, refer to the information under SIMPLE SENTENCE and JOINING TWO SENTENCES.

32.1 **Three simple, related sentences are joined by "and", "but", or "or."** Insert a comma (,) between two of the sentences, preferably between the pair which have a lesser relationship.

We tried our best to make them see the light, *and* Elmira even brought out the papers to prove it *and* they were still unable to grasp the truth.

Exception: **Sentences are quite short.** The sentences need only be separated by commas (,), but the last one should be preceded by a conjunction. The conjunction *but* is not used in this instance.

He wanted the football, I wanted the baseball, and she wanted a mink coat.

32.2 **Adverbial conjunction used.** An adverbial conjunction like *still* or *however*, which is always the second of two conjunctions, is used to help highlight a contrast between one sentence and another; a semicolon (;) should be inserted before it, and a comma (,) should follow it. In many cases the conjunction *but* may be used as well, but no comma follows it.

ADVERBIAL
CONJUNCTION: We tried our best to make them see the light *and* Elmira even brought out the papers to prove it; *however*, they were unable to grasp the truth.

BUT: We tried our best to make them see the light *and* Elmira even brought out the papers to prove it; *but* they were unable to grasp the truth.

32.3 **No conjunctions join the sentences.** Conjunctions which are omitted should be replaced by semicolons (;), but be sure the sentences are highly related.

We tried our best to make them see the light; Elmira even brought out the papers to prove it; they were nevertheless unable to grasp the truth.

32.4 **Three simple sentences begin with the same word(s).** Short sentences may be separated by conjunctions or semicolons (;). If the verb changes, however, use a conjunction/semicolon combination. But when the subject and verb are implied before the last two, only commas (,) are needed. Note: The words within brackets, found in the last example provided below, are implied.

SEPARATED BY...

Conjunctions: *One gave me* his word and *one gave me* a gift and *one gave me* a lecture.

Semicolons: *One gave me* his word; *one gave me* a gift; *one gave me* a lecture.

VERB CHANGES: She *felt* needed; she *was* elated; and she *started* to cry.

SUBJECT/VERB
IMPLIED: *There are* events to be planned, [there are] people to be called, [there are] spirits to be raised.

There are events to be planned, people to be called, spirits to be raised.

But regarding LONG sentences that share the same lead-in words, use the semicolon (;) to set them apart from one another.

It had been completed long before Augustus seized power on that day in May; *before* he married the beautiful and passionless Emiline on Philo Mountain; *before* in fact his father and mother had even conceived him.

Exception: **Only two sentences share the same lead-in words.** Insert a comma (,) between the two sentences which do not share the same lead-in words, which means it will appear after the first sentence or before the last one. Notice that in the second example the third set of lead-in words are implied.

I want you to understand that your action will have serious repercussions, and *there will* be some people who will despise you and *there will* be others who may throws rocks at you.

I want you to understand that your action will have serious repercussions, and *there will* be some people who will despise you and [there will be] others who may throws rocks at you.

Some will take any kind of drug and *some will* stick to only one type, or they are horrified by what it can do to their bodies and never even attempt to experiment.

32.5 **Strong pause follows the first of three joined sentences.** A colon (:) will probably be needed to separate it from the other two, which are no doubt functioning as a summary, explanation, conclusion, or elaboration, etc. Capitalization after the colon will not be necessary when the last two sentences are not dependent on the first one for their existence and their meaning will not be affected if the other sentence was absent The strength of the relationship between the last two simple sentences dictates the kind of punctuation needed between them—if any. Strong relationship: no comma when separated by a conjunction; contrasting sentences should be divided by a comma (,); weak relationship, insert a semicolon (;) between them.

RELATIONSHIP

Strong: It was obviously not going to work: two of them were pulling down on it *and* the other two were pushing up.

Contrast: My husband was ambivalent: he knew that I had a tendency to overwork myself, *but* he did not want to interfere in my career.

Weak: It was a bad scene: Twenty laborers were fired immediately; two bookkeepers were accused of juggling the books.

It has been a terrible day: I ran out of gas on the freeway; then I got fired when I finally arrived at work.

But if a conjunction separates the last two sentences and they have a weak relationship, the semicolon may be replaced by a comma (,).

It has been a terrible day: I ran out of gas on the freeway, *and* then I got fired when I finally arrived at work.

178

32.6 **Strong pause precedes the last of three joined sentences.**
A colon (:) should be inserted before it, because in most cases it has
been set up by the others to provide a conclusion, summary, explanation, etc. In the example which follows, a conclusion is being drawn.
Capitalize the sentence after the colon when it makes perfect sense
without the help of the other two

There is only one thing you can say about that, and I don't think any
sensible person would disagree: *Prejudice is a corrosive agent that
weakens one's potential and personality.*

32.7 **One of three joined sentences acts as an interruption.** In
this situation, the three sentences are not really joined, for the interruption—because it is easily removed and would not be missed—should be
encased in parentheses. Such a sentence may offer an opinion, explanation, identification, or some other type of personal comment that refers,
but may not relate directly, to the main thought being stated in the
other two sentences. Further, it should be capitalized, and the ending
punctuation should appear before the closing parenthesis. Keep in mind
that overuse of the parentheses can significantly reduce its effectiveness.

He fell a hundred feet to the ground. (I think he was drunk on blueberry
wine.) And Dr. Spunk maintains that it's still the county record.

Exception: **Greater emphasis needed.** The interruption should
be preceded and followed with a dash (—), and place a
conjunction before the last sentence.

He fell a hundred feet to the ground—*They say he went
head first into a cow pie*—and Dr. Spunk maintains that
it's given him a permanent tan.

Exception: **Second sentence proves a point.** All three sentences may be capitalized, with the second one set apart
by dashes (—). The first dash immediately follows the
period (.) which ends the first and second sentence. This
is a rare punctuation situation indeed and one which certainly should not be abused, because it is not customary
for the dash to follow a period. Although not as dramatic, use of the parentheses in the following situation
may be preferable. Moreover, it is perhaps debatable
whether or not the sentence shown below needs the emphasis which the dash provides.

The repetition which the advertising world subjects us
to can often work to its disadvantage.—*We have all
seen the Lo Kalorie Beer Commercial where the product
was so frequently hawked that we mentally turned the*

message off and swore that we would never buy it.—
But some advertisers fail to understand this.

32.8 **One of the three joined sentences is complex (has its own internal punctuation).** Special care must be taken to ensure that it not be confused with the other two. Generally this calls for the insertion of a comma (,) between those two sentences which have strong ties and are separated by a weak pause, but a semicolon (;) dividing those which have weak ties and strong pause between them. Shown below are examples of possible punctuation when the complex sentence (printed in italics for quicker identification) is first, second, and last.

FIRST: *His wig, yellow and worn, lay wadded on the table, its price tag still showing;* and when she reached out to examine it, she saw that it had two eyes.

SECOND: His wig lay wadded on the table; *she reached out to examine it, her heart pounding,* and then she saw that it had two eyes.

LAST: His wig lay wadded on the table; she reached out to examine it, *but then, suddenly, she saw that it had two eyes.*

Exception: **One sentences needs more emphasis.** Use the dash (—) to set it apart from the others. Again, the complex sentence has been placed in italics for quicker identification.

His wig lay wadded on the table, and her desire to pick it up was overwhelming—*but then, suddenly, she saw that it had two eyes.*

His wig, yellow and worn, lay wadded on the table, its price tag still showing—her desire to pick it up was overwhelming—and she then saw that it had two eyes when she reached for it.

32.9 **Two of three joined sentences are complex.** All three sentences are separated by semicolons (;). In the example which follows, the simple sentence has been italicized for quicker identification.

The team, having lost ten straight games, was desperate; and the stress, which was evident even in practice, began to manifest itself in the players' relations with their wives, press, and loyal fans; *it became clear that something had to give.*

Exception: **Simple sentence is last and is preceded by a conjunction.** If the pause before the conjunction is slight, a comma (,) may be inserted rather than a semi-colon, for the sentence flows easily after the one before it.

The team, having lost ten straight games, was desperate; and the stress, which was evident even in practice, began to manifest itself in the players' relations with their wives, press, and loyal fans, *and it became clear that something had to give.*

Exception: **Strong pause follows first sentence.** Whether the first sentence is simple or complex, insert a colon (:) after it, for the others are providing some kind of elaborating information (a summary, conclusion, etc.) which supports it. Separate the remaining two with semicolons (;) if they are complex sentences; but a comma (,) will suffice if one of them is of simple structure and preceded by a conjunction. In the examples which follow, the simple sentence is in italics.

    NO CONJ: *I will always remember that house:* it had a cool veranda on the left side, perfect for summer entertaining; the kitchen was enormous, offering plenty of counter space.

    CONJ: I will always remember that house, the one on Grand Vista; it had a cool veranda on the left side, perfect for summer entertaining, and *the kitchen was enormous.*

32.10 All three joined sentences are complex. A semicolon (;) is necessary between them. In this example, the add-on and interruptive phrases are shown in italics.

He had nothing, *or so it seemed,* that he could use as a downpayment; but that didn't stop him—*not for the moment, at least*—from making a bid; and he got scared, *as did his wife,* when the gavel banged down, *declaring him the buyer.*

Exception: **Last sentence needs to be emphasized.** If a dash has already been used, capitalize the last complex sentence.

He had nothing, or so it seemed, that he could use as a downpayment; but that didn't stop him—not for the moment, at least—from making a bid. *And he got scared, as did his wife, when the gavel banged down, declaring him the buyer.*

32.11 **One of three joined sentences interrupts as a quick opinion, comment, or explanation.** Place it inside a parentheses. Also, any semicolons (;) which may appear between the other two can be replaced by commas (,) when they have single rather than multiple add-on or interruptive phrases (*see* first and second examples).

OPINION: The journey was incredibly boring, much longer than I had expected (the meals they served were, unquestionably, worse), and I found myself going quite mad, becoming almost delirious in fact.

EXPLAINS: The journey was incredibly boring, much longer than I had expected (they had to take the mountain route because the soldiers had blocked the other roads) and I found myself going quite mad, becoming almost delirious in fact.

COMMENT: The journey was incredibly boring, much longer than I had expected, perhaps by six hours (I still don't don't understand why they took the mountain route); and I found myself going quite mad, becoming almost delirious in fact, what with the stench and quality of the food.

Joining Four Sentences, or More

For information regarding the meaning of simple, compound, and complex sentences, refer to the information under SIMPLE SENTENCE and JOINING TWO SENTENCES.

33.1 **Four closely related simple sentences have different lead-in words.** They should be separated by semicolons (;), as shown in the first example. Including interrupting or add-on phrases turns them into complex sentences, but it does not change the punctuation rule (*see* second example, which shows the interrupting and add-on phrases italicized).

I went to the circus down the street; she went to the movie which was playing uptown; he went to the last ballgame of the season; all the others stayed home.

I went to the circus down the street, *taking Marcia with me;* she went to see the new Garbo movie, *which was playing uptown;* he, *sad to say,* went to the last ballgame of the season; all the others, *in protest,* stayed home.

Exception: **Conjunction between last two sentences.** A comma (,) may be used to separate them when one is simple rather than compound.

I went to the circus down the street; she went to the movie which was playing uptown; he went to the last ballgame of the season, *and* all the others stayed home.

33.2 **Joining multiple simple sentences which are related.** Through editing, some simple sentences can be turned into phrases which introduce, interrupt, or are added to other sentences, turning them into complex sentences. The punctuation may be a combination of commas (,) and semicolons (;)—or semicolons alone may be used. As an illustration, here is a list of seven simple sentences which relate a tiny storyline and can be linked together. After them is an example of their being combined. The words in italics are those which have been added; those in brackets have been scratched. The semicolons represent the heavier pauses.

Sentence 1 The current rushed under me.
Sentence 2 I could only comply with its wishes.
Sentence 3 It suddenly turned with ferocity.
Sentence 4 I was buoyed by its liquid hand.
Sentence 5 I flew down the river.
Sentence 6 I was bouncing like a ball on the rapids.
Sentence 7 I hit the bridge abutment.

The current rushed under me, *and* I could only comply with its wishes; *then* it suddenly turned with ferocity *and*, [I was] buoyed by its liquid hand, I flew [down the river], [I was] bouncing like a ball on the rapids, *until* I hit the bridge abutment

33.3 **Strong pause follows the first of several joined sentence.** More often than not, a colon (:) will be needed at that spot, for the other sentences are probably providing information which help to elaborate, summarize, conclude, confirm, etc. Each of them should be separated with semicolons (;).

There is little we can do about it: they hold all of the important elective offices; their influence is all-powerful; and, the way I look at it, they have more talent than we do.

33.4 **Simple sentences have same lead-in words.** If the sentences are extremely short, use the comma (,) to separate them; but if the conjunction is removed before the last simple sentence, and all of them are a bit longer, insert semicolons (;) between them when the lead-in words are repeated. This is especially appropriate when the opening words are repeated each time and a stronger pause is needed between each sentence.

SHORT

Original:	He came. He saw. He conquered. He left.
Joined:	He came, he saw, he conquered, and he left.
Implied:	He came, saw, conquered, left.

LONGER

Original:	They entered the bar. They drank five beers. They sand old songs. They didn't tip.
Joined:	They entered the bar; they drank five beers; they sang old songs; they didn't tip.
Implied:	*They* entered the bar, drank five beers, sang old old songs, and didn't tip.

EVEN LONGER: Money in the hands of a bureaucrat will cause it to reduce in value; money in the hands of a financier will grow and prosper for him alone; money in the hands of relatives fosters jealousy; money in my hands is the same as throwing it out the window.

But when the last sentence is preceded by a conjunction, a comma (,) should be inserted before it if it doesn't confuse the reader. The conjunction which has been italicized in this example is the adverbial type.

Money in the hands of a bureaucrat will cause it to reduce in value; money in the hands of a financier will grow and prosper for him alone; money in the hands of relatives fosters jealousy, *yet* this doesn't mean it isn't worth pursuing.

Exception: **Repeated lead-in words do not begin successive sentences.** A keener editing task will be required. In the following example, the closely related sentences come in pairs, and the redundant words occur every other sentence. For the sake of brevity, notice how words within the sentence-pairs have been thrown out and replaced with commas (,) while semicolons (;) replace some periods (.).

I saw the canyon. ~~It was~~ beautiful as ever. ~~I~~ saw the ski slopes. ~~They were~~ beautiful as ever. ~~I~~ saw the cabin. ~~It was~~ beautiful as ever. ~~I~~ saw her. ~~She was~~ beautiful as ever.

Saw the canyon, beautiful as ever; saw the ski slopes, beautiful as ever; saw the cabin, beautiful as ever; saw her, beautiful as ever.

EDITED MORE: Saw the canyon, ski slopes, and cabin; beautiful as ever. Saw her, beautiful as ever.

Exception: **Repeated lead-in words follow a strong pause.** Insert a colon (:) after the first sentence, for the information which follows should be highly supportive. Remove the other lead-in words except the first ones, which may require adding a word or two to improve the flow. Do not capitalize the first word after the colon unless the first sentence adds nothing in the way of meaning.

The merits were considerable. *It had* a fifteen-year warranty on all parts. *It had* a reasonable price. *It had* a high trade-in value.

The merits were considerable: it had a fifteen-year warranty on all parts, a reasonable price, and a high trade-in value.

33.5 **Verb is repeated.** Rather than repeat the verb several times, it may be omitted and represented by a comma (,). The first two examples which follow indicate what editing may be required to prevent redundancy and tighten everything.

It came to pass that the seaman *found* a port; the politician *found* a cause; the minister *found* a sea of frustration, and the businessman *found* a way of making a profit.

It came to pass that the seaman *found* a port; the politician, a cause; the minister, a sea of frustration; the businessman, a way of making a profit.

33.6 **Complex sentences with the same lead-words.** Proper editing will permit such words to be implied rather than stated, with the semicolon (;) representing their absence. In the example which follows, rather than repeat *Joey, in an effort to get his mother to let him stay up late, decided that....*, only the LAST WORD of that group is used to launch each sentence thereafter.

Joey, in an effort to convince his mother to let him stay up late, decided that he would clean his room; *that* he would stay out of trouble all day, God willing, and certainly not fight with his sister; *that* it wouldn't hurt to clean out the garage, especially the junk he'd been collecting; *that* mowing the lawn would be in his best interests; *that*,

185

even though he dreaded the mere thought of it, apologizing to his brother in front of her might do the trick.

33.7 **Same conjunction begins several complex sentences.** The redundancy creates a sense of drama. In almost all cases it should be capitalized and follow a period (.), making each complex sentence stand alone. Note: this rule also applies to simple sentences which begin with a conjunction.

Frank Thomas, the coach, said it was impossible to throw the ball that far, but Jerry did. *And* wasn't he the same individual who, before last year's track meet, said it was unrealistic to think anyone could run that fast? *And* who, with a smirk, said that no one could ever eat that much? *And* can you, to the best of your ability, give me the name of the person who swore he was never wrong?

Exception: **Presenting a set of facts.** The same conjunction may be used repeatedly, but followed each time with a colon (:), and the word after the colon is capitalized. Admittedly, this is a unusual punctuation technique and one which should only be employed when even a greater sense of drama is desired, e.g., when you wish to convey an impressive weight of evidence. The conjunctions *and*, *or*, and *but* are best used in this situation.

Hamilton urged frugality rather than British imports, *and* he believed that raw materials were in such abundance that Americans would not need them when they realized the riches available to them. *And:* He knew that the continuous arrival of new immigrants, who were streaming into the country daily, were bringing the needed skills to erect and run production facilities. *And:* He was aware that France, despite what she said publicly, would intervene if England dared to start a war. *And:* He was of the opinion that people were equal and that government should not, and must not, tax them without representation.

33.8 **Paragraph of several sentences presents an interrupting opinion, comment, explanation, anecdote, or joke.** These related sentences can be simple, complex, or a combination of the two, and they should be encased in parentheses. Here's the way a single interrupting paragraph might look:

So when writing a résumé, you should keep in mind what the employer wants rather than what you want, although the latter is certainly critical to job satisfaction. But a key thing to remember is that the résumé is only designed to get you an interview; therefore, it is an advertisement.

186

(Take, for example, the products which are advertised on television and radio, including those in newspapers and magazines: none of the advertisers tell you what they want *from* you; instead, they tell you what the product can do *for* you—that is, make you happier, sexier, contented, and so on. They attempt to put the prospective buyer first and themselves last.)

But the overwhelming number of job hunters never see their résumés this way; consequently, most look like an accountant's ledger and they are filled with "I want this" and "I want that" type of language.

Exception: **Two paragraphs or more.** Place a parenthesis before the first word of each interrupting paragraph, but only insert the closing parenthesis after the last word of the interruption. In the following example, the interruption—which in this case is an anecdote—actually begins INSIDE of a paragraph which itself is not an interruption.

...and Reginald scoffed at the idea of their having anything in common, and found great amusement about the proposal for years after that. (Reminiscent of the story when Isadora Duncan suggested to George Bernard Shaw that they have a baby together.

("Just think," she proposed, "of a baby with your brains and my looks."

("Just think," he reflected, "of a baby with my looks and your brains.")

She took offense, of course, and never spoke to Reginald again.

33.9 **One of the joined sentences needs to be emphasized.** Dramatically separate it from the others by using a dash (—). In the examples provided below, the emphasized sentence leads off the first sentence; it interrupts in the second, and acts as an afterthought in the third. The words *I wrote about the Tinker family* are implied before each sentence except the first one.

LEADS: *I wrote about Grant Tinker, the undisputed head of the Tinker family*—the manuscript was never published, by the way, because no one wanted to offend him and risk being sued, and it's still tucked away in my desk drawer.

INTERRUPTS: I wrote about the Tinker family—*Grant Tinker, you might remember, started with five dollars and turned it into five million*—but someone talked my publisher out of doing it, although he says that's not true.

187

LAST:	I wrote about the Tinker family; that was before I published my book about the Wilsons, and it created quite a stir in their ranks, let me assure you—*the lawsuit alone was over ten million.*

33.10 Strong pause follows the first complex sentence. Insert a colon (:) to represent the pause, for the sentences which follow it are probably providing some type of elaborating information that helps to support it. Separate the other sentences with semicolons (;).

The world, from all indications, has never been at peace for several reasons: there is always some dictator who, despite the lessons of history, believes he is invincible; nations do not prepare for war and, therefore, are doomed to engage in it; and the will of the people, on average, has characteristically been one of weakness.

Motto, Epitaph, Inscription

Like book titles, every word of a motto, epitaph, or inscription is capitalized—except prepositions, conjunctions, and indefinite articles.

34.1 Follows a noun or pronoun. Insert a colon (:).

NOUN:	This was his *epitaph:* I Already Gave at the Office.
PRONOUN:	Truman's motto was *this:* The Buck Stops Here.
Exception:	**Needs emphasis.** Insert a dash (—) before it.

That was Harry S. Truman's motto—*The Buck Stops Here.*

Exception:	**"The" precedes it.** Punctuation is not necessary to set the motto, epitaph, or inscription apart.

The motto The Buck Stops Here seems to have lost favor nowadays.

34.2 Immediately follows a verb. Punctuation is not needed to set it apart.

On the monument was *engraved* The Buck Stops Here.

34.3 Interrupts a sentence and follows a pronoun. Requires a comma (,) before and after it, even though it may not immediately follow a pronoun. Use dashes (—) when you want to emphasize it. In the sentences which follow, *that* and *his* are pronouns.

That motto, The Buck Stops Here, is enjoying a comeback.
His motto—The Buck Stops Here—was written in large letters.

Dialogue

A line of dialogue, except for the "thinking" type and that which appears in stage and motion picture scripts, requires double quotation marks (" ") before and after it.

35.1 **Dialogue is accompanied by a verb such as "said" and "asked."** The group of words containing such a verb is set apart through the use of the comma (,), no matter if it precedes, interrupts, or follows the dialogue. But when the dialogue is interrupted, the first comma is inserted before the first closing quotation mark ("). In this situation, incidentally, there should be a four double quotation marks altogether (*see* third sentence example).

DIALOGUE IS...

Preceded: She *said,* "We can't go on like this."

He *asked* her innocently, "What did you have in mind?"

Interrupted: "How long can they keep up this charade," *Jerry* asked, "and still expect us to stand for it?"

Followed: "We should pull together," he *told* them that evening.

"We should pull together," *said* Bill.

Exception: **Dialogue has its own exclamation mark (!) or a question mark (?). No comma is needed between it and the nondialogue which follows it.**

"How do you expect to get a job in an office if you wear overalls and sneakers to the interview!" *she yelled.*

"Is this the door to the Men's Room?" *he inquired.*

35.2 **List of verbs which either precede or follow a line of dialogue.** Below, the manner in which the dialogue is spoken is shown at the left. Opposite it are the verbs in that category. A reminder: if the dialogue is immediately preceded by a noun or pronoun which repre-

189

sents the person speaking, insert a colon (:) between them; otherwise, a comma (,) is the required punctuation.

Said Herman: "The proof is in the pudding."
Jerry *replied*, "What's pudding got to do with it?"
"He's always talking about pudding," chimed in Robert.

Normal

ad libbed, commented, consoled, continued, expressed, joked, kidded, mentioned, noted, quipped, remarked, resumed, said, stated, teased, told, uttered, voiced, went on, wisecracked.

Lengthy: babbled, chattered, gabbed, gushed, jabbered, prattled, rambled, spouted, yacked.

Sound

Loud: bawled, bellowed, blared, blubbered, boomed, called, cried, exploded, howled, hollered, raged, ranted, sang, screeched, screamed, shrieked, shouted, sobbed, spouted, squawked, squealed, stormed, thundered, wailed, whooped, yelled, yelped, yowled

Soft : breathed, cooed, mumbled, murmured, muttered, purred, sighed, whispered

Tedious: droned

Windy: gasped, gulped, panted, puffed, wheezed

Positive

Agreeing: admitted, agreed, assented, conceded, concurred, complied, confirmed, corroborated, echoed, granted, subscribed, verified

Approving: approved, beamed, complimented, flattered, hailed, lauded, praised, rejoiced

Laughing: chuckled, giggled, guffawed, joked, laughed, rejoiced, smiled, teased, tittered

Other: assured, congratulated, counseled, encouraged, reassured, volunteered

Negative

Arguing: argued, contradicted, denied, disputed, interceded, objected, pointed out, protested, refuted

Disagreeing: differed, disagreed, dissented, reminded, remonstrated

Disapproving: accused; admonished; berated, bitched, charged, chided, complained, criticized, cursed, denounced, disapproved, fussed, griped, grumbled, huffed, lectured, rebuked, reproached, reproved, scolded, smirked, sqauwked, swore, threatened, upbraided

Ill Humor: growled, grunted, snapped, snarled, snorted

Sad: anguished, bemoaned, blubbered, cried, grieved, groaned, lamented, moaned, mourned, rued, sobbed, sniveled, wept, whined

Other: complained, criticized, griped, grumbled, hissed, impugned, jeered, nagged, razzed, ridiculed, snickered, whined

Responding

Interrupting: broke in, chimed in, cut in, interrupted, intervened, piped up, spoke up

Pleading: begged, beseeched, entreated, implored, pleaded, prayed

Question: asked, challenged, demanded, inquired, queried, questioned, requested

Replying: answered, assured, reacted, reacted, reassured, replied, rejoined, rebutted, responded, retorted

Providing Information

Advising: advocated, advised, cautioned, counseled, exhorted, lectured, recommended, sermonized, suggested, warned

Drawing a conclusion: alleged, believed, concluded, confirmed, decided, deduced, determined, hypothesized, judged, maintained, noted, observed, philosophized, testified, theorized, warranted

Emphasizing: affirmed, asserted, claimed, contended, declared, emphasized, insisted, maintained, stressed

Indicating: hinted, implied, indicated, insinuated, intimated, suggested

Informing: added, amplified, announced, apprized, confided, conveyed, explained, expounded, informed, proclaimed, recounted, related, reported

Predicting: calculated, estimated, forecasted, guessed, perceived, predicted, presumed, prophesized, reckoned, speculated, surmised, wagered

Reading Off: intoned, recited, reeled off

Telling a "Secret": blabbed, blurted, blurted out, confided, disclosed, divulged, gossiped, imparted, revealed, snitched, tattled, whispered

Mental

Thinking Aloud: agonized, anguished doubted, fretted, mused, resolved, deliberated, determined, hesitated, marveled, thought

Remembering: recalled, recollected, remembered, reminisced

Authoritative/Unauthoritative

Authoritative: commanded, decreed, demanded, demonstrated, dictated, directed, enjoined, instructed, ordered, preached, prescribed, pronounced, ruled, specified, spelled out, stipulated, summoned

Unauthoritative: acquiesced, capitulated, complied, consented, deferred, obeyed, quavered, recanted, submitted, surrendered, yielded

Other

Peculiar Speech Aspects: cackled, coughed, crooned, drawled, droned, lisped, panted, sputtered, stammered, stuttered, twanged, wheezed

Admitting: acknowledged, admitted, avowed, confessed
Bragging: blustered, boasted, bragged, crowed, exulted, gloated
Pretending: pretended, professed
Promising: pledged, promised, vowed, swore
Offering: advanced, offered, proffered, put forward, submitted, tendered

192

Persuading: coaxed, persuaded
Lying: amplified, enlarged, evaded, exaggerated, fibbed, lied
Surprised: exclaimed, gasped
Wheeling and Dealing: bargained, gambled
More Than One Person: buzzed, chanted, clamored, groaned, roared
Consulting: conferred, consulted

35.3 **Noun or pronoun precedes the dialogue.** A noun or pronoun immediately before a line of the dialogue demands a colon (:) after it. The nouns and pronouns are italicized in the following examples.

> Remarked the *leader:* "You haven't seen anything yet."
> Said *she:* "You're making this hard for all of us."
> Asked *Marlin:* "I say, is there any more soup back there?"

35.4 **Conjunction and sentence are added to dialogue.** Follow the dialogue with a comma (,) or a dash (—), but only use the latter when more drama is needed. The closing quotation mark (") is preceded by a comma (,), but the dash should be inserted *after* it.

> COMMA: She said, "I will never see him again," *and she meant it.*
> DASH: She said, "I will never see him again"—*and she meant it.*

> Exception: **Sentence added without a conjunction.** Place a semicolon (;) *after* the closing quotation mark, or place a period *before* it and capitalize the next word.
>
> > SEMICOLON: She replied, "I will never see him again"; it was something she would regret saying.
> >
> > PERIOD: She replied, "I will never see him again." It was something she would regret saying.

35.5 **Nondialogue phrase is added to the dialogue.** It should be preceded by a comma (,), to identify the pause which exists. The nondialogue phrase has been italicized in the following example.

> She said, "I will never see you again," *causing Wilbur's face to suddenly turn red with anger.*

> Exception: **Add-on phrase needs emphasis.** Drop the comma and insert the dash (—) after the closing quotation mark (").
>
> > She said, "I never saw him again"—*a bone-popping lie if there ever was one.*

193

Exception: **Dialogue ends with an exclamation point (!) or question mark (?).** No comma is needed between the dialogue and the add-on phrase.

She yelled, "I never saw him again!" *causing the defense attorney to gasp in disbelief.*

"Just what are you accusing me of?" *she demanded.*

35.6 **Dramatic pause in a line of dialogue.** If a dramatic pause is essential in a line of dialogue, represent that pause with a dash (—). In the examples which follow, note the placement of the separating commas (,) and double quotation marks (" ") when the nondialogue introduces, interrupts, and is added to the dialogue.

NONDIALOGUE
    Introduces: *Roger said,* "Not much can be done for him—or any of the rest of them, either."
    Interrupts: "Not much can be done for him," *said Roger,* "—or any of the rest of them, either."

    Added on: "Not much can be done for him—or any of the rest of them, either," *said Roger.*

35.7 **Showing hesitation, uncertainty, or confusion.** They appear in dialogue as pauses and are represented by three periods (...), called the ellipsis. In the first example shown below, the character speaking is trying to open a bottle of wine, and multiple pauses are used. In the second example, the same punctuation is employed to show confusion; in the final two, uncertainty. But in the last example, dashes (—) are used rather than the ellipsis, because the pauses are quicker.

    HESITATION: He wrestled with the cork top as he said, "You know, I didn't really get a good look at the fellow...Blimey, they must've put this thing in with a touch of glue...What was I saying?...Oh yeh, about that inspector fellow...Well, you know...Wait a minute...Uuumph!...Did you ever see such a cork?"

    CONFUSION: "But you said...I mean, I heard you....," began Buster Wiggins, with his eyes wider than saucers, trying to make sense of her denial.

    UNCERTAINTY: Jasper Jinkpot scratched his head and looked at her: "Gee, I dunno, Miz Maples...I guess I could...aw, but heck, you know how pa is."

Dash: *"I—you—uh—well,* all of us must share some of the blame, I suppose."

35.8   Quick transition of thought. The dash (—) is the most appropriate punctuation to use in this instance. Two examples:

"It is indestructible when—wait a minute, that can't be right."
"Patient? I think I am. In fact, I—Morley, turn that music down!"

35.9   Unfinished line of dialogue. It should end with four periods (....) if the character in the story or play pauses in his or her speech.

TAILS OFF: "I miss her," he said. "And there are times...." Then he stopped talking and looked away. It was the closest I'd ever seen him come to showing any emotion.

DISTRACTED: "I miss her terribly," he told the reporter, "and there are times...." The reporter waited for him to continue, but he was eyeing some woman in a red dress.

EXPECTANT: "And the winner is...."

But if the dialogue stops because the character is suddenly overwhelmed by emotion, or he or she is interrupted by someone else, a dash (—) is used instead. In the first example, emotion prevents the dialogue from continuing; in the second and third, it is interrupted by other dialogue; and in the last example below, a *general description* of what another character said performs as an interruption. The third example, incidentally, is a script format.

"I miss her. And there are times—" He tried, without success, to choke back an overwhelming sadness that had been with him ever since he had lost her to that terrible illness.

"My opponent has not lived up to his campaign promise and—"
"Now, hold it," interrupted the reporter, "that's not what I asked you."

EMMA: Are you telling me—
BURT: That's right.
EMMA: And all the time—
BURT: She's been skipping school.

"Let me tell you right now—" Sidney began, but Paula interrupted him. She let him know in no uncertain terms that she was the boss, not him.

Exception: **Begins the sentence rather than ends it.** Four periods (....) should be used. Insert them immediately after the opening quotation mark ("). This technique is often used to begin a new division of a story by capturing a character's dialogue at midpoint. Properly used, it can immediately cast the reader into the middle of a dramatic situation that is already in progress. But remember: quotation marks are not used in scripts for TV, movies, and the stage.

"....and I told'im that I wasn't gonna take it any more. I let'im know that he wasn't living up to the deal we made five years ago."

35.10 **Stuttering.** Duplicate the first letter of a word a few times and insert hyphens (-) between each of those letters.

"You are m-m-my s-s-s-sunshine, M-m-m-ary L-l-l-lou."

35.11 **Thinking dialogue.** That which a character in a story thinks rather than says is called thinking dialogue, and neither italics nor double quotation marks (" ") are necessary to set it apart. But a comma (,) is essential to separate thinking dialogue from nondialogue. However, if the nondialogue follows an exclamation mark (!) or question mark (?), the comma is omitted.

COMMA: I wonder what I should do, he asked himself.
He asked himself, Is this all there is?

NO COMMA: What to do! What to do! he wondered to himself.

Exception: **Real dialogue with thinking dialogue.** There are several options to identify the "thinking" part for the reader: the first example shows it encased in parentheses; in the second, it is typed in italics; and in the third example, the thinking dialogue and vocalized dialogue are placed in separate paragraphs. But in the final example, there is more thinking dialogue than actual dialogue; therefore, the spoken type is placed inside a parentheses instead. But it is worth noting that this reversal is rarely used.

No, I don't mind staying in the house with you today. (Wow, it's nice outside! I wonder how the fish are biting?) But shouldn't you get out and get a bit of sun?

No, I don't mind staying in the house with you today. *Wow, it's nice outside! I wonder how the fish are biting?* But shouldn't you get out and get a bit of sun?

> *Oh boy, it's really nice outside! I wonder how the fish are biting? I'll bet everybody's out at the lake.*
> "What? No, I don't mind staying in the house with you today."
> *Well, there's another lie. I don't know why she expects me to sit here and watch her sew on those curtains.*
> "Listen, I said I didn't mind. What more do you want?"

Wow, it's nice outside! I wonder how the fish are biting? I'll bet everybody's out at the lake. ("No, I don't mind staying in the house with you today.") I don't know why I have to sit here with her, watching her sew on those curtains and throwing gossip here and there. ("I said I didn't mind, didn't I?")

But in scripts for the stage, television and motion pictures, thinking dialogue is called an "aside," and that word is inserted between brackets and placed before the first word of the thinking dialogue. Two examples:

Yes, Marjorie, I love you. Yes, I want to get married. [Aside] My God, how am I going to get out of this? She bores me down to my socks. I've got it! [To Marjorie] Hey, Marj, I got an idea.

[Aside] To be or not to be, that is the....

35.12 **Remembering words once spoken.** Besides being preceded and followed by double quotation marks (" "), the dialogue recalled by a character should be encased in brackets. Note: Do not place a period (.) before the last bracket when the bracketed dialogue interrupts a sentence; however, if the recalled words carry their own ending exclamation mark (!) or question mark (?), it is essential to keep that punctuation.

The old man's words kept coming back to haunt him. ["None ofya will come back."] As he sat on the rock and ate his cold beans ["You're running after yellow metal, when the real gold is right here!"], he began to think that the old fool was right.

35.13 Adding dialect to dialogue. Dialect gives strict grammarians the absolute shudders, because it is considered to be an abomination of the English language; but if you are writing dialogue or quoting someone directly, capturing the actual flavor of that person's speech is usually to your advantage.

But writing dialect is easier than reading it. Anyone who would subject the reader to the tedious process of having to plod through one shortened or missing word after another may well deserve that reader's impatience. While it's a wonderful guide for actors, one must keep in mind that most people merely wish to be entertained without having to work hard at it. Including a smattering of dialect is quite acceptable, because it helps to prod the reader into identifying the key speech patterns of that person or fictional character, whether they are real or imagined. Therefore, use dialect as a seasoning, not as a main meal. In the first example which follows, too much dialect has been added.

TOO MUCH:	Da' ain't nobody up da', an' de do' is wide open. Sose y'all can be walkin' your mules up ta de ba'an and go sha-shayin' on up to de house when 'venient.
JUST ENOUGH:	Ain't nobody up there. Door's open. So y'all can be walkin' your mules up to the barn and go sha-shaying' on up to the house when it's convenient.

35.14 Omitting first letters of a word in dialect. The apostrophe (') is used to represent missing letters from the beginning of a word. If that word is normally capitalized, then capitalize it when it is part of dialect as well. In the first example below, the word being shortened is *away*, which shows the elimination of one alphabetic letter; in the second it is *beneath*, which shows the elimination of two letters. The opening quotation mark (") and the apostrophe point in different directions.

FIRST WORD:	" 'Way he went, Colonel. Fast as his legs could carry'im."
PARTIAL DIALOGUE:	And she said that "....'neath that ain't nothing but old newspapers."

35.15 Omitting middle letters of a word in dialect. An apostrophe (') is used to represent the missing letters in the middle of a word. Again, this is a practice that should not be overdone. In this example, the letters are being omitted from the word *suppose*.

"I *s'pose* you think you're right smart, don't you."

Exception: **Spelling altered.** This is a punctuation technique that should certainly not be used to excess. Nevertheless, here is an example of British dialect, where the spelling of *governor* and *half and half* are changed.

"Well, *guv'ner*, I'd say it's about 'arf and 'arf."

35.16 Omitting last letters of a word in dialect. The most common technique—and surely the one which readers most readily accept—is dropping one or two letters from the end of a word and replacing it with an apostrophe ('). Moreover, a southern U.S. dialect would also allow you to place the letter "a" before some words, followed by a hyphen. Commas (,), exclamation marks (!), and question marks (?) follow the apostrophe.

"While you was a-talkin', I was workin'!" said Slats.
Said Slats: "Ever' time you say you will, ol' man Rank gets richer."

35.17 Omitting first and last letters of a word in dialect. This is usually done when the word is the conjunction *and.* The missing letters are replaced by apostrophes (').

"Give me a can of pork *and* beans," Mary told the shopkeeper.
"Gimme a can of them pork 'n' beans," Mary told the shopkeeper

Exception: **Using one apostrophe instead of two.** This is a punctuation technique which is seen quite regularly. By using an apostrophe to substitute for the letter A only, it implies that the word is actually *an* rather than the conjunction *and,* because the letter D is not being represented. While this is incorrect, public acceptance of the single apostrophe may well make such punctuation of the word correct. Here is an example:

"And give me two orders of fish 'n chips," said Larry.

35.18 Combining words in dialect. Use an apostrophe (') to represent the missing letters when two words are combined. In the first example, the combined words are *another one;* in the second, it is the common expression *of course.*

"Then another'n almost knocked me over!" puffed Edgar.
"'Course, that was before I knew better," continued Betty.

35.19 Showing pronunciation. Rather than use dialect throughout an article or book with quoted passages and thereby risk boring the reader who is not all interested in slogging his way over a terrain consisting of missing letters and abundant apostrophes, you may simply want to

199

draw attention to someone's speech patterns just once and be done with it. For example, you might tell the reader that the person you are quoting has a habit of dropping the G's from the end of words, and in the very next quote you show him what you mean by placing the shortened word inside brackets. After you have drawn attention to it, it is up to the reader to take up the cause from then on. If he wants to imagine all the *G's* missing at the end of words in every quote, so be it.

"But I can't believe it's coming [comin'] to this, after all these years," replied Winslow.

35.20 **Joining related sentences in dialogue.** Insert a semicolon (;) between the when there is no separating conjunction. You may also insert a period (.) after the first sentence and capitalize the next one. The semicolon draws attention to the relationship of the two sentences, but either approach is acceptable.

SEMICOLON: "This is the way it will be; there are no alternatives."
PERIOD: "This is the way it will be. There are no alternatives."

35.21 **Dialogue follows one word.** A colon (:) is almost always the appropriate punctuation to use. In the first example below, the introductory word indicates a frame of mind and the nature of the dialogue confirms it. In the second example, it follows a proper name; but this latter technique is usually reserved for dialogue in scripts or as a quick insertion in an article or nonfiction book, in which case no double quotation marks are used. However, in some instances of fictional writing where one may choose to be less descriptive, it can sometimes be employed effectively.

Impressed: "No kidding!"

Bill: "Do it or pay the consequences."
Joe: "I'll take the consequences."

35.22 **Strong pause follows the first sentence of dialogue.** A colon (:) should represent that pause, for the opening sentence of dialogue is probably being followed by a set of instructions, summary, conclusion, confirmation, definition, or an explanation. Insert semicolons (;) between each of the related sentences thereafter. If the other information does not need the opening sentence to make sense, capitalize the first word. (*See* the first and second examples for a comparison.)

INSTRUCTS
Uncapitalized: "So, here's my plan: everybody on the first shift will slow down production at ten o'clock; the drivers will pull their trucks in front of the gate at ten-thirty; and Marvin, here, will unplug all of the refrigeration while that's taking place."

200

Capitalized:	"So, here's the plan: Our leader wants everybody on the first shift to slow down production at ten o'clock; the drivers should pull their trucks in front of the gate at ten-thirty; and he wants you, Marvin, to unplug all of the refrigeration while that's taking place."
EXPLAINS:	"He said it was true: said that no one in the department ever punched a time clock."
SUMMARIZES:	"That's about it: He has the money and we have the property."
CONCLUDES:	"I guess that's what we can look forward to if we stay here: she'll raise the rent and we'll argue about it; six months later she'll do it again, and again we'll raise a ruckus; she'll keep doing it until we move."

35.23 Person is being addressed. When addressing someone, that person's name is set apart from the other information—usually through the employment of the comma (,)—no matter if the name leads off, interrupts, or is added to the sentence. This also applies to colloquial names like *mom, grandpa,* and *dad,* including conventional terms of respect such as *madam* and *sir,* none of which are capitalized. However, when *sir* or any other title (Lady, Lord, etc.) are placed before an individual's name, then capitalization is mandatory. However, when more drama is required, the dash (—) is more appropriately used.

PROPER NAME:
First:	"*Mr. Jones,* please step forward."
Midsentence:	"You, *Burt,* are hard to understand."
	"No, *Madame Bovary,* it's me."
Last:	"Is that you, *Mrs. Elcott?*"
	"I wish you'd repeat that, *Sir James.*"

COLLOQUIAL:
First:	"*Mom,* I'm going to Jerry's house."
Midsentence:	"What, *sir,* do you mean by that?"
Last:	"You'd better listen to me, *sis.*"

DRAMATIC:	"*Jerry*—stop that!"
	"Who's coming—*Orville?*"

STANDS ALONE:	"*Grandpa!* "

Exception:	**"Yes" or "no" precedes the word "ma'am" or "sir."** No punctuation should divide them.

201

"*Yes sir*, that's what she told me."
"Well, *no ma'am*, I wouldn't like that at all."

Exception: **Pronoun "you" precedes a curse word.** No punctuation should divide them.

"*You bastard*, why didn't you tell me the truth?!"
"Because I didn't want to, *you SOB.*"

35.24 **"Hello", "goodbye", and their synonyms.** They should be set apart with commas (,) when attached to a line of dialogue; but if they stand alone, periods (.) or exclamation marks (!) are used. Foreign words, when possible to do so, should be italicized.

STANDS ALONE
    One word: "Farewell!"
    Foreign word: *"Au revoir."*
    In a series: "Farewell! Farewell! Farewell!"

BEGINNING
    Precedes one
    name: "Good afternoon, Mr. Mugwump."

    Precedes more
    than one name: "Hello, Mr. Anglehorst...Mr. Engleftwitt...Mrs. Williams. I'm so glad to finally meet all of you."

MIDSENTENCE
    Middle: "Well, how are you, Roger!"
    Follows pause: "Well—how are you, Roger!"

    Interrupts: "This hotel has more than a thousand rooms, and—Good-bye, Mrs. Endicott! I do hope your stay was a pleasant one!—now, let's see, what was I saying?"

                    "This hotel has more than a thousand rooms, and—Good-bye, Mrs. Endicott! I do hope your stay was a pleasant one! Now, let's see, what was I saying?"

END
    Follows name: "Mr. Westcott, good-bye."
    Strong pause: "Mr. Westcott—welcome."
    Elaborates: "Say what you always say: see you."
    Phone: "Hello—Mr. Mugwump?"

LETTER

Business:	Dear Mr. Soggs:
Personal:	Dear Thelma,

Exception: **Word needs highlighting.** When this occurs, it is no longer a greeting. And since double
quotation marks are already being used to encase
the dialogue, single quotation marks (' ') must
be employed to highlight the word. Another option is to italicize it.

"Did you actually say 'howdy'?"
"*Hello* did you say?"

Exception: **Acts as the subject of the sentence.** If
the greeting is the subject, it is functioning as a
noun and will need single quotation marks (' ')
to offset it in the sentence. But if it is not dialogue, use double quotation marks (" ").

"Karl, your 'good-bye' is considerably longer
than your 'hello.' "

"Hi" is not as formal as "Good day."

35.25 **Actor's directions in a script.** Directions which attend lines of
dialogue and provide key pieces of information for the actor with regard
to the character he or she is playing are encased in brackets (*see* the
fourth and sixth lines of dialogue below). Colons (:) follow each character's name. No double quotation marks are used before and after the
dialogue. Note: What you see below is how a play appears within a
book when it is published; it is not, however, the accepted format for
unpublished plays. In those instances, the name is centered and the dialogue is flush on the left-hand side. Shorter dialogue may be centered.

MARCIA: John?
JOHN: Mmmm?
MARCIA: Do you love me?
JOHN: [Looking up from paper] Huh?
MARCIA: I said, do you love me?
JOHN: [Throwing the paper down] Oh, for godsake!....
MARCIA: Well, you don't have to get mad about it!

35.26 **Stage directions in a script.** Unlike an actor's directions, these
are not bracketed. Instead, they are heavily indented at the left and
placed between the dialogue belonging to one character and the name of
the next character who is supposed to speak. The sentences in them
may be of a complex nature and demand commas (,). As opposed to

203

Rule 35.25, the format below is far closer to that which is preferred by directors and producers.

MARCIA
Well, you don't have to get mad about it!

> Enter Willie, Marcia's brother, from stage right. He is everything John hates in a human being: lazy, unkept, and having no taste for anything but beer and cigarettes.

WILLIE
Hey—who's got the paper? Huh?

35.27 Dialogue is in the form of a request. No question mark is needed after a line of dialogue which is framed in the nature of a request. But if the dialogue contains a comma (,) before such two-word phrases as *won't you* and *will you*, then a question mark (?) must be used.

NO QUESTION MARK: "Will you see what time it is."

WITH TWO-WORD PHRASE: "See what time it is, will you?"
    Name added: "See what time it is, will you, Bill?"

35.28 Nonwords. Nonwords often play an important role in the composition of dialogue, and members of this group have various uses which can be very effective in the right situation—and the punctuation which accompanies them is just as varied. Basically, to show emphasis use an exclamation mark (!), and place a period (.) after the nonword when it is not being dramatically inserted, keeping in mind that some nonwords—such as *poof* and *zowie*—are inherently dramatic and demand exclamation marks (!). Those nonwords which are attached to sentences and phrases may be followed and preceded by commas (,), dashes (—), and ellipsis (...), depending upon the circumstances.

SHOWING
COMPREHENSION: "*Ahhhh,* so that's what you were trying to do."

PAUSING: "But then Bertha...well, *uhhhhh,* she said we weren't allowed. But we went ahead, anyway."

ASKING FOR SOMETHING
TO BE REPEATED: "*Huh?* What did you say?"

204

"Then Nancy and I started to...*eh?*... That's right—Nancy Ainwright. Anyway, we started climbing...*eh?*...I'm sorry, I don't know where she lives."

ASKING FOR CONFIRMATION:	"So you really did it, *huh?*"
MEANS "I'M HERE" OR "WHAT DO YOU WANT?"	"*Yo!*"
DISMISSING THE POSSIBILITY:	"They wouldn't dare attack before breakfast. *Naaahhh!*"
AGREEING OR USED TO REPRESENT "I SEE"	"*Mmmm.* I suppose you're right." "*Um.* Whatever you say." "*Uh-huh.* And then what?"
THINKING:	"Hmmmm."
REPELLED:	"*Uuuu-!* Get it off! Quick!" "*Yuck!* What a mess!" "Well, there it is. *Yech!*"
LAUGHTER:	"*Ha-ha-ha-ha!* The joke's on you!"
DRUNKENESS:	"I wanted *(hic!)* to be there."

35.29 Changing the spelling of words. While this is not a punctuation problem, it's an important factor for some writers when they write dialogue. Just as in the case of writing dialect, which uses the apostrophe (') to represent omitted letters in a word, the practice of changing the spelling of some words should not be abused, for it can easily tire the reader who is either unaccustomed to or intolerant of such changes. How the word is changed depends on how you, the writer, hear it in your own mind. For example, "give me" can become *gimme;* "should have" can appear as *shoulda;* "how's that" can be written as *howzzat;* and "will you" can be changed to *willya.*

"*Gimme* that paper, *willya?*"
"You *shoulda* done what I told you to do."
"*Howzzat?* You want me to do what?"

Direct Quote

A direct quote matches, word for word, what someone said or wrote, which includes using the same spelling, punctuation, and capitalization.

However, errors in those quotes which are not famous, or which are quite dated, may be corrected to prevent confusion. The *corrections* must be inserted in brackets within the quote. Direct quotes are preceded and followed by double quotation marks (" ").

36.1 **"Said," "replied," etc. accompanies the direct quote.** When a verb such as these precede or follow a quote, its group of words is separated by a comma (,) from the actual quote, and that comma is inserted before the opening and closing quotation marks (" ") which accompany the quote—unless the quote is first or last (see first and third examples below), in which case only one separating comma is used.

DIALOGUE...

Leads off: "Defense is our first priority," *said* General Fandancer.

Interrupted: "This team," *fired back Coach Miller,* "will win or my name isn't—by the way, what is my name?"

At the end: Scrunch Suggs looked at the Crime Committee and *replied,* "Hey, all I do is run a simple little laundromat on Fifth Street."

Exception: **Quote follows an introductory verb.** This usually means the verb and the quote are forming an introductory phrase—one which will only need a comma after its last word.

Saying "I have no comment at this time," Governor Handsintill stormed past the reporters and slammed the door of his office.

Exception: **Quote comes from a famous person.** Look upon it as a formal quote and follow it with a colon (:), even though a verb directly precedes the quote.

President Tims remarked: "We must do our best."

Exception: **Long quote follows a verb.** Insert a colon (:) after the verb.

She *answered:* "A lack of fairness was the one thing I had not expected from you, Sir James, and I am shocked that you have done such a thing when so many people had been counting on you."

36.2 **Noun or pronoun precedes or follows a direct quote.** When either of them immediately *precedes* the quote, insert a colon (:) after it;

however, no punctuation is needed when the noun or pronoun *follows* the quote.

NOUN

Precedes: Said the *Secretary of State:* "High taxes have become a blight on this nation."

Follows: "High taxes have become a blight on this nation" *Secretary Hodges* said to him.

PRONOUN

Precedes: Said *she:* "My husband has worked hard for the city, and I would hate to see this indiscretion cost him his pension"

Follows: "I don't have the authority to do that" *he* said to the reporters, who were grouped around him.

Exception: **Quote has its question mark or exclamation mark.** Place either before the last double quotation mark (").

"Mr. Chairman, are you saying that high taxes are a blight on this nation?" Secretary Hodges asked him.

36.3 **Direct quote is preceded by a preposition.** Only double quotation marks (" ") need accompany the quote, unless more information is added; in that case, a comma (,) must be inserted before the closing quotation mark (*see* second example). In either situation, the quote is not capitalized.

PRECEDED BY
PREPOSITION: Opera star Jodi Machusi advises young singers *to* "refrain from trying to hit high notes in your teenage years."

Information
added: Opera star Jodi Machusi advises young singers *to* "refrain from trying to hit high notes in your teenage years," in order that their vocal chords be given time to mature.

36.4 **Direct quote extends beyond three typewritten lines.** There are two options: the quote can be treated as explained in Rules 36.1 through 36.3, or it may be placed in block form and isolated from the other information altogether. The latter technique is especially appropriate when the quote is being included as part of an essay or letter. To achieve the block form, follow these procedures: (1) insert a colon after the last word before the quote; (2) double space; (2) indent the quote's left- and right-hand margins and omit the double quotation marks; (3)

double space again; (4) type the next line of the nonquote without any left-hand indentation, unless you are beginning a new paragraph. Here is the way it would look on a page:

Before the Battle at Cutter's Creek, General Heartfelt wrote this in his diary:

> Our rations are growing dangerously low, and I do not know if we have enough bullets for our guns. Yet the morale of the men is remarkably high, and my hopes for victory remain undiminished.

The next day, the Twenty-Third Infantry Division lost nearly a third of its men in battle, and another third deserted, leaving the General....

Exception: **No pause precedes the quote.** If you still wish to keep it in block form, no colon is needed after the last word preceding the quote. And the quote itself does not begin with a capital letter. For example:

Vice-President of Marketing Herman Wickhouser is of the opinion that

> quality, while certainly desirable, should not stand in the way of producing products in quantity, for it is a highly competitive industry and becoming more precarious yearly.

Exception: **Part of the quote is in block form, part is not.** That which is *not* in block form should be placed between double quotation marks (" "), with a comma (,) inserted before the closing quotation mark. Then, double-space and put the rest of the quote in block form, using no quotation marks and capitalizing the first word. Note: Never use an ellipsis (...) before the first word or after the last one in a block quote.

"Quality, while certainly desirable, should not stand in the way of producing products in quantity," said Vice President of Marketing Herm Wickhouser.

> We are in a highly competitive industry which is becoming more precarious yearly, and if we do not respond to the needs of the marketplace, we are going to lose our share of it. You can count on it.

Exception: **Another quote inside a block quote.** It receives double quotation marks before and after (*see* italics in the following example), while the other quote receives none. In the sentence example below, notice that the question mark *follows* the closing quotation mark ("), because it is not a part of the quote itself.

The senator ended his discourse on corruption by saying this:

> I challenge any of my colleagues to find one thing in my background which they have not been guilty of themselves while serving the people of this great nation. Was it not Christ who said, *"He who is without sin cast the first stone"?*—which is something I think you should consider before censuring me.

Afterwards, the reporters bombarded him with questions about his association with Munny Hungri, noted crime syndicate boss.

36.5   Direct quote spans paragraphs. Precede it with a colon (:). If you are quoting a full speech, it will also be necessary to insert a colon after the salutation as well (e.g., *Mr. Chairman, Ladies and Gentlemen:*) Leave an extra space between the introductory sentence and the quote; then, indent each paragraph of the quote. While each paragraph begins with an *opening* double quotation mark ("), the *ending* double quotation mark (") is only inserted after the LAST WORD of the quote.

President Wilcox looked at his cabinet members and said:

"Gentlemen, I think the reason we have lost the confidence of the voters is that we have all forgotten what it really means to be a public servant.
"Let's take you, Secretary Smith. Ever since you have held office, your only concern has been to pad your own pockets, and I think everyone at this table would agree with that."

36.6   Direct quote is an entire letter or telegram. Always include the date—if one is available—and place a double quotation mark (") *before* it, not after; insert another quotation mark *before*, not after, the salutation (e.g., *Dear Sir*), and another before, though not at the end, of each paragraph, excepting *sincerely* or its various synonyms. Place a closing quotation mark (") after the person's name who wrote the original.

"January 5, 1875

"General Custer:

"Intelligence reports leads us to conclude that a potful of indians are waiting for you at Little Big Horn. You are advised not to saddle your horse and lead your men anywhere near that area.

"Secondly, General Putoff requests that you get a haircut immediately, if not sooner.

Sincerely,

Lt. J.P. Lickum"

36.7 **Succession of short direct quotes.** When they are heavily related, use semicolons (;) to separate the quotes form one another. All should retain their double quotation marks (" "). It is one of the rare times when double quotation marks follow one another. Note that the semicolons are inserted *after* the closing quotation mark.

"The police don't have sensitivity"; "The city government is out of touch with reality"; "The media is not trying to find the truth." These and other stupid statements were made by the individual members.

Exception: **Follows a strong pause.** If the pause between the introduction and the successive quotes is strong, insert a colon (:) to represent that pause; but when a verb similar to *said* and *asked* is used, a comma (,) is appropriate. However, should the quotes follow the word "as," the first quote is not preceded by a comma and the semicolons are replaced with commas. The separating semicolons and commas *follow* each closing quotation mark (").

AFTER THE
INTRODUCTION
Colon: In that situation, individual members made stupid statements: "The police don't have sensitivity"; "The city government is out of touch with reality"; "The media is not trying to find the truth."

Comma: Their individual members said, "The police don't have sensitivity"; "The city government is out of touch with reality"; "The media is not trying to find the truth."

210

Nothing: In that situation, individual members made such stupid statements as "The police don't have sensitivity", "The city government is out of touch with reality", "The media is not trying to find the truth."

36.8 **Direct quote needs to be shortened.** If it does not disrupt the original meaning of the quote itself, the omitted words can be replaced by three periods (...), called the ellipsis; but if the words are removed from the end of the sentence, they are replaced by four periods (....) rather than three. Should the quote contain more than one sentence, simply capitalize the first word of each sentence as you normally would and do not insert an extra period. In the second example, the word *therefore* begins the second sentence

ONE
SENTENCE: The mayor said, "All pedestrians...have a secret desire...to back up traffic during the rush hour."

TWO
SENTENCES: The mayor said, "All pedestrians...have a secret desire...to back up traffic during the rush hour....Therefore, we are going to pass laws which will forbid them from doing just that."

OMITTED AT
THE END: The soliloquy of Richard III began to come back to him, and suddenly the words floated out over the footlights: "Now is the winter of our discontent...."

Exception: **One or more sentences, or paragraphs, are removed.** Use four periods (....) rather than three to represent them.

Donaldson, who apparently looks upon him as his archenemy, said Smith is "....robbing the city blind with his political giveaways."

Exception: **Words removed between separate but related quotes.** This may sometimes be essential when editing information and space is crucial. Replace the missing words with a single word or a short phrase to retain the continuity, and encase that replacement in brackets. This tells the reader that the bracketed information is yours and not part of the actual quote.

WORD: "He said Spud couldn't hit left-handed pitching, and that they were going to trade him. [Consequently] I took [Spud] out to the

211

batting cage and wore him out with left-handed pitching, and at the end of the year he had batted .354 against southpaws."

PHRASE: "He was afraid of getting hit, that's all. But I made him stand there and not move. [In that way] he conquered his own fear about hitting against lefties, and it got so that he preferred them over right-handers."

36.9 **Part of direct quote is added to a complete thought.** Besides using double quotation marks (" "), a preceding dash (—) is required, including a comma (,) after it when followed by additional information. The first word of the quote is not capitalized.

They were so unalike: Tom was fat, slouchy, lazy; Bill was lean, intelligent, and ambitious—*"an active volcano of ideas on almost every subject imaginable,"* one of this friends recalled.

36.10 **Direct quote is interrupted by a comment, explanation, or identification, etc.** Encase the nonquotes in brackets. Question marks or exclamation marks needed must be placed inside the last bracket if you wish to emphasize something or express doubt (*see* first example). Quotes within a quote are set apart by single quotation marks (' ').

IDENTIFIES: He wrote, "Little Miss Muffet [an alias] sat on her tuffet [bottom?], eating her curds and whey, when all of a sudden she pulled out a plum, remarking 'Who put this in here?'"

COMMENT: "I heard him tell Corporal Dandy that he didn't want him to handle the bills of lading for the gun shipments [an odd request, since that had always been the corporal's job], because he wanted to assume the duty himself."

REFERS: "I think the farmers, out of anger, decided to form a group to protect themselves against unfair prices [refer to An Act of Faith, published in the April 1984 issue of this magazine—Editor], and it was from that point on that the environment of mistrust grew."

Exception: **Interruption is interrupted.** Place the original interruption in parentheses instead; next, encase the interruption-within-an-interruption in brackets. (It has been darkened in the example which follows.) Note: the interruption itself may have internal punctuation.

212

Said Bruce Smith: "I believe every man has a right to his own opinion." (It seems contrary to his private utterances, however [*see* **the May 3rd issue of the Sentinel, page 14**] and that of his management team), "for that is what this country stands for."

36.11 A direct quote within a quote. Insert single (') quotation marks before and after it to differentiate it from the other quote, which is encased in double quotation marks (" "). In the examples below, the quote-within-a-quote has been italicized so that you may quickly spot it. Notice that in the last example the single quotation mark immediately precedes the double quotation mark.

MIDSENTENCE: Replied Romeo: "When I said *'Hark, what light through yonder window breaks?'* I was just clearing my sinus passages."

END: "I heard the senator try to glide his way into their hearts by saying, *'Anyone here want a stick of gum?'* "

36.12 Error is found in the direct quote. There are two options available: (1) correct the error and place the correction in brackets; or (2) allow the error to stand and simply point it out to the reader by placing *sic* in brackets immediately after the error.

CORRECTED: Buffalo Bill said, "I only want a job that is com[mensurable] with my talents."

NOTING ERROR: Buffalo Bill said, "I only want a job that is commiserate [sic] with my talents."

36.13 Exclamation mark or question mark with direct quote. If either of these punctuation marks are part of the quote itself, insert the closing quotation marks (") *after* it. But if adding either of these marks yourself, it must *follow* the quotation mark rather than precede it.

PART OF
QUOTE: In the heat of battle General Putts yelled, "I can't find my pants anywhere!"

He turned to his Secretary of Defense and asked, "Where is Europe on the map?"

MARK
ADDED: Then the governor—imagine this—had the nerve during his speech to look at them and say, "I think I've earned your trust"!

Who was it that said, "Give me your tired, your poor, your huddled masses who yearn to breathe free"?

Exception: **Double question marks or exclamation marks.** When the quote ends with a question mark or exclamation mark, do not follow it with the same punctuation.

Is it true that he turned to his Secretary of Defense and asked, *"Where is Europe on the map?"*

36.14 Naming the source of the direct quote. It immediately follows the quote, and here are two ways of telling the reader the source:

1. *Encase the source in parentheses.* No period (.) is needed before or after the closing parenthesis. Place the name of the author first, and separate the additional elements with commas (,). The first example below shows a book title being added; the second, a job title. In the third example, however, only a general source is parenthesized.

   AUTHOR +
   Book title: "Life is but a school for the soul." (D.K. Tewk, *A Journey*)

   Job title: "Life is but a school for the soul." (D.K. Tewk, Professor of Theology, Christian University)

   GENERAL
   SOURCE: "Life is but a school for the soul." (African proverb)

2. *Separate the quote and the source by placing them on separate lines.* Quotation marks are not needed. Double-space between the quote and the source, and the line containing the quote's source should be flush with the right-hand margin. You may or may not precede the source with a dash (—). If more than one quote appears, triple space before each one, making sure to indent the name of the source at the same place as the one above it. Note: Such a quote may introduce an article, book, essay, etc., and in that instance it is called a "display quote." As part of a book, it is centered on a page and sets the tone for the information which follows; but as part of an article or essay, it precedes. In the five examples which follow, the source is followed by (1) a book title, (2) a book title and page number, (3) a book title below it, (4) the reason for the quote, and (5) a job title.

   Life has always been, and will continue to be, a school for the soul.

   — David K. Tewk, *A Journey*

214

Life has always been, and will continue to be, a school for the soul.

> — Donald K. Tewk, *A Journey*, page 191

Life has always been, and will continue to be, a school for the soul.

> — D.K. Tewk
> *A Journey*

He was an effective leader, in my opinion.

> Broom County Commissioner Samuel Snew, on former commissioner and brother Edgar Snew, who was the state's first serial killer.

Ask not what your country can do for you, but what you can do for your country.

> — John F. Kennedy
> 35th President of the United States

Exception: **Source is unknown.** In parentheses, type *source unknown*, capitalizing the word "source." Place the quote between double quotation marks (" ").

"Life is but a school for the soul." (Source unknown)

Exception: **Source wishes to remain anonymous.** This technique is frequently used in journalism to protect the identity of the person being quoted. The quote is set apart by double quotation marks (" ") and a comma (,), as shown in the first two examples below. If used as a display quote in a book, the quotation marks may be omitted altogether; instead, there is a double space after the quote and some sort of indented and identifying information is provided below it. In this instance, the quote may be italicized (*see* last example).

"The strategy was planned at the highest level," according to an anonymous source at the White House, on the government's gun-running policy in Utah.

According to an anonymous source at the White House, on the government's gun-running policy in Utah, "the strategy was planned at the highest level."

215

The strategy was planned at the highest level.

White House spokesman, on the government's
gun-running policy in Utah.

36.15 Common expressions: Biblical, common, and literary.
They are not set off by quotation marks. Those shown in the examples
below have only been italicized for your quick identification.

BIBLICAL: *Vengeance is mine,* saith the Lord.
LITERARY: How many of us have pondered *To be or not to be* ?
COMMON: Like they say, *you ain't seen nothing yet.*

36.16 Emphasizing some words in a direct quote. Type them in italics, but a two- to four-word explanation about why italics are being
used should be placed in parentheses at the end of that quote. In the
first two examples which follow, the original authors of the quote have
emphasized certain words in their own text; in the third example, however, the person who is quoting the author is inserting his own emphasis.

AUTHOR'S
EMPHASIS: Said the author: "I simply had *no desire* to continue pay-
              ing lip service to that kind of writing, so I turned to an-
              other form of expression." (Emphasis in original text.)

              "Can you imagine someone with that kind of background
              wanting to be *president?* " (Author's emphasis.)

QUOTER'S
EMPHASIS: Polly Parrot, noted movie starlet, said yesterday: "Gee,
              ain't everybody making *twenty million dollars a year like
              me?* " (Emphasis added.)

36.17 Foreign words in a direct quote. When a foreign word is inserted
into a quote that otherwise contains all English words, it needs to be
italicized; but a quote containing all foreign words is written without
italics. However, if the author has italicized one or more words—or if
you feel something in the quote should be emphasized—then italicize or
underline the words, but do not do both. Double quotation marks (" ")
are inserted before and after the quote.

ONE FOREIGN
WORD: "My life has not been happy," said Nobel Prize-win-
              ning author Peter Anunzio. "It is, as we say in Italy,
              tragico."
ALL FOREIGN
WORDS: "Ich hatte es vor. Aber es regnet, und wenn es so
              weiterregnet, bleibe ich lieber zu Hause."

216

Emphasized: "Der Tisch ist *lang.*"
"La mesa es larga."

36.18 Successive direct quotes from the same source. When using such quotes in succession without adding them to nondialogue, they should (1) be centered on the page, (2) share a common left-hand margin, and (3) be separated from one another by inserting three asterisks (***). Precede and follow them with double quotation marks ("). Here's the way it looks:

"If a dictator is placated because everyone wants peace, those doing the placating will only have to deal harshly with him later—if it is not too late."

* * *

"Only a fool or a maniac wants war; but if history has taught us anything, it should tell us that fools and maniacs have consistently dwelled among us."

36.19 Court testimony. Quotation marks are not used. There are two methods of presenting court testimony which are generally acceptable:

1. The words *question* and *answer* are represented by a capitalized "Q" and "A," followed by a period (.). An additional option is to indent the lines containing the answers (*see* second example).

Q. You saw her how many times?
A. Once or twice. I can't be sure.
Q. In the data processing area?
A. Yes.

Q. You saw her how many times?
 A. Once or twice. I can't be sure.
Q. In the data processing area?
 A. Yes.

2. Last names are provided, followed by dashes (—) or colons (:).

Johnson—You saw her how many times?
Witness—Once or twice. I can't be sure.
Witness—In the data processing area?
Johnson—Yes.

Johnson: You saw her how many times?
Witness: In the data processing area?
Johnson: Yes.
Witness: Once or twice. I can't be sure.

217

Exception: **Adding human responses or actions.** Place them between brackets. The reaction of the people in attendance, including what the principal speakers are doing, may be indicated.

Q. You mean you weren't spying?
A. Just looking, that's all.
[Courtroom laughter]
Q. Just looking, huh? [Shows him a document] All right, I would like for you to look at this and tell me if these are your notes.

36.20 **Direct quote precedes or follows a form of the verb "to be"** (e.g., *was, is,* etc.). No comma is needed. Double quotation marks (" "), however, are essential.

BEFORE VERB: "Everybody's in it for the buck" *was* the response I usually got when I surveyed voters in the First District.

AFTER VERB: His attitude *is* "Don't fire until you see the whites of their eyes."

36.21 **Remembering a quote.** To quickly insert the recollection of a quote, the technique is the same as it is in fiction: it should be encased in brackets, with double quotation marks (" ") inserted before and after it. Note: do not end the quote with a period (.) when it interrupts a sentence; however, an exclamation mark or question mark will be essential if either is part of the original quote

Playwright Edgar Snuggs said he stood before the memorial to President Kennedy, and as that memorable inaugural speech came to mind ["Ask not what your country can do for you, but what you can do for your country"], he felt sad, more for his lack of involvement than anything else.

Bob Shine had been there when FDR spoke [The only thing we have to fear is fear itself!] and he remembered how frightened he was of the depression.

Exception: **A quote is within a quote.** Precede and follow it with *single* quotation marks ('); the other quote, however, receives *double* quotation marks (").

Said Congressman Wooleyworm: "I stood before the memorial to President Kennedy and thought of his inaugural speech ['Ask not what your country can do for you, but what you can do for your country'] and I realized I had not been doing my best."

218

Indirect Quote

An indirect quote it is not set apart by double quotation marks, for it serves only to generally convey what someone has said or written. Accuracy is its casualty.

37.1 Examples of indirect quotes. None of the indirect quote examples which follow need double quotation marks to set them apart. The indirect quotes in the examples which follow have been italicized for quicker identification.

RUMOR: There are reports that he said *the company will not, under any circumstances, engage in a lawsuit.*

QUESTIONS: *Who will come? Who will go? Who will ensure their safety?* That's basically what the panel of journalists wanted to learn from the White House Chief of Staff.

RESPONSE: *Not true,* says the big man from Virginia.

Statistics prove that more people move from south to north (*a lie,* Wendell Wipe continually insists) and that this has been the trend for twenty years.

37.2 Indirect quote is preceded by "like" or "as." This is one of those rare instances when the indirect quote should be encased in double quotation marks (" "). When there are two or more quotes in succession, double quotations marks will follow one another.

1 QUOTE: He would always say things like "I didn't see anything. I didn't hear anything."

2 OR MORE: They said things like "I didn't see anything." "You'll have to talk to my lawyer." "I was out of town at the time." "I don't recall."

Exception: **Indirect quotes are questions.** Omit the quotation marks and capitalize the first word of each.

People who come into the store ask such questions as How much is that doggy in the window? Has it had its shots?

37.3 Indirect quote preceded by the word "that." When it immediately or subsequently follows "that," an indirect quote is not set off with double quotation marks. For your convenience, the indirect quote has been italicized in the following examples.

FOLLOWS...
<blockquote>
Subsequently: Author Gene Hadley said that he had *wanted to be a great writer for a long time.*

Immediately: Wasn't it Abe Lincoln who said that *the splitting of rails is a lot easier than splitting hairs?*
</blockquote>

But if the words *said that* are immediately followed by an indirect quote which has its own introduction, isolate the quote's own introduction with commas (,). In this example, *because the jail was overcrowded* is the quote's introduction.

Sheriff Cuggins said that, *because the jail was overcrowded, he was forced to let some prisoners out early.*

Cliché

38.1 **Explanation.** A cliché is usually a phrase (many common expressions, for example, are clichés), but it may sometimes be a full sentence, e.g., Shakespeare's wonderful metaphor *There's the rub*, which has subsequently become a cliché through overuse. Unless you are using one for a special reason—and there are many occasions when that will be the case—including too many of them in your writing should be avoided if at all possible. If you are not a poet who is adept at developing your own fresh metaphors (and few of us are), word replacements can be found in a thesaurus of synonyms.

38.2 **A cliché is the subject of the sentence.** It should be highlighted. Use italics or insert double quotation marks (" ") before and after it. Note that the cliché in the third example is not acting as as the sentence's subject and does not require either treatment.

<blockquote>
SUBJECT: "A chip off the old block" is the cliché that gave him the idea for his Oscar-winning movie.

Italicized: *A chip off the old block* is the cliché that gave him the idea for his Oscar-winning movie.

NOT SUBJECT: Knowing that Wilbur was a chip off the old block, I didn't even try to explain it to him.
</blockquote>

Proverb, Principle, etc.

39.1 **Synonyms explained.** There is little difference between the words *adage, proverb, old saw, old saying, maxim,* and *dictum:* they mean something has been accepted as the truth after a lengthy period—except that *maxim, proverb,* and *saw* reflect perhaps a bit more practicality; *dictum* is more authoritative. A *principle* is a generally recognized truth in specific areas: for example, the principle of Divine Right and Winehunder's Principle of Economics. An *axiom* and a *truism* are in the category of principles, but they are frequently preceded or followed by the word *that.* A *precept* is an accepted code of conduct, particularly in the area of morality; while a *doctrine* includes the teaching of a so-called truth.

39.2 **Capitalization.** Each word should be capitalized, except indefinite articles (*a, an, the*) and prepositions (*to, on,* etc.).

You know what they say: *Those Who Live by the Sword Will Die by the Sword.*

39.3 **Quotation marks or italics.** No quotation marks or italics are used to set off a proverb, principle, etc.

39.4 **Follows a strong pause.** When a proverb, etc. follows a full sentence and a strong pause, it needs a preceding colon (:), because it is supplying highly supportive information.

So, in a democracy it would be to everyone's benefit to keep that one thought in mind: *All Men Are Created Equal.*

39.5 **Follows a word like "proverb" or "principle."** In this situation it is acting as a noun and needs no punctuation before or after it.

The principle *Do unto Others As You Would Have Them Do unto You* is only practiced by a small handful in this world.

Quoting Poetry

40.1 **Quoting a poem as seen.** Set it completely apart from the other information on the page by double-spacing before its first and last lines, and provide comfortable margins on both sides. No quotation marks are necessary before and after the poem, but you may have to insert a colon (:) after the last word which precedes the poem, for in most cases the last sentence sets the stage for the poem and a heavy pause can be detected after it. If all lines of the poem do not start at flush-left, and a lack of space forbids copying the original format of the poem, it is acceptable to indent the lines equally on the left-hand side. Structurally, here's how it should appear:

> Permit me to quote Osgood Swizzlestik's great poem "The Rhyme of the Ancient Coalminer":
>
> > 1st line of the poem
> > 2nd line of poem
> > 3rd line of the poem, etc.
> >
> > A new and indented paragraph of information is
> then placed here.

40.2 **Quoting a poem in paragraph form.** The virgule (/) — or "slant," or "diagonal," as it it sometimes called — should be used to separate the lines from one another. All ending punctuation marks (e.g., periods, exclamation marks, etc.) are kept, and the poem is preceded and followed by double quotation marks (" ").

It was Stephen Crane who wrote "Upon the road of my life/Passed me many fair creatures/Clothed all in white and radiant./To one, finally...." and so on.

40.3 **Eliminating lines of poetry.** When the poem is in its natural vertical form, specific lines may be eliminated and substituted with equally spaced periods (.). Below the poem, in parentheses, encase the poet's name and the poem's title. But unless it is essential to draw attention to only specific lines of a poem, the omission of lines in poetry gains nothing; certainly little space—if any—and definitely not the appreciation of the poet. It looks like this:

> First line of poem is written
>
> . . . .
> . . . .
> One or more lines
>
> (Author's name, title of poem)

Exception: **In paragraph form.** Use the ellipsis (...) to indicate missing words and lines, or four periods after the last word when the poem is not quoted completely. Separate the lines with a virgule (/), and double quotation marks (" ") are essential before and after the poem.

> "I'd like to go by climbing a birch tree/And climb black branches up a snow-white trunk...That would be good...going and coming/ One could do worse...."

222

Time Period in a Sentence

41.1 **General rule for punctuating a time period.** Whether it is clock time or calendar time, a time period is usually led by a preposition (e.g., *At* six o'clock...) or an adverb (e.g., *Before* summer...) and Rules 17.2 and 20.1 provide substantial punctuation guidelines. Here is a quick overview:

INTRODUCES. When it is part of a short introductory phrase, it often does not need a comma unless the information which follows it is lengthy. *See* Rule 41.4 for amplification and exceptions.

INTERRUPTS. Punctuation is usually omitted when no pause precedes the time period. *See* Rule 41.5 for amplification and exceptions.

ADDED TO SENTENCE. Punctuation is again often eliminated, because the time period usually helps to round out the sentence. *See* Rule 41.6 for amplification and exceptions.

41.2 **Side-by-side time periods.** When a pause can be detected between them, or if confusion is possible, commas (,) are necessary for separation When the second time period begins with a preposition such as *at* or *of*, rarely is a comma needed to separate them. But insert a comma when the preposition is removed (*see* second example). In each example which follows, the second time period has been italicized for your quick identification.

PREVENT
CONFUSION: Two days before, *Monday,* he sent the letter to her.
You must be there at six, *Saturday.*

LED BY A
PREPOSITION: Friday *at noon* of my third week, I had had enough.
You must be there by Saturday *at six.*

Exception: **Confusion possible.** There are times when, through the use of a comma (,), a pause must be forced to prevent any confusion in the reader's mind. In the example below, the author means something will be finished. But without the comma, one might think that *Monday of next week* will be covered with something.

It'll be all over, *Monday of next week.*

41.3 **Possessive case of time period.** Insert an apostrophe S ('s) after the word which denotes time, but put the apostrophe *after* the letter S when you want to indicate more than one.

ONE: What I need is an *hour's* rest.
He only had a *minute's* warning to get out.
Just give me a *second's* notice, that's all.

MORE: It's several *hours'* drive from here.
Just give me a few *minutes'* head start.
All I want is a few *second's* of your time.
Yesterday's procrastination is *today's* due bill and *tomorrow's* hangover.

41.4 Time period introduces a sentence. If the "when" is important to the meaning of the sentence, the time period need not be set apart unless the information which follows it is lengthy—or if there is the possibility of some confusion. This is especially appropriate when the time period is vague (e.g., *During that time* I felt as if we could still pull it off). However, some grammarians prefer that a more specific time period be isolated when it introduces a sentence, except when its presence is crucial. Neither school of thought is incorrect, but perhaps the best way to work your way through this punctuation minefield is this: USE the comma (,) if you do not want to attach importance to the time period, and do NOT USE the comma when you think the time adds essential information.

TIME IS...

Important:	*At six o'clock* they captured the enemy's Third Battalion and ended the war.
Unimportant:	*At six o'clock,* they captured the enemy's Third Battalion and ended the war.
UNREMOVABLE:	*Since June* they have been in first place.
Exception:	**Emphasis needed.** Insert a dash (—) after it.
	December 7, 1941—how many remember what happened on that date?
Exception:	**Interruption follows.** A comma is not usually needed after the introductory time period.
	In 1714 he became, *much to the displeasure of the city fathers,* the first person to kick a pigeon in Venice.

But if the interruption immediately follows the time period, use the comma.

In 1714, *much to the displeasure of the city fathers,* he became the first person to kick a pigeon in Venice.

Exception: **Word or phrase is added to the sentence.** A comma is not usually needed after the introductory time period.

In 1714 he became the first person in history to kick a pigeon in Venice, *much to the displeasure of the city fathers.*

But if a long sentence separates the time period from the add-on, punctuation after the time period is usually desirable.

In 1714, he became the first person in history to kick a pigeon in Venice while walking in the town square in a red-striped bathrobe, *much to the displeasure of the city fathers.*

Exception: **Two simple sentences joined by a conjunction.** A comma is not needed after the introductory time period. In this example, the conjunction is "but."

In 1714 he became the first person in history to kick a pigeon in Venice, but no one would have dreamed of the repercussions.

Exception: **Strong pause follows.** A colon (:) is required when some type of elaborating information comes after the time period, but use a dash (—) for more emphasis.

Autumn: what a colorful time of year that is.
Monday—that's the only day I can come over.

Exception: **Long sentence follows.** Insert a comma (,) after the introductory time period, even though it may be crucial to the overall meaning and cannot be removed. The best way to test whether or not the sentence is long enough for the time period to be isolated, is to imagine it at the end of the sentence instead. If it sounds awkward, the comma is needed.

225

In 1989, they expect the economy to falter and begin a downward spiral toward breathtaking financial chaos that will last at least ten years.

41.5 **Time period interrupts a sentence.** An interrupting word or phrase that denotes time will require punctuation to set it apart when it can be easily removed without being missed. For example in the first sentence below, *when* it happened has little bearing: the fact that he was the *first* is really all that matters. In the second sentence, however, not only is there no discernible pause before the interruption, but the phrase *in 1714* also adds crucial information, for it immediately identifies *who*—that is, *the people who lived in 1714.*

REMOVABLE: He became, *in 1714,* the first person in history to slam-dunk a pigeon into a Venetian fountain.

UNREMOVABLE: But who *in 1714* would ever have imagined that such a thing could take place?

Exception: **Interrupts without a noticeable pause.** When it can be read without a pause before it, it usually does not need punctuation to set it apart.

And so *in January* he made up his mind to be the first member of his family to ask for a pension.

Congressman Wilbur Whippee said *Friday* that he would not call a special session.

He knows that *day after tomorrow* I'll be there.

Exception: **Follows a lead-off conjunction.** If no discernible pause precedes an interrupting time period, omit the comma before it but keep the one which follows it.

But *back then,* who would have thought prices would fall like they did?

Exception: **More emphasis needed.** Use a dash (—) to set it apart.

That was the year—*1714*—when he became the first person in history to drop-kick a pigeon in Venice.

41.6 **Time period ends a sentence.** An ending word or phrase that denotes time will require punctuation when it is easily removed without being missed. In the first sentence below, *on Tuesday* is not only an afterthought, but it is redundant: we already know it will be *seven days from now*. In the other sentence, though, it is vitally important: we now know that the person may not be safe at any other time *except Tuesday*. When the add-on time period needs to be emphasized, insert a dash (—) before it.

REMOVABLE: She will be arriving seven days from now, *on Tuesday*.

UNREMOVABLE: You will be safe here with us *on Tuesday*.

EMPHASIZED: Not tomorrow—*today!*

Exception: **Long sentence precedes it.** Insert a comma (,) before the time period when it is preceded by a long sentence.

The harvest was considered to be the best that had ever been seen in Redondo and all of the surrounding counties, *in 1989.*

Exception: **Strong pause precedes it.** A colon (:) is required when the time period identifies, summarizes, or explains that which precedes it; but use a dash (—) for more emphasis.

That's when it was signed: *July 4, 1776.*
Then came that fateful day—*April 15, 1981.*

41.7   Time period follows the pronoun "who" or "which." If the time period can be removed without being missed, set it apart with commas (,). Below are three examples: the first contains a time period that adds nothing to the meaning of the sentence, so it is set apart; in the second example, "which" would have been preceded by a comma anyway, but the phrase containing the time period is short and can be married to the pronoun without a preceding comma. However, in the last example below, the phrase containing the time period is not brief, and and so it—and the pronoun—must be preceded and followed by commas.

TIME PERIOD IS...
Unimportant: This is the person who, *in May 1970*, said he'd never do something like that.

Brief phrase: Credit goes to the Veterans' Club, which *in June 1985* initiated it.

227

Long phrase:	Then there was the rumor started by Elmer Doodle, who, *on or about the fifteenth of January*, said he saw Jasper Jenkins running in his underwear.

Time Elements

42.1 **Vague time.** When the element of time is vague, it is usually either a phrase or part of one, and it needs to be punctuated as such. When the phrase is removable, or when confusion is possible, a comma (,) is necessary to isolate it. The vague time used in the first two examples which follow needs to be set apart from the other information, because it could otherwise cause confusion; but notice that when it is placed at the end of the sentence it needs no preceding punctuation, for it round out the meaning. Also, refer to Rules 41.4 through 41.6 for additional information and possible exceptions to the rule.

FIRST:	*Ever since,* I've loved peanut butter.
INTERRUPTS:	So, *ever since,* my love for peanut butter has grown.
LAST:	I've loved peanut butter *ever since.*

Exception:	**Interrupts without a pause.** It does not need punctuation to set it apart in a sentence.

Although *back then* I didn't know anything.

Exception:	**No pause follows introduction.** This is frequently the case when vague time is part of an introductory phrase which begins with a preposition. The absence of a pause eliminates any need for a comma.

For a while I really thought she would come back.

42.2 **Hours, minutes, and seconds.** The colon (:) separates the hour from the minutes. If A.M. or P.M. is used, its capitalization is optional. Also, precede the number of seconds with a colon (:) when they are added to the minutes. A hyphen (-) is needed between the first two words of a time period when it is rounded off. Also, refer to Rules 41.4 through 41.6 for additional information and possible exceptions to the rule.

P.M. & A.M:	She will be there by *8:15 P.M.*
	She will be there there by *8:15 p.m.*
Implied:	She thought she could be there by *8:15.*

SECONDS:	He crossed the finish line at *8:15:59 p.m.*

ROUNDED OFF

3 words: By almost *half-past ten* we had everything in the boxes.

Exception: **Elapsed time.** The words *hour* and *minutes* may be abbreviated or spelled out. If spelled out, only separate them with a comma when the conjunction is missing. The first example shows them abbreviated; the second, spelled out; the third with no conjunction.

He ran there in *1 hr. 18 min.*
He ran there in *1 hour and 18 minutes.*
He ran there in *1 hour, 18 minutes.*

Exception: **Written number precedes "hour", "minute", or "second."** Use a hyphen (-) to separate the number from the hour, minute, or second when they precede a noun, for together they form a description (adjective). No apostrophe S is required. In the second example which follows no hyphen is needed, because it does not need precede a noun.

There will be a *six-hour* delay on all shipments.
There will be a delay of *six hours* on all shipments.

Exception: **Spelled out.** Use the hyphen (-) to separate the two- or three-word numbers; but if comprised of three words, insert the hyphen between the last two words only.

TWO: He said he'd have the contract and the pizza ready by *seven-thirty.*

THREE: You must arrive there at exactly *ten twenty-one* or the plan won't work.

Exception: **"O'clock" is used.** Only a one-word number may precede it, and it must be spelled out as well. Also, neither *a.m.* nor *p.m.* should be used. In the second example shown below, the conjunction "or" is missing and must be represented by a comma (,).

The festivities will be at their height by *nine o'clock.*
Eight, nine o'clock—it makes no difference to me.

Exception: **Vague time.** This is an acceptable alternative when the hour is already known. Like most phrases, it is separated by a comma (,) unless preceded by a verb (*see* last two examples). Note: this represents one of the few times when ending a phrase with the preposition *of* and *till* is perfectly acceptable

At half past, the train had still not arrived.
Then, *at a quarter of,* my boss gave me more work.
By a quarter till, it was evident she wasn't coming.
It's almost a *quarter till.*
You must be there by *a quarter of.*

Exception: **Military time.** Colons and the A.M./P.M. abbreviations are not used. Midnight is recorded as 2400 hours (12:30 A.M. would be 2430 hours), but the military clock falls back to 0100 hours when it is 1 A.M., and a hundred hours are added when each hour passes. High noon, for example, is 1200 hours; 6 P.M. is 1800 hours; and 11:59 P.M. is 2359 hours.

The general is scheduled to review the troops at *1430 hours.* Or is it *0430?*

42.3 **Specific day of the week.** When referring to a specific day of the week (e.g., Monday Tuesday, etc.) it can be a single word or part of a phrase; in either case, it is separated from the sentence when it can be removed without being missed. It is always separated from an actual calendar date. When phrases like *day after tomorrow* and *day before yesterday* act as interruptions to a sentence, they are usually set apart by commas (,); but as introductory or add-on phrases which accompany unpunctuated sentences, no commas need attend them if their removal would leave a serious gap. Also, refer to Rules 41.4 through 41.6 for additional information and possible exceptions to the rule.

REMOVABLE:
    One word: *Monday,* here's what I want you to do.
                       That's when it happened—*Monday.*

    Phrase: *On Monday,* here's what I want you to do.
                       The day after, all of us went skinny-dipping.

CAN'T REMOVE:
    One word: *Monday* we felt was probably better.
                       She said she was going to work *Monday.*

    Phrase: It felt like a morgue *day before yesterday.*

WITH DATE:
    Introduces: *Monday,* July 6, 1921, Bozo was born.
    Midsentence: But I think *Monday,* July 6, is too soon.
    End: It's scheduled for *Monday,* July 6, 1921.

42.4 **"Yesterday", "today", and "tomorrow."** Set any one of them apart with commas (,) when they introduce, interrupt, or are added to a sentence—yet could be removed without hampering the meaning of the sentence. However, as introductory words, do not isolate any of them when the information which follows is brief and the "when" which they provide is important. Also, refer to Rules 41.4 through 41.6 for additional information and possible exceptions to the rule.

BRIEF SENTENCE:
Important:	*Tomorrow* he will be here.
Unimportant:	*Today,* I just feel like staying in bed.

PAUSE PRECEDES: Then Betty, *yesterday,* surprised everyone.
It turned out to be a wonderful day, *yesterday.*

PHRASE: *Notwithstanding tomorrow,* let's have fun today.
I just think that, *today of all days,* you should have.
That's the whole story, *as of yesterday.*

SERIES: *Yesterday, today,* and *tomorrow* gives some people hope, some people sorrow.

42.5 **Week.** Unless an "ly" is attached to it and turns it into an adverb, this noun is always a part of a phrase, which relates *when* something happened or is about to occur; and a comma (,) is needed to set it apart when it can be removed without weakening the meaning of the sentence. Also, refer to Rules 41.4 through 41.6 for additional information and possible exceptions to the rule.

ADVERB:
Removable:	*Weekly,* I have found it to be entertaining.
Unremovable:	*Weekly* they come by and knock on my door.

PHRASE
Unremovable: *Next week* they will be here.
I think *next week* I'll take a drive up the coast.
Macy's is going to have a sale *the week of the 17th.*

Removable: *Last week,* Harry bought a Rolls Royce and wrecked it.
Then Jerry, *two weeks ago,* left for Montana forever.
There is Macy's sale to consider, *the week of the 17th.*

42.6 **Month.** Unless an "ly" is attached to it and turns it into an adverb, this noun is always a part of a phrase, which relates *when* something happened or is about to occur; and a comma (,) is needed to set it apart when it can be removed without weakening the meaning of the sentence. Also, refer to Rules 41.4 through 41.6 for additional information and possible exceptions to the rule.

ADVERB
Removable: *Monthly,* you can watch my bills increase.
Unremovable: *Monthly* the rain falls.
PHRASE
Unremovable: *Next month* no one will be allowed to cross that bridge.

It's important that we all do our best *this November.*

Removable: *Two months ago,* Millie said she would Rocky.
That time of year, *September and October,* is hectic.
It's not considered to be our best month, *January.*

42.7 **Month, day, and year (date).** If the sequence is month, day and year, place a comma (,) after the numbered day; but if the day comes first, no punctuation is necessary—the latter being the procedure used in the military. Also, refer to Rules 41.4 through 41.6 for additional information and possible exceptions to the rule.

MONTH FIRST: Nothing will move on *April 21, 1989.*
DAY FIRST: Nothing will move on *21 April 1989.*

Exception: **Preceded by a preposition.** When it introduces or interrupts a sentence, insert a comma (,) *after* the year as well as *before* it.

On July 10, 1991, he came to visit her.
Then, *on July 4, 1776,* they all signed it.

Exception: **Month represented by a number.** Divide the month, day and year by a virgule (/), which is often called a "diagonal" or a "slant." This is appropriate when the date is placed in these locations: (1) in the upper left- or right-hand corner of page containing columns of statistics, and where it acts as an overall date; (2) in a column with other dates. Here is an example of the second approach.

3/1/89 information is placed opposite the date
3/5/89 information is placed opposite the date

42.8   **Month and year only.** No punctuation is needed between the month and the year, but they are usually preceded by a preposition, causing them to become a part of a larger phrase, which more often than not *is* set apart by commas (,). Also, refer to Rules 41.4 through 41.6 for additional information and possible exceptions to the rule.

INTRODUCES: *In May 1969,* they were the first to win back-to-back championships.

INTERRUPTS: Finally, *in May 1969,* they won the championship.

42.9   **"Spring", "summer", "winter", and "fall."** Unless three of them combine to form a series, any member of this quartet of nouns is always part a phrase, and the comma (,) is used to set that phrase apart from the other information. But if the sentence is short, or if no pause can be detected before the phrase, the comma may be omitted as long as it does not confuse the reader. A year may also be added to any of them, and if the first two digits of the year are removed, replace them with an apostrophe ('). Also, refer to Rules 41.4 through 41.6 for additional information and possible exceptions to the rule.

PHRASE
    Removable: *In the fall of 1976,* Buster was tried and convicted.
                  Then, *that autumn,* I planted the seeds again.
                  That's the kind of season it was, *that winter.*

    Unremovable: *This winter* you won't see any robins.
                  Then *in the spring* our mission became obvious,
                  They felt isolated *all summer.*

YEAR ADDED: *During the spring of 1963* I moved to Yonkers.
                  But *in the fall of '63* I knew I had no other choice.

SERIES: I will love you in the spring, summer, fall, and winter.

42.10   **Year.** Never begin a sentence with a year, not even if it is spelled out—unless it is preceded by at least one word which is not time-related. A comma (,) is required when, as part of a phrase or not, it can be removed without disturbing the meaning of what is being conveyed; otherwise, no punctuation is necessary. Also, refer to Rules 41.4 through 41.6 for additional information and possible exceptions to the rule.

REMOVABLE: *In 1935,* it was they who first tried franchising.
                  It, *1929,* turned out to be a bust.
                  That was one long year of mistakes, *1929.*

UNREMOVABLE: *Last year* they lost twenty games in a row.

But who *last year* would have belived it?
I don't know if we can do that *a year from now*.

Exception: **Number follows the year.** A comma (,) is essential to prevent confusion.

In 1987, *1.8* chickens were sold in that area.

During 1975, *two-fifths* of the nation's banks failed.

Exception: **Year is spelled out.** Capitalize each word and place a hyphen (-) between the last two when it is comprised of five words. Do not begin a sentence with a spelled-out year (e.g., *Eighteen Hundred and Sixty-One* was...)

Didn't the American Civil War begin in *Eighteen Hundred and Sixty-One?*

Exception: **Removing first two digits.** They should be replaced with an apostrophe ('), but it is a technique that should be used quite sparingly.

I think the worst of it happened in '39.

However, if spelled out rather than written numerically, capitalize the words.

Who did you vote for in *Sixty:* Kennedy or Nixon?

Who did you vote for in *Sixty-Four:* Johnson or Goldwater?

42.11 Decade. When writing about a decade of years, the addition of the small letter S after the number is mandatory in order to show pluralism (e.g., 1930s). No apostrophe (') is needed. If the decade is spelled out, capitalize the word. Also, refer to Rules 41.4 through 41.6 for additional information and possible exceptions to the rule.

The *1990s* is going to make the *1930s* look like a fender-bender.
The nation experienced a depression during the *Nineteen Thirties*.

Exception: **First two digits removed.** Insert an apostrophe (') before the number. If the word is spelled out, capitalize it and do not use an apostrophe.

There was a depression in the *'30s*.

234

There was a depression in the *Thirties.*

42.12 **Century.** It is always part of a phrase (e.g., *In the sixth century...*) and is usually set apart by commas, unless to do so would seriously weaken the rest of the sentence. Also, refer to Rules 41.4 through 41.6 for additional information and possible exceptions to the rule.

REMOVABLE: *In the twentieth century,* drug smuggling has increased.

UNREMOVABLE: *Back in the nineteenth century* they rode around in wagons.

Exception: **Capitalization.** When spelled out, a century is not capitalized; but if the word *century* follows a numerically written number, it does require capitalization. This also represents one of the few times when such words as *third* and *fourth* can be abbreviated to *3rd* and *4th*.

They traced it back to the *3rd Century.*

Exception: **Adding B.C. or A.D.** When adding the abbreviations B.C. (Before Christ) or A.D. (After Death) to a century, no comma is necessary after the year. However, B.C. is placed after the year, while A.D. is inserted before it. But if the actual word "century" is used, they both follow the year. Finally, never use A.D. when it applies to both years.

That civilization lasted from 1002 B.C. until A.D. 41.

We know the nation existed from at least 2nd Century B.C. to the Eleventh Century A.D.

Time Span

43.1 **Time span of hours and minutes.** Employ the abbreviations *a.m.* or *p.m.* If the prepositions "to" or "until" are not inserted between the two sets of hours and minutes, use a dash (—) to separate them. This is also one of the few times when a dash may follow a period (.).

PREP: It will last from 10:45 a.m. *to* 1:30 p.m.

| Phrase: | *From 10:45 a.m. until 1:30 p.m.*, I watched them as they spread beans and honey all over the factory floor. |
| DASH: | It will last 10:45 a.m.—1:30 p.m. |

43.2 Time span of months. Separate them with either a preposition or a dash (—). To include the year as well, insert a comma (,) after the last month and then add the year. To also show that all months during that time span apply, another option is to use the word *inclusive*, and the same procedure applies.

SEPARATED BY...

| Preposition: | It didn't rain a drop from *May to September*. |
| Dash: | Then, *May—September*, it didn't rain a drop. |

| YEAR ADDED: | It didn't rain a single drop from *May to September, 1960.* |
| "INCLUSIVE" ADDED: | It didn't rain a single drop from May to September, *inclusive.* |

| Exception: | **Months are in different years.** A numerical year will have to be placed after each month. No punctuation need separate the month from the year. |
| | It didn't rain a single drop from *December 1960 to February 1961.* |

43.3 Time span of years. The hyphen (-) is the appropriate punctuation mark to indicate a span of years, but do not use the preposition *from* before it. Insert a dash (—) rather than the short hyphen when the time span is exceptionally long. However, commas (,) are employed when the years are displayed in succession.

HYPHEN:	He was in power *1955-60.*
DASH:	The period was *1202 B.C.—1109 B.C.*
COMMAS:	The years *1932, 1933, 1934, and 1935* were difficult.

| Exception: | **First two digits are removed.** Replace them with an apostrophe ('). But do not remove digits from years when the time span is lengthy. |
| | The years *''32, '33, '34, and '35* were particularly difficult. |

But if only two successive years are used, insert a hyphen (-) rather than a comma between them.

During the '72-'73 season they were in first place until the last week.

43.4 **Person's life span.** A person's life span is encased in parentheses and usually follows his or her name, with the years separated by a dash (—). This information is frequently used in biographical sketches.

Auturo Giovanni *(1829—1889)* was considered to be that country's greatest landscape artist.

Exception: **Birth or death is uncertain.** When the date given is only an approximate, insert a question mark (?) after the year about which there is doubt.

Auturo Giovanni *(1829?—1889)* is considered to be that country's greatest landscape artist.

Exception: **Individual is still living.** Within a parentheses include the person's birth, followed by a dash (—).

Christopher Peabody *(1961—)*, Director of the Art Institute of Rock City; Chairman of the Cleanup Committee; Volunteer Fireman; Member of the Scaredy Cats.

43.5 **Elapsed time.** No commas are needed to separate the various elements of time unless they are spelled out.

NO COMMAS: He was held prisoner for *2 years 8 months 21 days 6 hours and 14 minutes.*

SPELLED OUT: He lived for *thirty years, three months, and three days.*

Direct Question

44.1 **Stands alone.** Insert a question mark (?) after it. The question may even have missing, but implied, words. For example, in the second question below *Are you talking about* is missing before the first word.

How much is that doggie in the window?
The one with the waggly tail?
You call that a tail?
Wouldn't you?

44.2 **Question interrupted by a phrase or a sentence.** Set the phrase apart, using commas (,). The sentence, however, may well need a dash (—) before and after it to prevent confusion. If more than one interrupting phrase is used, insert a conjunction between them.

ONE PHRASE: Will they, *considering their dislike of him,* ever get to the place where they will trust him again?

TWO PHRASES: Will they, *considering their dislike of him and realizing they have vowed revenge,* ever get to the place where they will trust him again?

SENTENCE: Is he—*and I want you to carefully consider his actions before arriving at an answer*—the kind of person who says one thing but does another?

Exception: **Conjunction removed between two interrupting phrases.** Confusion on the part of the reader is far less likely when the dash (—) is used to set the phrases apart, particularly when both phrases begin with the same word.

Will they—*considering their hatred, their call for revenge*— ever get to the place where they will trust him again?

44.3   **Two-word question added to a simple statement.** This is a common practice, and the add-on question is preceded by a comma (,) and followed by a question mark (?). Questions of this nature begin with words like *isn't, could, may, wasn't, can't, does,* etc. Take a look at the first two examples below: if either of the add-on questions were removed, the information preceding either would become a simple statement. And even when another comma appears earlier in the sentence (*see* third example), the comma still appears before the add-on question. But such two-word questions added to some statements do not *always* create questions; and when they don't, they must NOT be followed by a question mark. *See* Rule 44.4.

You said you would, *didn't you?*
They have moved into first place, *haven't they?*
But listen, you'll give me a call when you get there, *won't you?*

Exception: **Ends with "not."** An add-on question which ends with this word is actually three words in length. Never precede "not" with another negative (e.g., *didn't you not,* which is the same as writing *did not you not*).

You said you would go, *did you not?*

<table>
<tr><td>Exception:</td><td>**Strong pause before the question.** Use a dash (—) instead of a comma. Another option is to make it stand alone.</td></tr>
</table>

<table>
<tr><td>DASH:</td><td>I can count on you—*can't I?*</td></tr>
<tr><td>STANDS ALONE:</td><td>I can count on you. *Can't I?*</td></tr>
</table>

44.4 **Looks like a question, but isn't.** In this situation, no question mark is required. There are four occasions when this will occur, and by mentally removing the so-called question it is easy to see that it is not what it seems. Imagine the italicized words did not exist in the following examples:

<table>
<tr><td>SARCASM:</td><td>*Did you,* indeed!
Tell us another whopper, *why don't you.*
And I'm the King of Siam, *aren't I.*</td></tr>
<tr><td>SHORT AND
INTERRUPTS:</td><td>We performed at our best, *did we not,* when no one expected much from us.</td></tr>
<tr><td>ADD-ON:</td><td>I suppose that's all you're going to give me, *isn't it.*</td></tr>
<tr><td>REQUEST:</td><td>*Will you* send me your picture.
Please, *would you* send me your picture.
Send me your autograph, *will you.*</td></tr>
</table>

44.5 **Question as an interrupting personal comment.** When interrupting a sentence with a question, encase it in parentheses without first-word capitalization; however, insert a question mark (?) before the last parenthesis. When the question-comment falls between two sentences, the same rule applies but the first word of the question should be capitalized. In the latter punctuation situation, the question may be preceded and followed by dashes instead of being placed within parentheses, but the capitalization is dropped.

<table>
<tr><td>WITHIN A
SENTENCE:</td><td>The fact that he twiddles his thumbs (actually, isn't thumb-twiddling their established policy?) may very well cost Throckmorton his job.</td></tr>
<tr><td>BETWEEN
SENTENCES:</td><td>Their wealth had suddenly reached absurd, almost frightening levels. (Wasn't it predictable, though, given their contacts?) This, oddly enough, only made them greedier.</td></tr>
<tr><td>Dash used:</td><td>They had lost again—*what else was new?*—and the stadium emptied like a funeral parlor.</td></tr>
</table>

239

Exception:	**Two or more questions interrupt.** They need to be dramatically separated from the other information through the use of the dash (—). Both are capitalized and end with a question mark. But if two questions are joined by a conjunction, a question mark is only required after the second one.

> They had lost again—*Why couldn't they hold a lead? Why didn't the coach get angry?*—and the stadium emptied like a funeral parlor.

> They had lost again—*Why couldn't they hold a lead and why didn't the coach get angry?*—and the stadium emptied like a funeral parlor.

44.6 **Successive questions share the same lead-in words.** Only the first question needs to be capitalized, and all of the other questions begin at the point where their words are not alike. Insert a question mark (?) after each. In the example which follows, the italicized words indicate those which are implied before the other questions.

> *Are you telling me that* she divorced Smith? married Jones? campaigned for Anderson? voted for Williams? shipped guns to Canada?

Exception:	**Questions need more emphasis.** Capitalize the first word of each succeeding question.

> But can you be sure of his past? His present? His future? His desire to do the right thing?

44.7 **Familiar question is quoted.** Although there are several situations where this rule may apply, it is particularly appropriate for a familiar question, i.e., frequently heard and usually quite brief. Such a question should be encased in double quotation marks (" "), and a comma neither precedes nor follows it. It is the kind of question which often acts like a part of speech itself (e.g., noun, adjective). In the first example below, the question is acting as a noun; in the second, an adjective.

> To avoid the eternal "What if?" avoid dwelling on your past so much. The "Why me?" syndrome is certainly something to consider.

Exception:	**Question is italicized.** No offsetting punctuation is required.

> *How* is what all of us want to know.
> *Who buys the oil* is probably a better question.

44.8 Question is immediately preceded by a word like "ask" and "wonder"—among which includes *inquire, demand, want to know, think, consider, ponder, speculate,* and *give thought to.* Insert a comma (,) after any of these words and capitalize the first word of the question.

It prompts one to *ask,* Where is all this going to lead us?
The new clues left me to *speculate,* Is she really guilty?

> Exception: **Introductory information is followed by a comma.** Omit the comma before the question, but retain its capitalization.
>
> Finally, it prompts one to *ask* Where will all this lead us?
>
> Given that, the new clues left me to *wonder* Is she as guiltless as she has led us to believe?

> Exception: **The question is followed by information which completes the original statement.** Double quotation marks (" ") should precede and follow the question, and no comma is needed after the question mark. If it is a question-within-a-question, two question marks (?) will be required. *See* second sentence.
>
> It seems to me that when you *ask,* "Where is all this going to lead us?" it unnerves everyone.
>
> Don't you think that when you *ask,* "Where is all this going to lead us?" that it unnerves everyone?

44.9 Question is immediately preceded by a word like "question." Other synonyms include *issue, problem, enigma,* and *puzzle.* Insert a comma (,) after that word, and capitalize the question.

Who among us can honestly answer the *question,* "Who didn't put the lid on the peanut butter jar?"

> Exception: **Word is followed by a strong pause.** Insert a colon (:) after it and capitalize the question. Sometimes, for the sake of brevity, you might simply want to use the word "question" only. *See* second example.
>
> I am plagued with this nagging *question:* Is this the year when the IRS will audit me?
>
> *Question:* Who was it that sailed the ocean blue?

241

> But for special effect—and this does not include court testimony, where this technique is used throughout—you may want to use the "question and answer" approach. Each question and answer is indented at the right.

> Question: Who was it that sailed the ocean blue?
> Answer: Christopher Columbus.
> Tougher question: Who thought he had discovered America, but found that someone else had beat him to it?

Exception: **Series of questions in a sentence.** Precede the first one with a comma (,) when a slight pause can be detected, and insert question marks (?) after each. To emphasize each question, capitalize them (*see* second example).

> You probably have such questions as, where do I sleep? when do I eat? who will be my group leader?

> You probably have such questions as, Where do I sleep? When do I eat? Who will be my group leader?

44.10 **Question is preceded by the word "not."** No comma is needed after "not." Nor are question marks, double quotation marks, or separating commas used; and the first word is not capitalized.

Ask yourself not *which is the most expedient.*

Exception: **Information follows the question.** Insert a comma (,) after the question.

> Ask yourself not *which is the most expedient,* for that will deter you from doing the right thing.

Exception: **Pronoun "I" precedes "not."** Insert double quotation marks (" ") before and after the question, and insert a question mark (?) before the closing quotation mark.

> I will wonder not "Which is the most expedient?"

> When heavily related information follows the question, no punctuation is needed to set it apart unless there is a strong pause; in that case, insert a semicolon (;) after the last quotation mark (*see* second example below).

> I will wonder not "Which is the most expedient?" for that will serve no useful purpose.

I will wonder not "Which is the most expedient?"; rather, I will pay closer attention to how it may help my fellow man.

44.11 Question is preceded by a strong pause. A colon (:) will be needed to represent that pause, and the question should be capitalized. Here are some instances when this occurs:

REPEATING: Once more: *Are we,* or are we not, *going to do something about this corruption?*

REPHRASING: Put another way: *Would you want your children to go to the same kind of school?*

SUMMARIZING: All told: *Can anyone in his right mind call that a safe investment?*

CONCLUDING: I am left with one nagging thought: *Who is going to pay for this disaster?*

44.12 Question is followed by complementary information. Place the question mark (?) immediately after the question.

Could he have lied? *John wondered.*
Why was he so late? *she wanted to know.*
How much money was there? was something we wanted to know.

Exception: **Heavy pause after the question.** Insert a dash (—) to represent that pause. In the third example below, the words *they are* are implied after the question.

ONE WORD: How?—that's what all we want to know.

LONG: Is he, or has he ever been, a member of the Doo Wah Diddy Club, which believes the sun rises in the west and sets in the east?—it's that simple.

IMPLIED
WORDS: Aren't they lovely?—a sight for sore eyes!

PHRASE
FOLLOWS: Why did she say that?—cautious as she normally is.

44.13 Question completes the sentence. Capitalize the question; then, insert a comma (,) before it and a question mark (?) after it. No quotation marks are necessary.

The first thing you're going to hear is, *How come you didn't do it the way it says to do it in the manual?*

Exception: **Information follows the question.** No comma is necessary after the question mark, but the question mark is retained.

While looking at them and thinking, *What did I ever see in this bunch of yo-yos?* he smiled and pretended that he was having lots of fun.

44.14 Question needs to be emphasized. Substitute the comma or the colon with a dash (—). The first word of the question is capitalized if it would normally follow a colon, but not when it is a commonly used question of two or three words, or when it performs as a contrast.

DASH REPLACES...
 Colon: Once more—Are we, or are we not, going to do something about this corruption?

 Comma: I wouldn't have done it—would you?

 CONTRAST: The county officials offered no support—*but* didn't they once say they would?

Indirect Question

45.1 One-word indirect question in a sentence. It does not require a question mark after it, but it should be italicized; otherwise underline it.

It's more appropriate to ask *what* rather than *who*.

45.2 Indirect question is longer than two words. An indirect question is an integral part of a sentence and cannot be removed without seriously damaging the meaning being conveyed. Therefore it needs no question mark, nor does it have to be italicized. To find out if your question is indirect: mentally remove it from the sentence to determine its importance; if the sentence becomes incomplete without it, the question is indirect. In this example, the indirect question has only been italicized for your quick identification.

It was not a matter of *who would pay the least for the most goods.*

List in Paragraph Form

When a LIST appears in paragraph form, it must not be confused with a SERIES. To discern the difference, ask if the elements being used can be listed vertically as well; if they cannot, they are functioning as a series. Therefore, refer to "series" in the index.

46.1 **List appears after the words "following" or "follows," though not necessarily immediately.** Insert a colon (:) before the list. In the first example below, the word *follows* immediately precedes the list; in the second example, however, the word *following* precedes an add-on phrase, which is itself set apart by a comma (,)—but note that the colon follows the phrase.

The members were as *follows*: Michael Works, Francis Miller, Ezra Thimble, and Wally Vinson.

The members were seated in the *following* order, left to right as one entered the room: Michael Works, Francis Miller, Ezra Thimble, and Wally Vinson.

Exception: **Phrases are added to the list entries.** Separate the entries with semicolons (;) rather than commas, but insert a comma (,) between each entry and its accompanying phrase. Here the add-on phrases follow the names of people in list, and they have been italicized for your quick identification.

The members were seated in the following order: Michael Works, *who said he would support the bill;* Francis Miller, *the avowed enemy of Pete Williams;* Ezra Thimble, *one-time mayor of Alvetta;* and Wally Vinson, *who loved to sleep during the hearings.*

46.2 **List follows a word like "namely."** A word—or word group—in this category (among which includes *for example, for instance, that is, that is to say, to wit,* and the abbreviations *e.g.* and *i.e.*) is always followed by a comma (,), but the punctuation which precedes it depends upon whether or not it follows a complete sentence. If it does, a semicolon (;) should be inserted before it; if not, then a comma is used instead. Each list entry is separated by a comma (,).

FOLLOWS
SENTENCE: They were all there; *namely,* the Chairman of Baldwin Motors, the Marketing Director of Hansel Clocks, the Manager of Dime Paper, and Arco's general manager.

SENTENCE: All of them, *namely*, the Chairman of Baldwin Motors, the Marketing Director of Hansel Clocks, the Manager of Dime Papermill, and Arco's general manager were there to take part in the festivities.

Note that a comma does not follow the interrupting list in the above sentence, because a verb immediately follows it and there is no pause.

Exception: **More emphasis is desired.** Use the dash (—) to separate the list from the rest of the sentence.

The situation in which I found myself—*namely*, the double-dealing, the lies, the total dishonesty of the program—had become intolerable.

I wanted no part of it—*namely*, the double-dealing, the lies, the total dishonesty of the program.

46.3 **List follows a strong pause.** When this occurs, the list is providing information which is elaborating in some way on that which precedes it, and a colon (:) should be used to represent that pause. Place commas (,) between the list entries when they are single words, and a conjunction may or may not precede the last entry. For more drama, the dash (—) may act as a substitute for the colon; but do not overuse this punctuation mark.

LIST HAS...
Single words: I have all I need: cot, blankets, skillet, flashlight.
I have all I need: cot, blankets, skillet, *and* flashlight.
I have all I need—cot, blankets, skillet, *and* flashlight.

But if at least one list entry has three or more words, separate each entry with semicolons (;). And if the list entries are accompanied by phrases which help to explain them, those phrases are set apart by commas. If a conjunction precedes the last entry, a comma (,) should replace the semicolon—unless phrases are added.

More than
3 words: I have all I need: a cot made by the Tewksberry Company; two heavy wool blankets; a cast-iron skillet that measures ten inches in diameter; a flashlight.

246

PHRASES ADDED: I have all I need: a cot made by the Tewksberry Company, *located in New Hampshire;* two heavy wool blankets; a cast-iron skillet that measures ten inches in diameter, *which my mother gave me*; and a flashlight.

46.4   **List of people and their associations.** Use a comma (,) to separate each person's name from his association, and place a semicolon (;) after the name of the organization unless it ends the sentence. When the conjunction "and" or "or" precedes the final list entry, replace the last semicolon with a comma (*see* second sentence). For quicker identification, the associations have been italicized in the examples below.

They invited Ted O'Connor, *of the Elks Lodge;* Mayor Sham Scurry, *of the Plattsburg Museum;* Marvelous Marv, *of the New York Mets.*

They invited Ted O'Connor, *of the Elks Lodge;* Mayor Sham Scurry, *of the Plattsburg Museum,* and Marvelous Marv, *of the New York Mets.*

Exception: **List follows a strong pause.** Insert a colon (:) after the word which precedes the list.

These people were invited: Ted O'Connor, *of the Elks Lodge;* Mayor Sham Scurry, *of the Plattsburg Museum;* Marvelous Marv, *of the New York Mets.*

46.5   **List of people, or groups, and their monetary donations.** The monetary donation of each list entry is preceded by a colon (:) and followed by a semicolon (;). For quicker identification, the monetary donations have been italicized in the sentence below.

Contributors were the Women's Press Club: *$5000;* the City Father's Group: *$2500;* the Refurbishers: *$6000;* the Historical Society: *$1800.*

Exception: **List follows a strong pause.** Insert a colon (:) after the word which precedes the list and use commas (,) rather than colons between the names and donations.

The highest contributors included the following: the Women's Press Club, *$5000;* the City Father's Group, *$2500;* the Refurbishers, *$6000;* the Historical Society, *$1800.*

46.6   **List of people and their hometowns.** Use a comma (,) to separate each person's name from his hometown, and insert a semicolon (;) after the town. However, when the geographical locations are indelibly linked to the names listed, no commas are needed to separate the individuals' names and the places from which they hail (see second sentence below). For quicker identification, the "hometown" phrases have been italicized in the sentences below.

Everyone showed up except Mel Murder, *of Atlanta;* Jim Jumper, *of Boston;* Hal Houdini, *of Los Angeles.*
Morbid Jones had loved Lovely Louisa *of Louisville,* Marvelous Mary *of Memphis,* Darling Della *of Dallas,* and Sweet Sarah *of St. Louis.*

Exception: **List follows a strong pause.** Insert a colon (:) after the word which precedes the list.
Everyone but these people showed up in court to testify against him: Mel Murder, *of Atlanta;* Jim Jumper, *of Boston;* Hal Houdini, *of Los Angeles.*

46.7 **List of people and their job titles.** Use a comma (,) to separate each person's name from his job title, and insert a semicolon (;) after the job title. A conjunction precedes the last entry in the second sentence; therefore, the semicolon is replaced with a comma. For quicker identification, the job titles have been italicized in the sentences below.

In attendance were Tim Frick, *President of Fixit Motors;* Earl Butts, *President of Big Canoe;* William Moot, *President of Compunet.*

Those industry leaders who did not attend included Burt Thompson, *President of Fixit Motors;* Earl Williams, *President of Big Canoe,* and Alexander Moot, *President of Compunet.*

Exception: **List follows a strong pause.** Insert a colon (:) after the word which precedes the list. In this example, too, a sentence is added to the list and is preceded by a semicolon (;) because of its high relationship to what precedes it.

In attendance were these people: Burt Thompson, *President of Fixit Motors;* Earl Williams, *President of Big Canoe;* Alexander Moot, *President of Compunet;* each of whom was given a set of alphabet blocks.

46.8 **List of cities and states.** Use a comma (,) to divide the city from its state, and separate the list entries from one another by using semicolons (;).

The cities which have opted to curtail all garbage pickup during certain periods of July include *Dayton, Ohio; Indianapolis, Indiana; St. Louis, Missouri; Boise, Idaho.*

Exception: **List follows a strong pause.** Insert a colon (:) after the word which precedes the list.

These cities have opted to curtail all garbage pickup during certain periods of July: Dayton, Ohio; Indianapolis, Indiana; St. Louis, Missouri; Boise, Idaho.

But if dates are added, the semicolons (;) are retained, Insert a colon (:) before each date. This is one of the few times when one colon may follow another.

These cities have opted to curtail all garbage pickup during the month of July: Dayton, Ohio: *July 1-7;* Indianapolis, Indiana: *July 8-15;* St. Louis, Missouri: *July 16-23;* Boise, Idaho: *July 23-30.*

46.9 **List of dates.** Use a comma (,) to divide the days from the years, and separate the dates from one another by using semicolons (;). Should you decide to insert a conjunction before the last entry, the comma should substitute for the last semicolon (see second sentence) If the list follows a strong pause, *see* Rule 46.3 for guidelines.

It happened on *March 2, 1952; May 4, 1952; June 17, 1955; July 7, 1956.*

It happened on *March 2, 1952; May 4, 1952; June 17, 1955,* and *July 7, 1956.*

Exception: **List follows a strong pause.** Insert a colon (:) after the word which precedes the list. If a conjunction precedes the last date, precede it with a comma (,).

Over a ten-year span, this famous jazz group appeared four times in Houston: *June 2, 1959; May 14, 1965; October 1, 1970* and *June 3, 1972.*

46.10 **Phrase or sentence follows the list.** A comma (,) is used when there is no danger of an add-on phrase or sentence being confused with the last entry of the list; if such confusion *is* possible, use a semicolon (;) instead, for it will establish a stronger break than a comma. In the first sentence which follows a conjunction leads off an add-on sentence, and a preceding comma is acceptable.

CONFUSION...
Unlikely: In attendance were Burt Thompson, President of Fixit Motors; Earl Williams, President of Big Canoe; Alexander Moot, President of Compunet, *and every one of them agreed that something had to be done to make American manufacturing more competitive in the world.*

Possible: In attendance were Burt Thompson, President of Fixit Motors; Earl Williams, President of Big Canoe; Alexander Moot, President of Compunet; *in black suit and black tie.*

List in Vertical Form

47.1   **General guidelines for punctuating a vertical list.** Besides punctuation tips, here is also information pertaining to the numbering, capitalization, indentation, and spacing of entries in a vertical list.

NUMBERING, ETC. Items listed vertically may be preceded by numbers, letters, dashes, or graphics. Whichever is chosen, it is best to use the same format throughout your written work; so if you start out using numbers, continue doing so thereafter (for an exception, review Rule 47.5). Refrain from using the asterisk (*), however, for this punctuation mark is for footnotes and other special situations. Here are examples, using the same sentence:

NUMBER: 1. They kept their inventory low
DASH: — They kept their inventory low
GRAPHIC: • They kept their inventory low
LETTER: a. They kept their inventory low

CAPITALIZATION: First words of complete sentences in a vertical list are capitalized; others, such as phrases and words, are written in lowercase letters. Therefore, it is best not to have a combination of sentences and phrases in a list.

INDENTATION: The vertical list which follows the introduction should be indented several spaces from the left, so the reader can quickly see that the two are related. For instance:

The preceding paragraph of information sets the stage for the list, like so:

1. The number, letter, etc. preceding each entry in the list is indented at the left-hand margin.

MIXTURE OF PHRASES, SENTENCES, OR WORDS: Rewrite the list, so that it will be uniform; that is, it should contain all phrases, sentences, or words

PARENTHESES: Not acceptable in a vertical list. Some insist that a half one (*parenthesis*) may be used after an alphabetic letter which precedes each list entry, but this is not a good practice.

250

PERIOD (.): Only use it after a number or letter that precedes each list entry; otherwise refrain from employing this punctuation mark, even if the entries in the list are complete sentences.

SPACING: Double-space before the first list entry, and double space again after the last entry and before the next paragraph.

47.2 **List immediately follows a verb.** Do not follow the verb with any punctuation, but be sure that the verb is implied before each list entry. In this example, the verb *were* could be placed before each subsequently line.

The Cincinnati Reds of the National League were

1. the first professional baseball team
2. world champions in 1975, 1976 and 1990
3. purchased by Marge Schott

Those animals not a part of the zoo include

- cows
- squirrels
- house cats
- dogs

Exception: **Numbers, letters, or graphic marks are not used.** Insert a colon (:) after the verb preceding the list. (This, incidentally, is one of the rare times when a colon may follow a verb.) Next, drop down one space and type the vertical list *to the right* of the colon.

Those who attended were as follows:
Harlo Hump
Wally Wistful
Buster Bluebump

47.3 **List does not follow a verb.** Insert a colon (:) after the word which immediately precedes the list. While the list may follow several different parts of speech, the more commonly used words are *following, as follows,* and *namely.*

The members were as follows:

1. Michael Works
2. Francis Miller
3. Ezra Thimble
4. Wally Vinson

But in the following example, notice that a phrase is added before the colon and requires its normal preceding comma (,). The colon is therefore delayed and placed instead after the last word of the phrase.

The members were seated in the following order, *left to right as one entered the room:*

1. Michael Works
2. Francis Miller
3. Ezra Thimble
4. Wally Vinson

Exception: **Numbers, letters, or graphic marks are not used.** Insert a colon (:) after the last word which precedes the list. Next, drop down one space and type the vertical list *to the right* of the colon.

The members were seated in this order:
$$\qquad\qquad\qquad\text{Michael Works}$$
$$\qquad\qquad\qquad\text{Francis Miller}$$
$$\qquad\qquad\qquad\text{Ezra Thimble}$$

Exception: **Phrases are added to the list entries.** Separate each entry from its phrase with a comma (,). The phrases in this example have been italicized for your quick identification.

The members were seated in the following order:

1. Michael Works, *supporter of the tax bill*
2. Francis Miller, *an avowed enemy of taxes*
3. Ezra Thimble, *one-time mayor of Alvetta*
4. Wally Vinson, *long-time oppponent of Miller*

Exception: **Phrases begin with capital letters.** If there are only two or three list entries, the dash (—) may be used to dramatically set the phrases apart.

The Sixth Street Gym has turned out famous fighters:

1. Max Grunt—*Heavyweight Champion in the '80s*
2. Crim Puff—*Lightweight Champion in 1975*

47.4   **Major headings comprise the list.** When major headings are substituted for numbers, graphics, or letters, they should be darkened or underlined or totally capitalized; however, do not use a combination of any of these techniques. The heading itself should be immediately followed by a dash (—), period (.), or colon (:)—do *not* use a combination—and its explanatory information comes after that.

HEADINGS ARE...

Capitalized: Let us take a look at some of the similarities which have been found between the 1920s and 1980s:
ECONOMY: The predominant economic philosophy was *laissez-faire* and it created economic misery.

SCANDAL: The same government offices were affected, and there was criminal activity in the banking industry.

Darkened: Let us take a look at some of the similarities which have been found between the 1920s and 1980s:

Economy. Information follows it and is not indented.

Scandal. Information follows....

Underlined: Let us take a look at some of the similarities which have been found between the 1920s and 1980s:

Economy Information follows the heading and is not indented.

Scandal Information follows....

47.5 **One list leads to another.** This represents one of the few times when different techniques may be employed before the list entries. In the example below, a numbering system is followed by a lettering system.

The curriculum is designed to provide a well-rounded education. Among the courses include the following:

1. **History.** An essential course of study for college students, because it gives the following:

    a. an appreciation of the past
    b. a grasp of current events
    c. a chance to goof off

2. **Psychology.** The knowledge gained in this field will deepen the student's grasp of human nature. In turn, it will promote this:

a. patience in dealing with others

b. total confusion

47.6 **Showing relationship between entries in a vertical list.** To indicate that one or more entries in a list share, or do not share, the same characteristics, the asterisk (*) may be placed in front of them. However, bullets (•) would be better. But an explanation regarding their use must be supplied, usually within a parentheses.

Here are the competing teams (winners of their divisions are identified by bullets):

- Chicago Cubs
  New York Mets
  Philadelphia Phillies
- Atlanta Braves
  Oakland Athletics

47.7 **List of complete sentences.** The sentences should follow a colon (:), and each should be capitalized; however, none require an ending period (.)

There are several reasons why the company was successful, among which were these:

1. They kept their inventory low
2. Their customer service was above-average
3. All employees had a profit-sharing plan

47.8 **List of partial sentences.** This occurs when the words preceding the list are implied before each entry. In the example which follows, the words "what you will find is" are implied before all list entries, none of which are capitalized. These partial sentences are preceded by a colon (:), and require no following punctuation mark, such as a period (.).

What you will find is this:

1. a shocking display of mismanagement
2. corruption from top to bottom
3. an unshakable and stifling bureaucracy

47.9 **List of recipe ingredients.** You may, if you wish, use ditto marks (") beneath certain words to prevent redundancy.

Add one dash pepper
" " " salt
" " " curry powder
Stir together until smooth

254

47.10 List of monetary donations. When the person or group precedes the monetary donation, they should be separated by a comma (,).

Among the contributors were the following:

a. Women's Press Club, $5000
b. City Fathers Group, $2500
c. The Refurbishers, $6000
d. Boys in the Band, $2.50

47.11 Vertical list of dates. Besides following a colon (:), numbers, graphics, or alphabetic letters should be placed before them.

We expect you to report on these dates:

1. May 13, 1979
2. June 15, 1979

Number Appears Before...

48.1 Number appears before a noun. While not a punctuation problem, the situation is being included here because of its widespread misuse. It is this: when two separate numbers appear before a noun in the same sentence and the second one is larger, spell out the first number and write the second one numerically. However, if the first number is larger than the second one, then the opposite is true.

FIRST NUMBER IS...

Larger: Give me 100 *twelve-inch* rulers.
            I need 20 *ten-cent* stamps.

Smaller: We bought *five* 10 cent stamps.

Exception: **Before two nouns.** If it joins a noun to describe another noun, it is part of a two-word adjective and needs to be followed by a hyphen (-), whether the number is written numerically or not.

            NUMERICAL: It was a *50*-acre farm.
            SPELLED OUT: It was a *fifty*-acre farm.

            But if the number is comprised of two digits and is spelled out, the hyphen (-) is placed between the numbers rather than before the noun.

            It was a *fifty-five* acre farm.

255

48.2   **Number appears before words in a series.** Encase the numbers in parentheses and separate the words with commas (,). Single words are separated by commas (,), and the conjunction may be omitted before the last number. If a strong pause precedes the first parenthesized number, a colon (:) will probably be needed to represent that pause, because the series is expanding upon that information which precedes it. In that case, insert semicolons (;) between the words.

NO COLON: She *was* (1) calm, (2) cool, and (3) collected.
She *was* (1) calm, (2) cool, (3) collected.

COLON: She had these feelings about what had happened to her: (1) regret; (2) relief; (3) revenge.

48.3   **Number appears before sentences in a series.** Encase the numbers in parentheses and separate the sentences with semicolons (;). A conjunction before the last number demands a preceding comma (,); but if it is eliminated, put a semicolon (;) in its place. If there is a strong pause before the first number, the information before it should be a full sentence. Insert a colon (:) to represent the pause, and place semicolons between each of the sentences.

NO COLON: He said that (1) he wasn't near the train depot that night; (2) he was left-handed; (3) the bootprint didn't match his, and (4) he had Agnes as an alibi.

Without conj: He said that (1) he wasn't near the train depot that night; (2) he was left-handed; (3) the bootprint didn't match his; (4) he had Agnes as an alibi.

COLON: He gave me these reasons: (1) he wasn't near the train that night; (2) he was left-handed; (3) he had Agnes as an alibi.

Exception: **Numbers are spelled out and the sentences are long.** Capitalize the numbers and insert a colon (:) after each. End each sentence with a period (.).

One: Management will no longer tolerate tardiness that extends beyond the two-minute mark. *Two:* Overtime pay will only be extended to those with seniority.

But shorter sentences, especially those which begin with the same word, can be separated by semicolons (;) rather than periods (.). Insert a comma (,) after each number, and capitalize the first one only.

256

The product has three advantages: *One, it* is long-lasting; *two, it* is pleasing to the eye; *three, it* only costs pennies to operate.

48.4 **Number appears before partial sentences in a series.** Encase each number in parentheses, and separate the partial sentences with commas (,). No punctuation is needed before the first number. In this example, the words *they were discovered to be* are implied before each group that follows a number.

They were discovered to be (1) unreceptive to breakthrough ideas, (2) militarily weak, and (3) rich beyond anyone's wildest dreams.

Exception: **Conjunction eliminated before the last number.** Substitute the commas with semicolons (;).

They were discovered to be (1) unreceptive to breakthrough ideas; (2) militarily weak; (3) rich beyond anyone's wildest dreams.

48.5 **Number appears before phrases in a series.** Encase each number in parentheses, and separate the phrases with commas (,).

I have been led to believe that because Arnold Aardvark (1) callously disregarded his chronic ear wax problem, (2) scratched his sensitive parts in public, and (3) used facial tissue as a writing tablet, he found himself to be an outcast in his immediate family.

Exception: **Numbered phrases follow a strong pause.** A full sentence should appear before the pause, and a colon (:) should be inserted to represent that pause. The phrases, which should elaborate on the sentence in some way, must be separated with a semicolon (;).

These features have always set him apart: (1) callously disregarding a chronic ear wax problem; (2) scratching his sensitive parts in public; (3) using facial tissue as a writing tablet.

48.6 **Number appears before a numbered street address.** When the name of a street is a number rather than a regular noun, the street number before it should be separated from it by a hyphen (-). Make sure to insert an extra space before and after the hyphen.

They live at *386 - 17th* Street.

48.7 **Number appears before an abbreviation.** It is acceptable to place numbers before abbreviations when they stand alone or are not part of a sentence, and punctuation rarely if ever separates them. But a

257

noun which introduces them is followed by a colon (:). However, if the number and the abbreviation combine to serve as an adjective that describes a noun, it is essential that a hyphen (-) separate them (*see second example*).

STANDS ALONE: Length: *10 in.*   Weight: *25 lbs.*
ADJECTIVE: I once owned a *16-mm* camera.

Large Number

49.1   **Billions or millions.** Exact numbers involving millions or billions of dollars are divided at every three digits, starting from the right and using the comma (,).

MILLIONS: The total was 2,654, 801.
BILLIONS: The total was 1, 203, 716, 499.

Exception: **Number is rounded off.** Insert a decimal point (.) between the billion or million figure and a single-digit number which represents the rounded-off number. For even greater generality, such words as *about* or *in the neighborhood of* may be used to introduce it, but this will require spelling out the number and using only the billion or million figure (see second example).

ROUNDED OFF: There are *16.2 million* people who have yet to receive their benefits.

GENERAL: I believe there are more than *two billion* rocks on that beach.

49.2   **Thousands.** Beginning at the right, insert a comma (,) every three digits.

HUNDREDS OF
THOUSANDS: The exact head count was 409, 613.

THOUSANDS: They say that 2,500 people showed up at the festival.

Exception: **Four-digit number is divisible by fifty.** The comma may be eliminated..

They say that *2500* people showed up at the festival.

Exception: **Page number.** No comma is needed.

You will find the answer on page 1108.

258

49.3   **Patent number.** Beginning at the right, use the comma (,) to divide the number at every three digits. *Number* is abbreviated to *No.*

Patent No. 1, 695, 103, 294

49.4   **Serial numbers and kilocycles.** They are not divided by commas.

SERIAL NUMBER: My serial number is 15566499.
KILOCYCLES: The company uses 142796 kc per week.

Small Number

50.1   **Fraction.** Written numerically, the numbers in a fraction are separated by a virgule (/); but if spelled out, a hyphen (-) is used. Also, when spelling it out, drop the letter S from the end of the fraction when it is being used to indicate a physical measurement (e.g., inch, foot, yard, etc.)

NUMERICAL: She lived 1 3/4-miles up the road from him.
SPELLED OUT: She lived *one and three-fourths* miles from him.

PHYSICAL
MEASUREMENT: It has a *three-fourth* inch head.

Exception: **Fraction contains three-words.** Write it numerically rather than spell it out, and insert a virgule (/) after the first number. Below is the correct and incorrect way of punctuating it.

INCORRECT: It has a.two *sixty-fourths* tolerance.
CORRECT: There's a *7/64* tolerance.

Exception: **One-word fraction.** Spell it out rather than write it numerically. It is acceptable to add the letter S when the fraction is plural.

PLURAL: Divide the pie into *fourths.*
SINGULAR: It's only missing by an *eighth.*

50.2   **Decimal fraction.** Decimal points (.), which are nothing but periods, always follow either zeroes or whole numbers; the fraction follows the decimal point.

LESS THAN "ONE":   The tolerance is less than *0.11* inches.
NUMBER + FRACTION: The tolerance is about *1.11* inches.

259

Exception: **Decimal fraction acts as an adjective.** A hyphen (-) is required after the decimal fraction. Never use half ditto marks (') or ditto marks (") to represent inches or feet.

There is less than an *0.11-inch* tolerance.

50.3 **Percentage.** If the percentage is less than one percent, insert a decimal point (.) *after* a zero; otherwise, it follows a whole number. Do not use the percent sign (%) in a sentence.

LESS THAN 1%:   My income has risen *0.3 percent.*
                     My income has risen *0.06 percent.*

MORE THAN 1%:   My income has risen *2.05 percent.*
                     My income has risen *33.86 percent.*

Exception: **Number is not statistical or scientific.** Spell out the word *percent* after the number rather than use the percent sign (%). Double numbers before the word *percent* are hyphenated (*see* second example below).

My income has risen *forty percent.*
My income has risen *forty-one percent.*

Monetary Number

51.1 **Billions or millions of dollars.** Beginning at the right, use the comma (,) to divide the number at every three digits

MILLIONS: I believe you owe me *$1,659,402.*
BILLIONS: Or was it *$1, 101, 659, 402?*

Exception: **Figure is rounded off.** Follow the millions or billions number with a decimal point (.), and round off the second figure to a single-digit number. For even greater generality, words like *more than* can be used to introduce it, and no punctuation is needed. Note: If the dollar sign ($) is used, the word *dollars* should not follow the number; but if the dollar sign is not used, spell out the number. A hyphen (-) is needed when *dollar* is preceded by a two-word adjective.

ROUNDED OFF: He paid *$102.2 million* for the rights.
GENERAL: There was at least *six million dollars.*

It's a *one-million* dollar contract.

51.2 **Thousands of dollars.** Use the comma (,) to separate the last three digits from the preceding numbers.
The balance due is *$726,818*
The balance due is *$6,818*

> Exception: **Four-digit figure is divisible by fifty.** The comma may be omitted.

> I paid them *$4800,* but they wanted more.

51.3 **Dollars, but no cents.** There is no need to add a period (.) and two zeroes after the number. Insert a dollar figure ($) before it.

I paid *$35* for that piece of junk.
That junk cost *$35!*

51.4 **Less than a dollar.** The cent sign (¢) should be reserved for advertisements and other special areas. For example, employing it on a store coupon is much better than spelling it out.

Colonel's Corn Flakes $1.90. Save *60¢.*

Here are other punctuation guidelines pertaining to monetary figures that are less than a dollar:

ONE NUMBER: A cent figure comprised of one number should be spelled out.

> INCORRECT: All she had was *40 cents.*
> CORRECT: All she had was *forty cent.*

TWO NUMBERS: A cent figure comprised of two numbers should be written numerically rather than spelled out.

> INCORRECT: He gave her *twenty-one* cents
> CORRECT: He gave her *21* cents.

THREE NUMBERS: A decimal point (.) and dollar sign ($) are used when the cent figure contains three numbers.

> The balance on the bill read *$0.00.*
> The balance on the bill read *$0.27.*
> The balance on the bill read *$1.64.*
> It amounts to a *$0.394* savings.

51.5 **Approximate and rounded-off monetary figures.** An approximate monetary figure should only be written numerically. Rounded-off figures, on the other hand, can be spelled out or written numerically. If the latter joins other words and acts as an adjective, a hyphen (-) will be needed between it; but a hyphen is not placed between a spelled out number and the word *dollar* (*see* last example below). In either case, the dollar sign ($) should only be used when the number is not spelled out.

APPROXIMATE: It was worth about *$500.*

ROUNDED OFF: He's got a *million bucks* to blow.
He was a *$100-per-week* clerk going nowhere.
He was a *hundred dollar-a-week* clerk—at best.

51.6   **Indicating terms of payment.** When not included in a sentence, the number should be separated from the payment terms by a hyphen (-). This represents one of the rare times when a numerically-written figure may be seen first.

SENTENCE: There will be a *twenty percent* charge on checks arriving after the due date.

No sentence: 20%-checks arriving after due date.

SENTENCE: You will be paid three hundred dollars each Friday of every month.

No sentence: $300-each Friday of every month.

Measurement

52.1   **Showing dimensions, using "by."** Hyphens (-) are needed when the dimension helps to describe a noun (*see* first example below). However, no hyphens are necessary if the dimensions are not being used to describe anything.

DESCRIPTIVE: It was a *20-by-20-inch* picture.

NOT DESCRIPTIVE: It measured *20 by 24 inches.*
It measured *1 foot by 6 inches.*

52.2   **Showing dimensions, using the letter "x."** The lower-case "x" is never accompanied by hyphens (-) when used to show a dimension of something. However, exact amounts of feet can be shown through the use of the cipher ('), and inches are represented by the ditto mark ("), which is NOT a double quotation mark, though they are frequently confused with one another. When the dimension ends a sentence, the period (.) comes *after* the cipher or ditto mark, not before.

USING...
    Abbreviations: It measures 2 ft. x 6 ft. x 10 ft.
                      It is a 2 3/16 in. x 6 3/8 in. picture.
    Cipher: It measures 2' x 6' x 10'.
    Ditto marks: It is a 2 3/16" x 6 3/8"

52.3 **Indicating height, length, or width.** A comma is not needed to separate feet from inches. You may use ditto marks (") to represent the word *inches* and ciphers (') to represent the word *feet* (*see* second example). When the dimension ends a sentence, the period (.) comes *after* the cipher or ditto mark—not before.

A woman *7 feet 4 inches* tall was the first draft pick.
A woman *7' 4"* tall was the first draft-pick.
Her height was *7'4"*.

Miscellaneous Numbers

53.1 **Showing odds.** Whether the odds are spelled out or written numerically, they are separated by hyphens (-). A preposition is invariably in the middle.

    SPELLED OUT: You have a *million-to-one* shot of winning.
    NUMERICAL: The odds are *6-to-5*.

53.2 **Plural number.** The apostrophe (') may or may not be used to indicate more than one of the same number.

    APOSTROPHE: There were five *6's*.
                      He asked for her *seven's* and won the game.

    NO APOSTROPHE: I saw five *6s* on the table.
                      He asked for her *sevens* and won the game.

    Exception: **Number represents a time span.** No apostrophe is needed for a span of time in a person's life, but the word should be capitalized when it refers to calendar time.

                      PERSON: He was somewhere in his *thirties*.
                      CALENDAR: That happened back in the *Thirties*.

53.3 **Ratio.** Written numerically, the two numbers in a ratio are divided by a colon (:). When spelled out, they deserve hyphens (-) between them, with the preposition *to* in the middle.

    NUMERICAL: I'm told that it's a 15:4 ratio.

SPELLED OUT: The ratio is fifteen-to-four.

53.4   **Score.** The two numbers in a score are separated from one another by hyphens (-), even when the preposition *to* is inserted between them.

The Cincinnati Reds were behind *7-6* ballgame in the ninth; right now, the score is *8-to-8*.

Exception: **Team's name precedes each number.** No hyphen is needed, but a comma (,) should be inserted after the first number, which is always the highest of the two—unless, of course, the score is tied.

The score in the seventh is *Dodgers 3, Pirates 1.*

53.5   **Numbers in a series.** Each number is separated by a comma (,). The last number may or may not be preceded by a conjunction.

The winning lottery numbers today are 5, 16, 18, 34, 35, and 42.
The winning lottery numbers today are 5, 16, 18, 34, 35, 42.

53.6   **Consecutive numbers.** The hyphen (-) is the most frequently used punctuation mark which is placed between two numbers in order to show that the consecutive numbers between them are implied as well. Now while this is still the acceptable procedure, the hyphen, especially when the text is prepared in small type, can get lost; therefore the dash (—), which is longer and bolder, is a worthwhile option. Finally, to ensure the reader understands that the first and last number are meant to be included, the word *inclusive* may be added after the last number, preceded by a comma (,). Also, the word *numbers* may be abbreviated to *Nos.*

HYPHEN: Nos. 401-409
DASH: Nos. 401—409, inclusive

53.7   **Confirming the exactness of a spelled-out number.** To confirm that the number you have spelled out is the number you intended, insert its numerical equivalent within a parentheses and place it immediately after that number which has been spelled out.

NOT MONEY: The seven hundred and forty (740) people who showed up weren't enthusiastic.

MONEY: You owe me exactly one hundred ten dollars and twenty-five cents ($110.25).

53.8   **Showing the frequency of something happening.** No hyphens are needed between those words which indicate how often something is occurring. Numbers in this situation are usually divided by such words as "in" and "out of."

One in six prefer Jasper Toiletries over the leading brand.
Two out of ten will not even bother going to the polls.

53.9   **Numbers in a temperature span.** Separate the two numbers with a hyphen (-). There is no need to precede the numbers with words like *between* and *from*. If you do not use the degree symbol, spell out the word *degrees* after the last number. And if the hyphen is not used, the preposition "to" is almost always its replacement.

DEGREE SYMBOL: They say it's going to be 80°-100° tomorrow.
NO SYMBOL: The temperature will be 80-100 degrees tomorrow.
NO HYPHEN: They say it's going to be 80 to 100 degrees tomorrow.

53.10   **Person's age follows his or her name.** Inserting someone's age after his or her name requires that it be set apart by commas (,). But if the age acts as a surprising comment by itself, encase it in parentheses (see second example).

Their chief executive officer is Robert Peters, 62, a take-charge financial whiz who gained his reputation in Wall Street.

But still in the field when the sun went down was Wilma Mathers (92), picking the last row of beans.

Literary Title

In this section, guidance is provided on how to list and punctuate titles (literary, art, music) within bibliographies and footnotes.

54.1   **When to italicize.** In the left-hand column below is a list of literary sources. The "yes" and "no" indicators in the three columns to the right indicate when the title should be underlined, italicized, or placed it between quotation marks. Several provide you with dual options, but always adopt one approach and stick with it when writing: in other words, don't begin using italics for titles and later decide to switch to underlining. When a number appears alongside one of the list entries, additional information can be found at the end of this section. When it is suggested that a title be italicized, but you are unable to comply because you are handwriting it, or because you don't have the proper equipment, underlining is acceptable.

	ITALICS	QUOTATION MARKS	UNDERLINE
book	yes	no	yes
booklet	yes	no	yes
brochure	no	no	yes
collections of...			
• books	yes	no	yes
• manuscripts	no	yes	yes
• poetry	yes	no	yes
diary	no	yes	no
dissertation	no	yes	no
essay	no	yes	no
journal	yes	no	yes
legal case[1]	yes	yes	yes
magazine, name of	yes	no	yes
magazine article[2]	no	yes	no
movie	yes	no	yes
newspapers	yes	no	yes
• Sections published separately	yes	no	no
pamphlet	yes	no	yes
papers at meetings	no	yes	no
periodical	yes	no	yes
play[3]	yes	no	yes
poetry [2, 4]			
• Long, published separately	yes	no	yes
• Short	no	yes	no
proposal	no	yes	no
radio show	no	yes	no
report[5]	no	no	yes
short story[2]	no	yes	no
sculpture	yes	yes	no
speech[2]	no	yes	no
television show	no	yes	no
thesis	no	yes	no

[1] **Legal case.** The names of the plaintiff and defendant are separated by the small letter V, which is followed by a period (.)

Johnson v. Johnson was a landmark case.

[2] **Poem, magazine article, speech, or short story.** If an established title is made part of a *new* title, a single quotation mark (') before and after the established title is required—in addition to the double quotation marks (" ") which encases the whole title. But if you have the ability to produce italics, italicize the entire title and insert double quotation marks before and after the title-within-a-title.

266

NO ITALICS:	It is titled "The Hidden Myth in 'The Rhyme of the Ancient Mariner.'"
ITALICS:	It is titled *The Hidden Myth in* "The Rhyme of the Ancient Mariner."

3 **Act and scene numbers in a play.** While the title of a play should be italicized, the words *scene* and *act* should be in regular type and presented in upper and lowercase letters. The numbers which follow them, however, should be in Roman numerals.

Act I, Scene II

4 **Title of several poems.** Type all of them in italics. However, when also citing a poem's canto and stanza (the divisions given to some long poetry), do not italicize them.

In his English class he studied *The Eve of St. Agnes, Beowulf, Venus and Adonis,* and *Paradise Lost.*

5 **Report.** Underlining a report is appropriate when the work is important enough to stand on its own. But when a section of the report is being referred to, place it between double quotation marks (" ").

The "Effect of Fatty Diets on the Brain" section of the <u>Federal Report on General Nutrition</u> starts on page 491.

54.2 **Capitalization of titles.** With the exception of prepositions, conjunctions, and indefinite articles, each word of a title is capitalized.

INDEFINITE ARTICLE:	He wrote *Who's Minding <u>the</u> Store?* in less than a month.
PREP:	Roger Wickwack, author of the *Magician <u>of</u> Herald Square,* was the winner of the National Book Award.
CONJ:	*Battling Your Habits <u>and</u> Vices* was a very boring book.
Exception:	**Preposition, conjunction, or indefinite article acts as the first word.** In this case, it must be capitalized as well. In the first example, the title begins with an indefinite article; in the second, a preposition.
	Peter Fratt wrote *The Long and Short of It* in ten days. The shortest novel I ever read was *Of Thee I Sing.*

Exception: **Title has a hyphenated word.** Capitalize the first word but not the word which follows it, unless unusual circumstances prevail

They have quit stocking *The Death-defying Leap of Woodrow Wacko.*

Exception: **Ends in a preposition.** Capitalize the preposition.

What We're Working For sold a million copies in less than a month.

Exception: **Contains the name of a previously published book.** Only the title of the original book is typed in italics, and the entire title of the new book is encased in double quotation marks (" "). In the example which follows, *Gone with the Wind* is the original book title which has been placed inside a new title.

Her book, "*Gone with the Wind*—and Back Again," is simply a rehash of old magazine articles about that Clark Gable-Vivien Leigh film.

54.3 **Author's name precedes the title.** An apostrophe S ('s) is always added to the author's name, and a comma is not required when no other words separate it from the title.

Percival Hugenot's *Prunes and Manure* has caused no movement among book buyers.

But if another word, such as *book* or *novel*, follows the author's name, a separating comma (,) will be needed—unless the author has written more than one in that same literary category: e.g., two books, two magazine articles, and so on.

MORE THAN
ONE TITLE: Hemingway's novella *The Old Man and the Sea* was instrumental in helping him win the Nobel Prize for literature.

ONE ONLY: Percival Hugenot's book, *Prunes and Manure,* has caused no movement book among book-buyers to date.

54.4 **Author's name follows the title.** When the author's name follows a literary title, it is part of an interrupting or add-on phrase and the comma (,) must be employed to set the phrase apart. But if a verb is the next word, there is no pause and no comma is required.

COMMA:	*Down Under,* a novel written by Hans Krinke about seafaring, only sold five copies.
	I think I read *All About Cooking,* Jim Grady's book.
NO COMMA:	*A Time to Look* was authored by John Steele.

54.5 **Subtitle added to title.** The subtitle is separated from the other title, using a colon (:). In the following example, *A Study of Man's Decisions* is the subtitle.

It is documented in *The Course of Events: A Study of Man's Decisions,* written by Thomas Ewell, of Smart University.

54.6 **Year or time span added to title.** A year or time span added to a title needs to be separated by a comma (,); in the case of a span of time, though, a hyphen (-) will be needed to separate the two years.

ONE YEAR FOLLOWS:	I read *The Year That Changed Us All, 1963* in one afternoon.
TIME SPAN:	*The Prairie Years, 1820-1860* was not what you would call a smashing big seller.

54.7 **Phrase is dramatically added to the title.** When a phrase is dramatically added to a title, precede it with a dash (—).

He bought six copies of *The Unauthorized Biography of Peter Piper—and What He's Doing Now.*

Bibliography

55.1 **General information on bibliographies.** A bibliography contains a list of the source materials used to create a book manuscript. It is comprised of titles, authors' names, dates, page numbers, and other pertinent information. Although customarily found under the heading "Bibliography" at the rear of a book manuscript, the source materials may appear instead as individual footnotes at the bottom of a page, more particularly where they are being cited; in this instance they are provided with numbers which match those in the text above them. Periods (.), commas (,), semicolons (;), and hyphens (-) are the most commonly used punctuation marks in bibliographies.

55.2 **Magazine articles in a bibliography.** An entry in a bibliography usually begins with the author's last name, first name, middle initial; title of the article; the name of the magazine in which it appeared;

and the date it was published. Below is how additional information is added. Observe the placement of commas, periods, quotation marks, parentheses, and hyphens.

AUTHOR
& TITLE: Frenchwine, Priscilla W. "The Hydrogen Problem." *Journal of American Medicine* (May 1975).

PAGE NO: Frenchwine, Priscilla W. "The Hydrogen Problem." *Journal of American Medicine*, **40** (May 1975).

PAGE NOS: Frenchwine, Priscilla W. "The Hydrogen Problem." *Journal of American Medicine*, **pp. 40-44** (May 1975).

Exception: **No author can be named.** Simply begin with the article's title instead. This is often the case when it has been written by the staff members of a magazine.

                "The Hydrogen Problem." *Journal of American Medicine*, pp. 40-44 (May 1975).

Exception: **Information is from different sources.** It is better to place the various sources cited under one general heading, as shown below (e.g., Electioneering).

                ELECTIONEERING, the 1944 Presidential Campaign

                The Reporter (New York), 1941-1945; *The Prime Weekly* (Washington), 1942-1945.

55.3   **Books in a bibliography.** An entry in a bibliography usually begins with the author's last name, followed by his first name, middle initial; the title of the book; the city where the publisher is located; name of the publisher; and the year it was published. The darkened lettering below indicates how additional information is added. Observe closely the placement of commas, periods, quotation marks, parentheses, and hyphens.

AUTHOR, TITLE,
CITY, PUBL.,
YEAR: Clark, Robert E., *Your ABC's.* Boston: Truth Press, 1980.

VOLUME: Clark, Robert E., *Your ABC's,* **Vol. 2,** Boston: Truth Press, 1980

> But if page numbers are added, drop the abbreviation *vol.* and insert the number before the page numbers, followed by a colon (:).

PAGE NOS.   Clark, Robert E., *Your ABC's* 2:**18—21,** Boston: Truth Press, 1980

> But when there is no volume number, use the abbreviation *pp.* before the page numbers. If there is only one page number, drop *pp.*

Clark, Robert E., *Your ABC's* **pp. 18-21,** Boston: Truth Press, 1980

EDITION: Clark, Robert E., *Your ABC's.* pp. 18-21, **3rd edition,** Boston: Truth Press, 1980

55.4   **Separate books, but same author.** Rather than include the author's name two or more times and risk redundancy, an underline may be used instead, followed by a comma (,). The only problem with this technique, however, is that the reader may well think the author is unknown.

Smith, James, *The King.* New York: Action Press, 1971
_____ , *The Queen.* New York: Action Press, 1971

55.5   **Book has more than one author.** If there are two authors, separate their names with a conjunction; but if there are three or more, separate their names with semicolons (;). Last name is separated from the first by a comma (,).

2 AUTHORS: Park, Wilma and Futz, Frank. *The Talk of the Town,* New York: Prime Sellers, 1968

3 AUTHORS: Park, Wilma; Futz, Frank; and Murr, James. *The Talk of the Town,* New York: Prime Sellers, 1968

55.6   **Author cannot be identified.** Use only the name of the book, including the publisher and the place where it was published. A colon (:) precedes the publisher's name.

The Layman's Dictionary, Chicago: Diet Press

55.7 **Speeches in a bibliography.** The order in which the entries are listed, including their required punctuation, is as follows: the author's last name, first name, middle initial; the word *Speech* or *Address*, capitalized; an ellipsis (...); theme of speech, beginning with the words *on the;* and the city and year, in parentheses.

Allen, August C., Speech...on the Natural Conflict Between the Branches of Government (Cincinnati, 1952).

Exception: **Audience or locale, or both, supplied.** Insert this information immediately after the word "speech" or "address," and begin it with the capitalized word *Delivered.* In this example, the speaker's middle name is spelled out as well.

Miller, Rashmelda Agnes, Address *Delivered before the Phi Beta Kappa Society of Harvard University*...on the Legacy of the Jackson Era (Boston, 1981).

Exception: **Bibliographic information is grouped under the heading of "speeches."** First, the reader must be made aware that a grouping of speeches in a bibliography pertains to the same person. Below are four options, but keep in mind that a list should contain one type and not a mixture. In the first example, the *location* where the speech was delivered is listed first; in the second, the *subject matter* leads off; but in the third and fourth examples, the word "speech" comes first. Place "speech" or "address" in italics when either word is listed first. Please note the insertion of commas (,), semicolons (;), and ellipsis (...).

Speeches

Haven Hall; Jasper,Virginia; May 19, 1971
On the Texas Question...Jasper, Virginia, 1971
Speech...Haven Hall, Jasper,Virginia, May 19, 1971
Speech on the Texas Question ...Jasper, Virginia, 1971

Footnote

56.1 **Explanation regarding footnotes.** Footnotes can frequently be viewed as mini-bibliographies. Their punctuation and order of their information is not unlike bibliographies found at the end of a book. The important thing to remember about a footnote is this: it must be preceded by a number or special graphic which corresponds with the same in the text where that source is cited.

```
|  ............  |
|  ............  |
|  ............  |   <<< Footnote mark in text
|  ...........   |
|  ...........   |
|  ...........   |
|  _____  |
|_____  |   <<< Footnote at bottom of page
```

56.2 **Footnote marks in the text.** Several different footnote marks are available. If there is just one on a page, the asterisk (*) is undoubtedly the easiest mark to use, and it is inserted after the last word of that which pertains to the cited information. If there is more than one footnote on a page, employ a numbering system instead, beginning with "1," and give each subsequent footnote the next highest number. When possible, type the number slightly above its normal position. Here are two examples of how a footnote might be cited in the text.

ASTERISK: In his diary Judge Rice wrote, "I am not very happy with the defense attorney." *

NUMBER: In his diary Judge Rice wrote, "I am not very happy with the defense attorney." [1]

Note: There are other footnote options available to you. Rather than use the asterisk or a numbering system, the marks shown to the left below may be inserted in their place. Good computer programs can produce these footnote marks; but if you are using a typewriter, the information listed at the right of the footnote marks will explain how to achieve them.

§   Type one small S; backspace; type another S slightly above it.
≠   Type a slant (/); backspace; type an equal sign (=).
†   Type a lowercase L; backspace; type a hyphen (-).
¥   Type a capital Y; backspace; type a hyphen (-).
//   Type two slants (/).
Ø   Type the letter O; backspace; type a slant (/).

56.3 **Footnotes at the bottom of a page.** A single unbroken line should extend from the left margin to the right margin and separate all the footnotes from the text above them. Three, sometimes four, footnotes may appear at the bottom of a page. Here is the general format, sequence, and required punctuation:

1. Indent the first line of each footnote five to eight spaces.
2. Insert an asterisk, number, or other footnote notation *before* it and slightly *above* the typewritten line, leaving no space between the

mark and the first word of the footnote. If using a numbering system, place the numbers in smaller type whenever possible. Whichever number or mark is used, it should match that which appears somewhere in the text above it.

3. Include the name of the author, followed by the name of the book, article, etc. The author's first or last name may be typed first. Spelling out the middle name is also optional. (In the first example shown below there is no need to insert the author's name, because it is already part of the title.)

4. In parentheses include the following: the publisher's location, followed by a colon (:), the publisher's name, a comma (,), and the year of publication. After the last parenthesis, insert a comma (,) when a page number follows.

5. Include the page number(s) where the information being cited can be found. Preceding the page number(s) with the abbreviation *p.* for "page," or *pp.* for "pages" is optional. But if more than one page is being cited, separate the numbers with a hyphen (-).

Below are two examples. For information regarding books, articles, etc., please see the rules in this category which specifically applies to them.

[1]Diary of Judge Whoop, 1891-1895 (Nashville: Baker Press International, 1935).

[2]John R. Stix, *On Target,* p. 23.

56.4 **Citing a book in a footnote.** The title is typed in italics, and if the book is from a collection of the author's work, it should be in italics too. But when the work has been translated or edited, the editor's or translator's name should be included after the last title, preceded by the abbreviation "ed." for editor and "trans." for translator. When there is more than one volume, only the one being cited as a source material is used, and it precedes any mention of the editor's or translator's name. However, insert the total number of volumes available inside the parentheses and just before the publisher's geographical location. The comma (,) separates these various parts. Underlining a book's title is acceptable when italics is not available. The words have been darkened in the examples below to provide quicker identification.

EDITOR'S NAME
IS ADDED:

[1]John R. Stix, *On Target,* in *The CompleteWorks of John Stix,* **ed. by Hans Dabrow,** (Memphis: Bibbs Publishing Company, 1991), p. 23.

TRANSLATED: [1]John R. Stix, *On Target*, **trans. by Betty Culver**, (Memphis: Bibbs Publishing Company, 1991), p. 23.

MORE THAN
ONE VOLUME: [1]John R. Stix, *On Target*, **Vol. 2 of** *The Complete Works of John Stix*, ed. by Hans Dabrow, (4 vols; Memphis: Bibbs Publishing Company, 1991), p. 23.

56.5   Citing a magazine article in a book. When a magazine article has been republished and made part of a book, its title should be placed between double quotation marks (" ") and precede the title of the book. The comma (,) separates these various parts. Underlining the title is acceptable when italics is not available.

[1]Joe Broom, "Going to the Circus," *The Fascinating World of the Circus,* pp. 21-22.

56.6   Citing a magazine article in a footnote. The title should precede the name of the magazine and be placed between double quotation marks (" "); it may be in italics or underlined, followed by its volume number. The publication date follows the volume number and is in parentheses. The comma (,) separates these various parts.

[1]Zane Watt, "Canyon War," *Historical Perspective, Vol.* IX (Summer 1963), p. 91.

56.7   Two footnotes citing the same work on the same page. Rather than repeat the same information, there are two options available: (1) use the Latin abbreviation *Ibid* for the second footnote, but be sure to include the page number where the information can be found, even when both footnotes refer to the same page. If you do not have the equipment to type italics, you will have to underline *Ibid.*, a distinct disadvantage when using the abbreviation in succession; (2) type the author's last name, and add the page number where the information can be found in the material being cited. In the examples below, the first one is a book; the second one, a magazine article. The words have been darkened for quicker identification.

Ibid.   [1]Joseph Blow, *Ronnie and George, Pals,* (New York: Empire Publishing Co., 1989), p. 91
[2]*Ibid.*, p. 92.

LAST NAME: [1]Joseph Blow, "Predictions for the 1980s," *Politics,* II (May 1959), p. 65.
[2]**Blow**, p. 67.

56.8 **Citing same literary work on another page.** To show that a literary source has been cited in a footnote on a previous page, you may (1) type the author's last name and insert the italicized abbreviation *op. cit.* , or (2) simply use one word to represent the title, but in that previous footnote you must tell the reader what you are going to do (*see* "hereafter" in the first example below). In either case, the new page number should follow.

[1]Joseph Blow, "Marc Antony and Cleopatra Were Just Good Friends," *Politics*, II (May 1959), p. 91. Hereafter referred to as *Marc*.

USING...
Author's last name:	[1]Blow, *op. cit.*, p. 93.
First word of source:	[1]*Marc*, p. 175.

56.9 **Footnote cites two authors of the same literary work.** Include both names (last names may be first or last) and separate them with the conjunction "and." In the first example below, the author's last name follows his first one; in the second example, it precedes it.

[1]John G. Shane and Alex W. Cumquat, *The Shame of Our Environmental Policy*, pp. 321-325.

[1]Shane, John G., and Cumquat, Alex W. *The Shame of Our Environmental Policy*, pp. 321-325.

56.10 **Footnote cites three authors of the same literary work.** Include all three names, and insert a conjunction before the last name. In the first example below, the author's last name follows the his first one; in the second example, it precedes it.

[1]John G. Shane, Alex W. Cumquat, and James Tiller, *The Shame of Our Environmental Policy*, pp. 321-325.

[1]Shane, John G.; Cumquat, Alex W.; and Tiller, James *The Shame of Our Environmental Policy*, pp. 321-325.

56.11 **Footnote cites four or more authors of the same work.** Rather than include all of them in the footnote, choose only one; then write "and others," which should be preceded and followed by a comma (,).

[1]John G. Shane, and others, *The Shame of Our Environmental Policy*, pp. 321-325.

56.12 **Author is an organization or group.** The footnote in this instance usually pertains to a book, and, more often than not, the "author" is the publisher as well. The group's name comes immediately after the footnote notation and is followed by a period (.). The italicized name of the book is followed by a comma (,) and then the page number(s).

[1]National Horse Club. *Thoroughbreds in Kentucky*, p. 95.

56.13 Footnote is your personal comment. When the footnote takes on the character of a personal comment, punctuate it as you would any sentence.

[1]To see how his views changed, read pages 101-105 in his autobiography *My Life, My Times.*

Person's Title

57.1 Job title or rank. It should be set apart from the person's name, using commas (,).

PRECEDES NAME: *The Secretary of Agriculture,* Osgood Morganputh, said they were wrong.

INTERRUPTS
SENTENCE: Then Pete Smash, a *staff sergeant* attached to Biker's company, called him a flipping sissy.

FOLLOWS NAME: That is the expert opinion of Jim Black, *General Manager of Vita-Kim.*

Exception: **Indefinite article "the" is omitted from title.** When the title immediately precedes the person's name, no comma is needed to separate the two.

     Director of Marketing James Watkins claims that the company had a great year.

Exception: **Job title is informal and no hesitation follows.** A separating comma is not needed.

     The *reporter* Kwite Knozy wanted the truth.

57.2 Job title begins with the word "vice." A hyphen (-) may or may not be inserted immediately after it.

HYPHEN: He was promoted to the position of *Vice-President* of License Plates.

NO HYPHEN: He was promoted to the position of *Vice President* of License Plates.

Exception: **Vice President of the United States.** No hyphen is required.

57.3 **Job title begins with the word "under."** A hyphen (-) must be inserted after it. Capitalize *under* when it is followed by either the name of the person or the department to which the title applies. In the first example, the person's name follows; in the second, the department; in the third, the person's name precedes the title.

It was *Under-Secretary* Hugh Knox who spoke.
Knox was named *Under-Secretary of Bad Affairs.*
Is Knox the new *under-secretary?*

57.4 **Military rank placed in a list.** When the names of individuals and their military ranks are placed in a list, the ranks may be abbreviated.

Maj. Gen. Hopalong Cassidy
Gen. Buck Shootem
Lt. James Passabuck

Other Titles

58.1 **Titles of artwork.** Drawings, etchings, paintings, sculpture, and statues are either italicized or underlined. No quotation marks are needed.

We saw the *Mona Lisa* and the *Statue of David* on Wednesday.

58.2 **Music titles.** Types of music is listed in the left-hand column below. To the right are guidelines on how to present them on a page.

	ITALICS	QUOTATION MARKS	UNDERLINE
Classical	no	no	no
Motet	yes	no	yes
Opera	yes	no	yes
Oratorio	yes	no	yes
Short	no	yes	no
Song (popular)	no	yes	no
Tone poem	yes	no	no

Exception: **Specific classical music titles.** While concertos, symphonies, etc. receive no special punctuation, specific titles such as "The Rites of Spring" and the "Grand Canyon Suite" require double quotation marks (" "). When a classical music title includes divisions, insert a comma (,) between each. Further, the divisions—such as *opus* and *number*—may be abbreviated.

She has the lead role in the ballet "Romeo and Juliet."
It was Smith's Sonata No.5, Op. 36.

58.3 **Objects of technology.** When a ship, train, spacecraft, etc. is given a special name, that name should be underlined. However, the preceding abbreviation (e.g., U.S.S.) does not receive the same treatment.

We're going to set sail on the U.S.S <u>Americana</u> tomorrow.

Person's Name

59.1 **Nickname.** Highlight it by inserting double quotation marks (" ") before and after it. But if the nickname is well-known and it's a name the person uses consistently, it does not need quotation marks (*see* second sentence).

"Mugsy" Muldoon declined to comment.
Mugsy Muldoon declined to comment.

59.2 **By-name.** It is descriptive and receives no quotation marks around it, and when it immediately precedes or follows the person's name, a comma (,) must set it apart. Also each word is capitalized, except indefinite articles and prepositions that are not first words. The examples below have only been italicized for your quick identification.

SET APART: Charlie Chaplin, *The Little Tramp*, was America's favorite.

We will all remember Desmond, *The Dancer in the Dark.*

59.3 **First name omitted.** Use underlining to represent the missing name. If a comma would normally precede the name, retain it.

After that, ____ Smith said he would buy it.

59.4 **Last name omitted.** A dash (—) or an underline may represent the missing last name. If a comma would normally follow the name, retain it.

DASH: Alice—, the woman who blew the whistle on the corporation, is now in custody.

UNDERLINE: Bart ____ is the first baseman.

59.5 **Name identified.** When a word or phrase precedes or follows a person's name and serves to identify that person in some way, it is set apart by commas (,).

SHORT: Eugene Frimp, *the new fire chief,* hired six more firemen on Wednesday.

LONG: Eugene Frimp, *recipient of the Fire Chief of the Year Award in 1981,* hired six more firemen on Wednesday.

ADD-ON: That is the opinion of Eugene Frimp, *the fellow we all count on.*

AS SUBJECT: *The fire chief,* Eugene Frimp, hired six more firemen on Wednesday.

Exception: **Identification acts as a quick side comment.** Put it inside a parentheses.

Eugene Frimp (fire chief) gave his opinion as well.

Exception: **Identification needs emphasis.** Insert a dash (—) before and after it.

Eugene Frimp—the fire chief who won Fireman of the Year in 1981—was indicted yesterday for theft.

59.6 **Followed by "of."** No comma is needed between an individual's name and the preposition *of* when the information which follows is traditionally linked to that name—or when there is no discernible pause. Observe the last sentence example: see how the addition and repositioning of words creates a pause before the "of" phrase and demands commas (,) to set it apart? When *of* is followed by a geographical location, see Rule 59.8.

NO COMMA
Linked to name: The always unpredictable Engleburt Ink *of* Inglewood said he wanted to be the mayor of Flattsburg.

| No pause: | Jim Kelly *of* the FBI made the arrest. |

COMMA

| Not linked: | I think you can safely say that Engleburt Ink, *of the notorious Ink family*, was the most ruthless of them all. |

| Pause: | Actually it was Jim Kelly, *of the FBI*, who arrested him. |

59.7 Name is linked to an organized group. The information containing the name of the group is almost always part of an introductory, interrupting, or add-on phrase and needs to be set apart by a comma (,). Such a group could be almost anything: an employer, an association, a loose confederation of those who believe in the same thing, etc.

A member of the FBI, Jim Kelly retired with a full pension.
Jim Kelly, *FBI officer*, retired with a full pension.
Retiring with a full pension was Jim Kelly, *an FBI officer.*

59.8 Name is linked to a geographical location. Set the two apart, using the comma (,).

| STATE: | Standing there was Daniel Boone, *of Kentucky*, with a beanie under his coonskin hat. |

| CITY & STATE: | Jasper Jenkins, *of Denver, Colorado*, said he used the soap for thirty days and suffered no after-effect. |

| NATION: | José Rodrigo, of Mexico, was awarded the top prize. |

| Exception: | **Name and geographical area are traditionally seen together.** No punctuation is needed between them. |

He had loved the notorious *Alice of Atlanta* for as long as he could remember.

Now, let's hear it for the Doo Wah Diddy Boys *of Dallas.*

59.9 One name linked to another. When two names are separated by a word which indicates their relationship to one another, the second name is set apart by at least one comma (,). Strict grammarians may well insist that one-of-a-kind relationships do not need to be separated, but the fact remains that (1) a definite pause can always be detected before the second name, and (2) confusion might easily result if you do not set the names apart. In the three examples below, the words "brother" and "next-door neighbor" are the separating words.

281

TWO COMMAS:	Jack's *brother*, Timothy, won the Hugo Award.
	Arnold's *next-door neighbor*, Mrs. Willoughby, called the police.
ONE COMMA:	The person who called was Arnold's *next-door neighbor*, Mrs. Willoughby.

59.10 Person's name is immediately followed by a question. Place a colon (:) between the name and the question, and capitalize the first word of the question.

Hank Hefford: *Isn't he one who bowled a 300-game last week?*

Exception: **Person is being directly addressed.** Use a comma (,) instead, and do not capitalize the first word.

Hank, *did you go bowling with Harry last week?*

59.11 Milestone information. When preparing milestone-type information about someone for a magazine, first determine the nature of the information which is causing the piece to be written. Is it his or her resignation? promotion? marriage? What exactly is the *key word?* The key word will begin the information and will stand alone.

Suppose, for example, a relatively well-known person was resigning from his or her job; therefore, the key word in this case would be *resigning.* Capitalize all the letters of that word and insert a period (.) after it. Follow it with the person's name, age, and brief identification, using commas (,) to separate each of them. Use semicolons (;) to set the other entries apart from one another.

RESIGNING. Melvin Smedly, 35, director of the Baylor Gallery who was charged with larceny; in Chicago.

APPOINTED. Willa Barney, 21, wife of the 1988 Democratic candidate for mayor of Hadleyville; to the Disease Control Committee; by Governor Fish; in Denver, Colorado.

59.12 Death notice. While the format may change slightly from newspaper to newspaper, the sequence and punctuation of the information included is remarkably similar. Below is the sequence of questions, and underneath each is an italicized response; note the placement of the commas (,). Next is an example of how it looks when the answers to the questions are put together.

1
Last name
WATT

2
First name and middle initial?
"nee")
Beaulah T.

3
maiden name, if female (precede with
(nee Thomas),

4
Wife or husband of who?
wife of Dr. Henry J. Watt,

5
Mother or father of who?
beloved mother of Andrew Watt,

6
Sister or brother of who?
sister of Barney J. Thomas,
nieces,

7
Survived by who?
survived by several grandchildren,
and nephews,

8
Date of death?
Thursday, April 9, 1990.

9
Age? (capitalized)
Age 85 years.

10
City where he or she lived?
Residence: Indianapolis.

Thursday,

11
Directions for mourners?
Friends may call at the Anderson
Funeral Home, 619 Bridge Rd.,

April 11 at 10 A.M.

12
Memorials?
Memorials may be sent to the American Heart Association.

WATT

Beaulah T. (nee Thomas), wife of Dr. Henry J. Watt, beloved mother of Alexander Watt, sister of Barney J. Thomas, survived by several grandchildren, nieces, and nephews, Thursday, April 9, 1990. Age 85 years. Residence: Indianapolis. Friends may call at the Anderson Funeral Home, 619 Bridge Rd., Thursday, April 11 at 10 A.M. Memorials may be sent to the American Heart Association.

59.13 **"Junior" follows the person's name.** Use the abbreviation *Jr.* and insert a comma (,) before it.

His name is Felix Fiddlehaufer, Jr.\

Company's Name

60.1 **Company trade name.** It may, or may not, be placed entirely in capital letters. But if totally capitalized, there is a danger of undue emphasis being attached to it. The trade name below has only been italicized for quicker identification.

Apple's *MACINTOSH* computer has been major turning point in the industry.

Apple's *Macintosh* computer has been a major turning point in the industry.

60.2 **Company name is followed by "Inc."** The comma (,) should be inserted before such abbreviations as *Inc.* or *Incorporated* when they follow the name of a business firm, but it may be omitted if the name has been officially registered without the comma. However, add-on words or abbreviations preceded by "and"—such as *and Co.* or *and Company*—are not preceded by a comma.

The new firm was registered as Wimple, Wimple, and Wimple, *Inc.*

The offices were decorated by Smith *and Co.*

Punctuation Marks

61.1 **Accent (´).** This punctuation mark is only used with words which have a French origin, and it is always placed over the letter E.

I paid over two hundred dollars for this *résumé*.

61.2 **Apostrophe (').** Below are the most common ways this punctuation mark is used. When your typewriter or computer cannot produce a true apostrophe, then the cipher (') will have to serve as a substitute.

As a substitute for one or more missing letters:	*'Fore* you do that, come see me first.
As an indicator that words are joined:	It *wasn't* what I really wanted.
To set off a quote-within-a-quote	The Governor said, "My father always told me, *'Don't put up your dukes unless you aim to fight,'* and that applies here as well."

61.3 **Brackets [ ].** Below are the most common ways this punctuation mark is used.

Encases directions
in a script: [Angrily] Why did you do that, Buford!

Interruption within
a parentheses: The Queen wrote to Commander Jack Jumpen (remember, he was the revolutionary who led the August Rebellion [1798] in an effort to end the monarchy system), and asked him for his help.

Highlights an
error in a quote: "I will give you [advise], not arms and supplies."

Shows the error
corrected in a quote: "I will give you [advice], not arms and supplies."

Encases information
that interrupts a
quote: "I will give you advice, not arms and supplies [as it turned out, he didn't even do that], for he is my friend as well."

61.4 **Cipher (').** This punctuation mark is inserted after a number and acts as a substitute for the word *foot* or *feet*. Ending punctuation *follows* it rather than precedes it. When your typewriter or computer is unable to produce a single apostrophe ('), which is curved, it may substitute for that punctuation mark also.

It measured 12' x 6'.

61.5 **The colon (:).** It should never immediately follow a verb like *is*, *are*, *was*, *were*, *have*, *has*, and *be*. Below are the most common ways this punctuation mark is used.

Second sentence
elaborates on first one: His dilemma was obvious: he would be damned if he did and damned if he didn't.

Before a list: Those who attended were the following:

                      1. President Argo Jump
                      2. Vice President Whip Lash

These organizations were counted among them: the Blue Blazers; the Royal Shafters, from Whitlow County; and the Movers and Shakers.

Before a formal quote:	Said the King: "Where is the Queen?"
Between numbers:	At 6:15 p.m. there was a 10:1 ratio.

61.6 **The comma (,).** This is the real workhorse of all the punctuation marks, and it is abused and underused. Below are the most common ways it is employed.

Indicates the inclusion of unimportant words:	*Really*, you should be more careful.
Indicates the inclusion of unimportant phrases:	You should be more careful with your money, *knowing how you lost it the last time.*
Between sentences and before a conjunction:	She didn't say anything about the car, *and* I didn't think it was my duty to tell her.
Represents a missing word:	He was angrier, more violent than I ever remember seeing him.
Separates words or phrases a series:	Bring me some *chicken*, *mashed potatoes*, *lemonade*, and *cookies*.

61.7 **The dash (—).** This punctuation mark is quite dramatic. Like the colon, it represents a strong pause—actually substituting for the other in some instances—but it is highly adaptable and can be used in places where the colon cannot. The danger is in putting it to work too much, for overuse definitely weakens its effectiveness. Below are the most common ways it is employed.

Represents a strong pause:	Wait a minute—who's side are you on, anyway?
	He had two reasons—a fear of poverty and a lust for riches.

| Represents quick pauses in dialogue: | But—well, he said—or was that—gee, I don't know. |

| Group of words interrupt a sentence: | Then he said—listen to this—that I was late Friday morning. |

| Emphasizes an introduction: | Really—he said it in all earnest. |

| Emphasizes an add-on | Go ahead, fill it up—for all the good it'll do. |

61.8 **Ditto mark (").** Only use it as a quotation marks (which are curved) when the opportunity to produce the latter is not available on your typewriter or computer, for the purpose of a ditto mark is to act as either a symbol for the word *inches* or to prevent the same information from being repeated in successive, separate lines within a list. Periods (.), question marks (?), and exclamation marks (!) always *follow* a ditto mark at the end of the end of a sentence—unless it is acting as a quotation mark.

INCHES: The card measures 8" x 9".

LIST: In the beginning, God created Earth.
             "   "   "   "   "   Man.

61.9 **Ellipsis (...).** Consists of three periods and is used to show that information has been purposely omitted from a quote, in order to present the main thought in as few words as possible. But four periods (....) are used after the last word when you wish to indicate that the quote is not finished. The ellipsis can also be effectively used by dramatists to indicate undramatic pauses in dialogue.

QUOTE: Today Abraham Lincoln said, "Four score and seven years ago, our forefathers brought forth...a new nation...dedicated to the proposition that all men are created equal...."

DIALOGUE: But....oh, I dunno....maybe it's just me.

61.10 **The exclamation mark (!).** Sometimes it is called the exclamation *point*. Mark or point, it adds more force than a period (.) and is placed after a stand-alone word or full statement that needs more emphasis. Using it can indicate surprise, disbelief, sudden happiness, anger, relief, excitability, or one of many other displays of emotion. It may even follow a question mark (?), although never a period (.) or a dash (—). Adding an exclamation mark to a quote in order to express irony or sar-

casm is quite acceptable, but it must follow the last quotation mark (")
and a period (.) cannot precede it.

AFTER....
a word:	Wow!
a question mark:	Did you see that?!
a phrase:	As if you didn't know!
a sentence:	Never again will I trust you!
quotation mark:	The minister said, "Our church believes the Golden Rule has become outdated"!

61.11 The hyphen (-). The trend in the late twentieth century has been to employ this punctuation mark as little as possible. Nevertheless, there are still many situations where it is extremely important. Specifically:

One-letter prefix: I hit an *E-flat* on my clarinet just as she hit the *S-curve* in the road.

> NOTE: When the prefix is a single alphabetic letter, capitalize it but not the word which follows it. But if the prefix is more than one letter, don't capitalize it unless it begins a sentence.

Prefix: The *pro-defense* lobbyists were lined up on the left; on the right were the *anti-defense* lobbyists.

Dividing a word at its syllable   She respected him for not having had an *extra-marital* affair in his life.

> But it is advisable that you check your dictionary for a word's syllable breaks rather than guess where you think it is. *SEE* THE EXCEPTION TO THIS RULE.

Successive hyphen-ated words, sharing the same words:

two: It's a *five-* or *six-story* building.

three: All *one-*, *two-*, and *three-act* plays will be read by Miss Hensley.

DO NOT insert a hyphen...   ...after one alphabetic letter at the end of a line.

...before a two-letter syllable at the beginning of a line.

...between an abbreviation
    a proper noun
    a number
    two words between quotation marks

...between two normally hyphenated words when they *follow* either a noun (**Bill White** was *well educated* and rich) or pronoun (**You** will find him to be *well educated* and rich).

...between a two word adjective that precedes a noun, when the first word ends in "ly" (That *frequently used* ploy won't work this time.)

Exception: **Normally hyphenated prefix falls at the end of a typewritten line.** Take a look at the first sentence below, which shows the prefix *pro* at the end of one line and its follow-up word at the beginning of the next. Could not the reader easily assume that *pro* and *democratic*— were they not on separate lines—would otherwise be joined as one word? Computer programs which automatically hyphenate do not often recognize this subtlety and will make the division after the hyphen. Try to restructure the sentence so the prefix and the word which follows it will be on the same line.

In such a dictatorship, it is extremely hard to be *pro-democratic* without getting into trouble.

In such a dictatorship, it's hard to be *pro-democratic* without getting into trouble.

61.12 The parentheses ( ). It encases what might otherwise be called "throwaway information"—that which usually interrupts and would not be missed at all if removed. It is used to set apart the insertion of a personal comment, explanation, identification, instruction, or question. Question marks (?) and exclamation marks (!) before the last parenthesis is acceptable, but in these two instances the first word of the parenthetical information must be capitalized. Periods (.) may only be inserted after the last word of the parenthetical information when it is placed between two complete sentences or after a period at the end of a paragraph. In those situations, too, its first word is capitalized.

COMMENT: General Pflugenpuss (I can't say that name in public without laughing) was the commander of all the forces in Hussenfessen.

289

EXPLANATION:	All of the bearded folk (ministers) were against it.
INSTRUCTION:	The rafenblagen (refer to page 21 for discussion of this creature) have been dying off in this century.
QUESTION:	I wanted to see that movie very much (Didn't everyone?), and I had saved my nickels and dimes to make sure that I could.
BETWEEN SENTENCES:	There was no more money in the till. (Well, after all, what did they expect: they had been borrowing against it for years.) Yet they screamed bloody murder when the bank decided to foreclose.

61.13 The period (.) Except when used at the end of an abbreviation, this punctuation mark tells the reader to come to a full stop before continuing. It can follow a single word, a phrase, or a sentence.

WORD:	*Yes.* But just how did you know that?
PHRASE:	*Of course.* And then she'll want something else.
SENTENCE:	These are the times that try men' souls.
ABBREVIATION:	Las Vegas: 40 *mi.*

61.14 The question mark (?). It may follow a word, a phrase, or a sentence. Whatever the case, its insertion tells the reader that a reply is being demanded, even when the answer may already be known. It never follows a request, which often appears to be a question.

WORD:	Who?
PHRASE:	With that in mind?
SENTENCE:	Are you still going to deny that it rained?
REQUEST:	May I have your autograph.

61.15 Double quotation marks (" "). These are not to be confused with ditto marks ("), which are not curved. Yet, ditto marks will have to be used if your typewriter or word processor is incapable of making the distinction. Below are the most common ways this punctuation is put to use.

BEFORE & AFTER	
A quote:	Said President Ambura today: "The cost of our defense program is going to bankrupt this country."
Dialogue:	"I love you," said Wanda, smiling at him.
HIGHLIGHTING	
Word:	That "vacation" almost killed me.

Phrase: Whenever he looks up from his speech and says "in short," you can be sure he will talk for another hour.

61.16 Single quotation marks (' '). They are used to separate a quote which is inside another quote. (Observe the italics in the example below). It should not be confused with the cipher ('), which is not curved; however, the cipher may be employed when your typewriter or word processor does not have a key for a single apostrophe.

"When Shakespeare penned *'Now is the winter of our discontent,'* I think he felt the heartbeat of all societies that were to follow the Elizabethan era," said Professor Snodgrass.

61.17 The semicolon (;). The pause it represents is stronger than that which the comma is able provide, but one which is not as powerful as the conclusive stop which the period (.) carries. It marries words, phrases, or sentences in a series, usually without benefit of a conjunction. In the first sentence below, the semicolon takes the place of the conjunction *because.* In the second example, it separates complete thoughts which relate to a sentence that precedes a colon (:).

He wouldn't do business with Smith; the injury that had been done to his family long ago still nagged him.

He had reasons for not doing business with Smith: the man was nearly bankrupt; there was a rumor that the bottom was going to drop out of the saucer market; the insult he had suffered long ago still nagged him.

61.18 The virgule (/). This is not a commonly used punctuation mark; in fact, many grammarians frown upon it when it is used for anything much more than separating numbers in a date (e.g., 4/16/81). When placed between words, it presents two alternatives. In the example below, the writer means that a budget will be presented and consequences will be suffered; also, that consequences will be suffered if a budget is not presented.

Either way, we will present a budget *and/or* suffer the consequences.

The Prefix

The punctuation mark used after a prefix is the hyphen (-), but referring to an up-to-date, comprehensive dictionary or contacting your librarian should indeed be considered when you are unsure about when to use the hyphen. Provided below are punctuation guidelines with regard to the most frequently used prefixes, which are listed in alphabetical order.

Keep in mind, however, that numerous exceptions to the rules may well exist.

62.1   **Afro.** This prefix is always capitalized and followed by a hyphen.

62.2   **Anglo.** This prefix is always capitalized and followed by a hyphen (-).

62.3   **ante.** No hyphen is needed after it unless the next word is either capitalized or begins with a vowel (A, E, I, O, U). Exceptions include *ante bellum* and *ante-war*.

62.4   **anti.** No hyphen is needed after it unless the next word is either capitalized or begins with a vowel (A, E, I, O, U); but a hyphen (-) is needed when this prefix helps to form these concepts: *anti-defense, anti-knock, anti-rent, anti-slavery, anti-tank,* and *anti-war*.

62.5   **arch.** No hyphen is needed after it unless the first letter of the next word is capitalized or begins with the letter H.

62.6   **be.** No hyphen is needed after it unless the next word is either capitalized or begins with a vowel (A, E, I, O, U).

62.7   **bi.** No hyphen is needed after it unless the next letter is "i" or "h," or the word following it is capitalized.

62.8   **bio.** No hyphen is needed after it unless the next word is either capitalized or begins with a vowel (A, E, I, O, U).

62.9   **co.** Inserting a hyphen after the prefix *co* is optional, except when a capital letter follows; in that case, a hyphen (-) is demanded. If the letter O immediately follows and you are not using the hyphen, a dieresis (ö) should be inserted above the second O. However, if you do not have the proper equipment to provide a dieresis, combining the prefix and the word without any punctuation mark is acceptable.

HYPHEN:	I don't want to be your *co-worker*.
NO HYPHEN:	All right, I'll be your *coworker*.
DIERESIS:	Who's going to *coördinate* this?
NO DIERESIS:	Never *coordinate* anything for me again.

62.10   **de.** No hyphen is needed after it unless the next word is either capitalized or begins with a vowel (A, E, I, O, U).

62.11   **ex.** When this prefix combines with a word to indicate the former status of someone or something, insert a hyphen (-) after it.

62.12   **fore.** Except for *fore-and-aft* (a nautical term), this word is always joined to another without a hyphen.

62.13 hyper. No hyphen is needed after it unless the next letter is capitalized.

62.14 hypo. No hyphen is needed after it unless the next letter is capitalized.

62.15 Indo. This prefix is always capitalized and followed by a hyphen (-). However, the words *Indochina* and *Indochinese* are written as one word.

62.16 infra. No hyphen is needed after it unless the next word is either capitalized or begins with a vowel (A, E, I, O, U).

62.17 inter. No hyphen is needed after it unless the next letter is capitalized.

62.18 intra. No hyphen is needed after it unless the next word is either capitalized or begins with a vowel (A, E, I, O, U).

62.19 mal. No hyphen is necessary after this prefix.

62.20 meta. No hyphen is needed after this prefix unless the next word begins with the letter A.

62.21 micro. No hyphen is needed after it unless the next word is capitalized or begins with the letter O.

62.22 mini. No hyphen is needed after it unless the next word is either capitalized or begins with a vowel (A, E, I, O, U).

62.23 mis. No hyphen is needed after it unless the next letter begins with either the letters H or S.

62.24 neo. No hyphen is needed after it unless the next word is either capitalized or begins with a vowel (A, E, I, O, U); however, *neo-classic* and *neo-classicism* are always hyphenated.

62.25 non. No hyphen is needed after it unless the next letter is capitalized. But if the word following it begins with the letter N, a hyphen (-) is warranted (e.g., *non-negotiable*).

62.26 Pan. This prefix is always capitalized and followed by a hyphen (-).

62.27 para. No hyphen is needed after this prefix.

62.28 pre. No hyphen is needed after it unless the next word is capitalized or begins with the letter E. However, *pre-cast, pre-cool, pre-heated, pre-military, and pre-shrunk* are always hyphenated.

62.29 pro. This prefix is followed by a hyphen (-) when favoritism toward someone or something is being expressed (e.g., One candidate was *pro-taxes,* which cost him the election).

62.30 **quasi.** This prefix is always followed by a hyphen (-) and should precede a noun.

62.31 **re.** This prefix requires a following hyphen (-) in the instances shown below and to the left.

FOLLOWED BY...
Capital letter:	He had to be *re-Americanized.*
Letter E:	He was *re-educated* in their social customs.
Letters RE:	We must *re-regain* the ground we've lost.

CONFUSING	I plan to *recover* that couch.
Better:	I plan to *re-cover* that couch.

62.32 **semi.** No hyphen is needed after it unless the next word is either capitalized or begins with a vowel (A, E, I, O, U).

62.33 **serio.** No hyphen is needed after it unless the next word is either capitalized or begins with a vowel (A, E, I, O, U).

62.34 **sub.** No hyphen is needed after it unless the next letter is capitalized.

62.35 **trans.** No hyphen is needed after it unless the next letter is capitalized.

62.36 **tri.** This prefix is always joined to the word which follows it. But if the first letter of the next word is "i," insert a hyphen (-) between them. A hyphen should also be used when it helps to form the name of something.

JOINED:	It has a *triangular* shape.
"I" FOLLOWS:	His *tri-ideology* was stupid.
NAME:	How big is *Tri-Star* Pictures?

62.37 **ultra.** This prefix does not require a hyphen (-) after it unless the next word is either capitalized or begins with a vowel (A, E, I, O, U).

62.38 **un.** No hyphen is needed after it unless the next letter is capitalized.

62.39 **Vice.** This prefix is capitalized, and it may or may not be followed by a hyphen. However, when writing about the Vice President of the United States, a hyphen is never used.

But the *Vice-President* of Tuttle Motors said they planned no reorganization.
What was *Vice President* Alben Barkley's home state?

Hyphemes & Solidemes

Hyphemes and solidemes are often confused with prefixes, because some of them require a following hyphen (-) in certain situations. Among the most frequently used are those which are listed here in alphabetical order. If in doubt, check a comprehensive dictionary or call your local librarian.

63.1 **aero.** No hyphen is needed after it.

63.2 **agro.** No hyphen is needed after it.

63.3 **air.** A hyphen should follow it when it helps to form a description Exceptions: *airlike, airward, airwise, airproof, airtight.*

63.4 **auto.** Does not require a hyphen when it is joined to another word and creates a totally new one (e.g., *autoanalysis*).

63.5 **by.** The hyphen (-) accompanies *by-and-by, by-line, by-pass, by-path, by-play,* and *by-product.* Other concepts are joined as one word.

63.6 **counter.** As the first word of a two-word description, no hyphen need follow it unless the next word begins with the letter "i" (e.g., I have always enjoyed *counter-intelligence* work). Rather, it is joined to the other word. But when it is followed by *jumper, offensive, reconnaissance,* or *revolution* it is a noun which needs a hyphen.

63.7 **double.** As the first word of a two-word description, a hyphen (-) should be used after it. A hyphen is also needed when it precedes one of these words and forms a noun: *bass, bassoon, cross, dealer, decker, duty, entendre, header, quick, take,* and *time.* The verbs *double-cross* and *double-date* are hyphenated, too.

63.8 **ever.** It requires a hyphen (-) after it when it joins another word to form an adjective (e.g., The *ever-increasing* sound began to grate on my nerves). However, *everbearing* and *everliving* are not hyphenated.

63.9 **glass.** A hyphen (-) should follow it when it joins another word; but should the word be *bead, furnace, house, making, wall, ware, window,* or *work,* it is separated without a connecting hyphen.

63.10 **heart.** A hyphen (-) is essential after it when it joins another word to describe a noun. Exceptions include *heartheavy, heartsick, heartsickening,* and *heartbroken.*

63.11 **home.** A hyphen should follow it when it helps to form a description (e.g., He married a *home-loving* wife). But the adjective *homeward* is not separated. When followed by the word *builder, defense, folks, lover, owner,* or *brew,* it helps to form a noun and requires a hyphen after it.

63.12 **ill.** It should be followed by a hyphen when it joins another word to describe a noun (e.g., It was a *well-conceived* plan). *Ill-nature,* a noun, is also hyphenated.

63.13 **long.** It should be followed by a hyphen when it joins another word to describe a noun(e.g., It had been a *long-awaited* event).

63.14 **macro.** No hyphen is needed after it unless the next word is capitalized or begins with the letter O. (e.g., *macro-organisms*).

63.15 **man.** Except for *mankilling,* all two-word descriptions which this word forms should be hyphenated. These nouns require hyphens as well: *man-about-town, man-at-arms, man-child, man-eater,* and *man-of-war.*

63.16 **mega.** It is never separated by a hyphen when it joins another word to form a noun (e.g., *megabucks*).

63.17 **mid.** Some say it should never be followed by a hyphen; others say it should. All agree, however, that a hyphen is necessary when the next word is capitalized or begins with the letter "d." Otherwise, choose whatever school of thought you wish, keeping in mind that today's trend is to eliminate the hyphen whenever possible.

At *midlunch,* I received a call from him in the lobby.
Boris accused Hansel of sleeping during *mid-debate.*
Did you say the *mid-Roman* era was exciting?

Exception: These words are never hyphenated: *midafternon, midautumn, midevening, midmonth, midmorning, midseason, midsentence, midspace, midstory, midweek, midwinter,* and *midyear.*

63.18 **milli.** No hyphen need follow it when it joins a word to form a noun (e.g., *millisecond*).

63.19 **multi:** It is only followed by a hyphen when the first letter of the next word is "i" (e.g., *multi-infections*) although there may be instances when a hyphen must be inserted before other vowels as well.

63.20 **over.** No hyphen is needed after it unless the next word is capitalized. Exceptions include the descriptive combinations *over-all, over-the-counter,* and *over-used.*

63.21 **proof.** It is joined to another word without a hyphen when it helps to form a new word. But if it creates an adjective which indicates a measurement, the words are separated (e.g., You can hardly find *hundred proof* whiskey nowadays); however, the nonadjectives *proof read* and *proof positive* are written separately.

63.22 **psuedo.** It is joined to the other word when it helps to form a technical word; otherwise it is set apart.

TECHNICAL: *Psuedomigraine* headaches will be tonight's topic.

NONTECHNICAL: The *psuedo sportsman* probably plays chess.

63.23 **self.** Except for *selfless* and *selfsame,* this word is always followed by a hyphen (e.g., *self-pity*).

63.24 **step.** This word is joined to the words *son, mother, father, brother, sister,* or any other noun that represents a family member. *Step-down, step-up, step-in,* and *step-parent* demand hyphens (-).

63.25 **under.** It is joined to another word without a separating hyphen when it creates a new concept. However, if the next word is capitalized, a hyphen is essential. Other exceptions include job types, such as *under-clerk* and *under-treasurer,* and the adjectives *under-age* and *under-arm.*

NO HYPHEN: Wilma is an *underachiever.*
CAPITAL LETTER: The *under-Socialists* went underground.

Other Words

When two words combine to help describe a noun or pronoun, a hyphen (-) is usually required to separate them. This is especially true when the other word ends in *ed, en, d,* or *ing,* or when the first word is a number which is spelled out. But if the first word ends in *ly,* do not place a hyphen between them. Some of these words can join other words to form nouns and verbs as well.

64.1 **all.** As the first word of a two-word description, a hyphen (-) should follow it (e.g., This *all-encompassing* program doesn't do enough).

64.2 **best.** It should be followed by a hyphen when the word after it precedes a noun (e.g., It was the best-acted *play* I have ever seen).

64.3 **better.** It should be followed by a hyphen when the word after it precedes a noun (e.g., It was a better-made *house* than the other).

64.4 **black.** The hyphen (-) is used with *black-and-blue, black-and-tan,* and *black-hearted.*

64.5   **blood.** The hyphen (-) is used with *blood-and-thunder*, *blood-curdling*, and *blood-red*.

64.6   **blue.** The hyphen (-) is inserted after it when either the word *eyed* or *penciled* immediately follows it (e.g., They *blue-penciled* all of the curse words in the manuscript).

64.7   **book.** The hyphen (-) is used when either the words *end* or *learning*. immediately follows it (e.g., He's a *book-end* without books.)

64.8   **clear.** The hyphen (-) should be used when the words *cut*, *eyed*, *headed*, and *sighted* follow this word (e.g., It left him *clear-headed* and shocked).

64.9   **close.** A hyphen is needed after it when the next word is *bodied*, *fitting*, *mouthed*, *order drill*, or *up*. However, if it acts as a verb and joins *up*, they are written separately (e.g., I want you fellows to *close up* your ranks).

64.10   **cross.** Insert a hyphen after this word when it is followed by one of the following: *bedded*, *country*, *examine*, *fertilize*, *figure*, *hair*, *hatch*, *head*, *index*, *over*, *peen*, *pollinate*, *purpose*, *question*, *reference*, *section*, *stitch*, *talk*, *thread*, *tie*, *town*, *wind*, *wire*, or *word puzzle*.

64.11   **cut.** The three-word adjective *cut-and-dried* needs to be hyphenated. A hyphen must also be inserted when it is followed by one of these words: *in*, *off*, *out*, *over*, *price*, *rate*, *throat*, or *up*.

64.12   **degree.** As the second word of a two-word description, it only needs a hyphen (-) before it when it is preceded by spelled-out numbers like *first*, *second*, and *third* (e.g., She suffered *first-degree* burns on her arms and legs).

64.13   **extra.** As a prefix in a two-word description, it is joined to the second word without a hyphen—except when a capital letter or vowel (*a, e, i, o*, or *u*) follows it. Exceptions include *extra-bold*, *extra-condensed*, *extra-curricular*, and *extra-professional*. The adjective *extraordinary* is not hyphenated, even though the letters A and O are side by side.

64.14   **fellow.** With the exception of *fellowship*, this word is separated from another when it helps to form a new concept (e.g., You should treat your *fellow workers* like members of your family).

64.15   **fire.** The word *fire-eater* is hyphenated; otherwise this word is separated from, or combined with, other words.

64.16   **first.** The two-word combinations *first-born*, *first-fruit*, and *first-rate* are hyphenated.

64.17 fold. As a suffix, it is only preceded by a hyphen (-) when a numerically written number precedes it; but when the number is spelled out, it is joined to the other word without a hyphen (*see* second example below).

NUMERICAL: There was a *5-fold* increase in the population.
SPELLED OUT: There was a *fivefold* increase in the population.

64.18 folk. Except for *folklore*, this word is written separately and is not followed by a hyphen.

64.19 foot. As the first word of a two-word description, it is followed by a hyphen (e.g., *foot-stomping* crowd); but it is joined to the other word without a hyphen when it helps to form a noun. Exceptions include *foot brake, foot ladder,* and *foot soldier.*

64.20 foster. This word does not need a hyphen after it when it precedes the words *mother, father,* or *child.*

64.21 fourth(s). Should it be the second half of a spelled-out fraction, a hyphen must precede it (e.g., It was *three-fourths* full or *one-fourth* empty).

64.22 free. Insert a hyphen (-) after it when it is followed by one of these words: *born, handed, hearted, living, spoken, trader,* or *lance. Free-for-all* is also hyphenated.

64.23 good. A hyphen should follow when it precedes one of these words: *fellowship, looking, tempered,* and *will. Good-for-nothing* is also hyphened.

64.24 half. Insert a hyphen (-) after it when it is the first word of a two-word adjective or noun. Nouns which are not hyphenated include *halfback, half blood, half gainer, half note, half pint, half relief, half tide, half time,* and *halftone.*

ADJECTIVE: Where exactly is the *half-way* mark?
NOUN: A *half-dozen* ran a *half-mile.*

64.25 hand. When *knitted* or *made* follows this word, a hyphen should be inserted after it. *Hand-to-hand, hand-to-mouth., hand-in-glove, hand-in-hand, hand-out* and *hand-pick* are also hyphenated.

64.26 hard. A hyphen should be inserted after it when it is followed by one of these words: *bitten, boiled, earned, featured, fought, looking, mouthed,* or *spun.*

64.27 high. As the first of two words which combine to form a description, it is followed by a hyphen (e.g., It was a *high-profile* job in a low-pro-

299

file company). Nouns which receive a separating hyphen include the following: *high-binder, high-flier,* and *high-hat.*

64.28 jet. *Jet-propelled* requires a hyphen; other combinations are written separately.

64.29 like. A hyphen (-) is necessary after it when it acts as the *first* word of two joined words. But when it performs as the *second* word of a two-word description, it only requires a preceding hyphen in these instances: (1) three Ls appear in a row; (2) first word is capitalized; (3) it follows two other words which are separated by a hyphen.

FIRST WORD: They were *like-minded* in almost every way.

THREE Ls: It had a *bill-like* mouth.

> In some cases, two Ls in a row may demand a hyphen as well, to prevent confusion. For instance:

It moved *eel-like* through the water.

CAPITAL LETTER: There was a *Faulkner-like* flavor to his writing.

TWO HYPHENS: It had a *half- dollar-like* feel to it.

64.30 little. It should be followed by a hyphen when the word after it precedes a noun (e.g. It was that little-known *fact* about him which would prove to be his undoing).

64.31 low. As the first word of a two-word description, a hyphen (-) should follow it (e.g., The *low-sounding* music drifted across the field).

64.32 odd. No hyphen is needed before this word unless it follows a number which is spelled out or written numerically (e.g., Some *twenty-odd* years ago I felt the same way). *Odds and ends* requires no hyphen.

64.33 post. When this word precedes another, no hyphen is needed unless a capitalized word follows it. But the adjective *post-paid* is hyphenated, as is the case when it forms a noun and the second word is *horse, house, mortem, note, office, position,* or *terminal.*

64.34 super. When it precedes another word to help form a two-word adjective, the words are joined without a hyphen. But if a capitalized word follows it, a hyphen is needed (e.g., Reaganomics was *super-Coolidgenomics*).

64.35 third(s). Precede it with a hyphen when it follows another word to form a fraction (e.g., He was *two-thirds* finished, when he had to start over).

64.36 well. It should be followed by a hyphen when the word after it precedes a noun (e.g., It was a well-conceived *plan* that pulled that off).

64.37 wide. If it combines with another word to form a two word adjective, insert a hyphen (e.g. It is going to have *wide-ranging* effect). Otherwise combine the two words as one unless, unless the word is followed by *a, e, i, o,* or *u,* or the two words have political or geographical implications (e.g., *wide area*).

64.38 wise. There is no need to precede it with a hyphen when this word acts as a suffix, (e.g., Tax*wise*, I'm not in very good shape).

Referring the Reader

When instructing the reader within a paragraph to refer to a specific part of a magazine article, book, or poem, the punctuation rules vary in relation to what kind of material—as well as what part—is being cited. Such references are not to be confused with bibliographies or footnotes.

65.1 Preceding the reference with the word "see." This word should be italicized, even when it is capitalized.

UNCAPITALIZED: As an example, *see* Figure 1 on page 23.
CAPITALIZED: *See* the photo on page 14.

Exception: **Word which follows is italicized.** Do not italicize "see."

For an example of this, see *The Healthy Breakfast* in Chapter Six.

65.2 Referring to a poem. If referring the reader to consecutive verses in a poem, separate the verse numbers with a colon (:). But if the verses are separate rather than consecutive, insert a hyphen (-) between them.

CONSECUTIVE
VERSES: In verses 11:15 of Ted Christwell's epic poem, *The Withered Chair,* the imagery is rather powerful.

DIFFERENT
VERSES: Read verses 11-21 in *The Withered Chair.*

65.3   **Referring the reader to a book.** Here are just a few punctuation samples, keeping in mind that the possibilities are nearly as vast as the rules discussed earlier in this reference book regarding single words, phrases, and the joining of sentences.

CHAPTER:	Read Chapter One of *History II*. Read *For the Life of Me*, Chapter Ten.
SECTION or PART:	
First:	The answer can be found in Part 5, Chapter 10, of *The Last American Cowboy*.
Last:	Read *Ground Zero*, Chapter Ten, Section 5.
Follows title:	In *World War II*, Section 5, Chapter 10, some reference is made to that.
Section titled:	Read the section titled "The Coolidge Era" in *The Uproarious Twenties*.
VOLUME:	
First:	In Volume 10, Chapter 2 of that series, you will learn there is very little evidence to support what you are saying.
Last:	It's all there in black and white: page 52, Section 3, Chapter 1, Volume 18.
PAGES:	
One page	In Chapter 7, page 389, of the book, reference is made to the fact he never sought that office.
Consecutive:	Please *see* Chapter 8, pages 401-403.
Unonsecutive:	In Criswell's book *False Images*, pages 29, 74, and 205-208, you will see what I'm talking about.
BIBLE	In Genesis, I ask you to turn to Chapter I, Verse One, to get a better idea of how it all started.
	And that's how it started (Gen.1:1).

65.4   **Referring the reader to a magazine article.** Whether citing one or more page numbers in a magazine, precede the information with the volume number of that particular magazine whenever possible. In the sentence examples below, the volume number is shown two ways: numerically and spelled out. If a number, follow it with a colon (:); if spelled out, follow it with a comma (,).

NUMERICAL:	You will find it in *The American Journal*, 5:137-139.
SPELLED OUT:	In Volume Five, pages 137 to 139 of *The American Journal*, you can read about what they actually did.

Headings and Captions

66.1   **Headings.** The words placed above one or more paragraphs of information—usually seen in larger, bolder print—are not followed by a period (.) or any other punctuation mark. The words should also be capitalized; however if a hyphen (-) appears between two of the words, do not capitalize the second one. For example:

The Dust-covered Army

66.2   **Captions.** Except for the key opening words, which may be seen in bolder type, the information which follows it and which can be placed under, above, or beside photos, illustrations, etc., is not followed by a period (.) or any other punctuation mark. For example, imagine that a photo was opposite the words below.

Take that! This crushing blow is the last thing Tiger Thompson remembered in the first round of last night's fight.

Military Commands

67.1   **Stands alone.** A military command frequently stands alone and represents a full sentence, even though not all of the parts of speech are in evidence; the other words are simply omitted and implied. For example, *about face* could be an abbreviated version of *I want you to do an about face*. And except for *as you were* and *at ease*—both of which end in a period (.)—a command is followed by an exclamation mark (!).

EXCLAMATION MARK:	Left face!
PERIOD:	At ease.

67.2   **Dramatic pause.** Some commands contain dramatic pauses, which are represented by a dash (—). This is particularly true when the command *march!* is added.

To the right flank—march!
Forward—march!

67.3 **Followed by a noun.** A noun may be attached to the commands *as you were, at ease,* and *attention.* When this occurs, separate the command from the noun, using a comma (,). Insert an exclamation mark (!) after the noun when the command is being used emphatically.

BEFORE A NOUN: *As you were,* Private.
     Emphatic   *Attention,* Corporal!

67.4 **Counting cadence.** The elements are strung together in a series and separated by commas (,) and the ellipsis (...), with the latter representing pauses in the drill instructor's command

Left, right, left...go to your left...your left...your left, right, left....to the rear—march!

67.5 **"March" is shortened.** Few if any drill instructors can be heard pronouncing the consonant M when they say *march.* For authenticity when writing dialogue, consider dropping the letter and replacing it with an apostrophe ('); but retain the letter if the word leads off the sentence.

To the left flank—*'arch!*
March, soldier!

67.6 **Lengthening a word.** To convey the actual sound of some parts of a military command when writing dialogue, lengthening the word by adding identical letters and hyphens (-) can be effective. In some cases the changing of spelling is also acceptable.

Forrrr-waaaard—'arch!
For-r-r-r-rwa-a-r-r-rd—march!
Atten—shun!

Capitalization

Capitalization is not a punctuation problem, but doubt about when to capitalize words after certain punctuation marks certainly arises; therefore, here is some general information which should prove to be helpful.

68.1 **Capitalization after a colon.** If the information which follows the colon (:) is a complete sentence and is "formal" in nature—that is, it can stand alone and does not need any preceding information to help introduce it (*see* the first example)—capitalization is necessary. However, if you do not have a full sentence, but you wish to emphasize it, capitalization of the first word is also encouraged (*see* the second example).

The outcome was predictable: *Two* politicians with no scruples, placed in a desperate situation to produce votes, will produce mudslingling of monumental proportions.

Verdict: *Guilty.*

68.2 **Capitalization inside a parentheses.** The first word within a parentheses is usually not capitalized, unless it begins a question or is a proper name that must be capitalized. But if the parenthetical statement demands an exclamation mark (!) at the end, capitalizing the first word is essential if the information is lengthy. Here are examples:

QUESTION: His associate, Michael Woodpuff (*Isn't* he the one who was indicted for fraud?), said the company would look into the matter at its earliest convenience.

PROPER NAME: Everyone was there (*Norman* Cashew, of course, wouldn't have anything to do with the proceedings) and I'm glad I went, but I didn't know it was to be formal.

EXCLAMATION MARK:
  Short: He (*the* lazy bum!) sat in the car while his wife changed the flat tire.

  Lengthy: Admiral Bowinkle (*That's* the fellow, by the way, who said submarines were just a fad!) was asked to resign by the Joint Chief of Staff.

QUOTE: Mayor Switch (*"Trust* me and I won't let you down"*) was indicted for fraud today.

68.3 **Capitalizing poetry in paragraph form.** Doubt about capitalizing poetry sometimes occurs when its lines are placed in paragraph form. Use the slant or virgule (/) to separate the lines from one another, and capitalize the words as you would if it were in its traditional vertical format.

68.4 **Capitalizing a person's title.** An official title is always capitalized when it immediately precedes someone's name. But if a person's name does not follow it, and the title neither pertains to a recognized leader of a nation nor anyone else who was was elected or appointed to government office, it is NOT capitalized.

<table>
<tr><td>PRECEDES
NAME:</td><td>It was *President* Sam Snerd of the Bow Weevil Company who wore polyester underwear.</td></tr>
<tr><td>NOT FOLLOWED
BY OFFICE NAME:</td><td>The *president* of Ford Motor Company said that all of the executive's expense accounts had been reduced.</td></tr>
<tr><td>ELECTED OFFICE:</td><td>But key members of Congress said that the *President* was being unreasonable in his demands.</td></tr>
<tr><td>Exception:</td><td>**Reverend.** Always capitalized, and so is the indefinite article *the* which must precede it. (This word, by the way, may only be abbreviated—i.e., *Rev.*—when addressing an envelope.)</td></tr>
<tr><td></td><td>Didn't *The Reverend* Jesse Jackson run for President in 1988?</td></tr>
</table>

68.5 **Capitalizing geographical areas and directions.** Geographical areas are always capitalized, but directions are not.

AREA: In the *Southwest,* we don't have much of that.
DIRECTION: Traveling *southwest,* you'll see this fork in the road.

68.6 **Capitalizing family relationships.** A word that shows family relationship is always capitalized, but not when it immediately follows a pronoun.

CAPITALIZED: No one, not even *Aunt* Wilma, knew the answer.
Good morning, *Mother.*

FOLLOWS
PRONOUN: She told *her* father that she'd be late.

68.7 **Changes in capitalization within legal documents.** Changes in capitalization, whether going from lowercase to capitalization or vice versa, are placed within brackets.

The [c]ity admits that it must discharge its duties accordingly.

....and shall hereafter be known as the [S]eller in this contract.

68.8 **Capitalizing single alphabetic letters.** Single alphabetic letters should not be capitalized when followed by an apostrophe S. Instead, italicize them if you have the proper equipment to do so.

I want to be sure to dot all of my *i's* and cross all of my *t's.*

68.9 Capitalizing signs and notices. When making reference to a sign or notice that appears inside a building or anywhere else, *all* of its letters should be capitalized when it is used in a sentence.

On the door was the sign EMPLOYEES ONLY.

Closing Phrase in a Letter

69.1 Business letter. The closing phrase just above the name at the bottom of a letter is followed by a comma (,). Two double spaces are usually inserted before the name is typed. Below the letter writer's name in a business letter, and separated by a comma, should appear his or her title and the name of the department. However, one-of-a-kind titles— such as *president* and other positions where there is little likelihood of confusion—need not be followed by a department name. The name of a country may also follow the title of someone who holds a prestigious government office.

Sincerely,   *Respectfully,*

Homer Hickock   Homer Hickock
Vice-President, Sales   Secretary of State, U.S.A.

69.2 Personal letter. The closing phrase just above the name at the bottom of a letter is followed by a comma (,). Two double spaces are usually inserted before the name is typed. There is no need to include the last name when there is friendship between the writer and recipient of the letter.

Trite Word Combinations

70.1 Explanation. In this category is a list of word combinations which are frequently used to shape sentences and phrases in business letters; however, many of them are stilted and all are trite. So before using one of them in your letter, consider replacing it with something that doesn't sound so stuffy and which does not add more words than is actually needed.

acknowledging receipt of	enclosed herewith
as per your inquiry	enclosed please find
at the present writing	I am in receipt of your inquiry of
in due course	I wish to acknowledge
in regard to	it is our belief
in reply to yours of	may we direct your attention to

in reviewing our files
in the event that
pursuant to
referring to your inquiry of
thanking you again
thanking you in advance
attached hereto
attached herewith

please advise
please be advised
this is in reply to
this is to inform you
this will acknowledge
we are [not] in a position to
we wish to take this opportunity

Wrong Combinations

71.1 **Explanation.** Below is list of often-used word combinations, some of which act alone as phrases and others of which simply serve as the opening words of phrases and clauses. Some are grammatically incorrect. Others contain redundant words. Catching redundant words in commonly used phrases, by the way, is more difficult than one might imagine; this is primarily because we have heard or read them so often that we automatically accept them—and use them—without ever thinking how absurd they are. Even dog-eared clauses such as *Enough is enough*, which carries a humorous tone of finality, is brutally redundant. After all, if *enough* is not enough, then what is it?

71.2 **aiding and abetting.** *Aiding* and *abetting* mean the same thing.

71.3 **as best as.** Rewrite it and eliminate *as*.

71.4 **both alike, both together, equally alike,** or **equally together.** Omit the word *both* or *equally* from these match-ups, or the word which follows them, to eliminate superfluousness.

71.5 **buoyed up.** It's hard to buoy *down*.

71.6 **by leaps and bounds.** If you *leap*, you *bound*. Choose one of them.

71.7 **climbing up.** One can't climb *down*, so get rid of *up*.

71.8 **consulting together.** If one could consult with oneself, *together* would not be redundant.

71.9 **contemplating on** or **contemplating over.** *On* or *over* is implied and does not need to be added.

71.10 **continuing on** or **continuing to remain.** *On* or *to remain* are superfluous.

71.11 **converted over.** *Over* is already implied in the word *converted*. Why add it?

71.12 **cooperating together.** Omit *together*, unless you know of a way of where one might cooperate with one's self.

71.13 **could of.** Use *have* rather than *of*.

71.14 **depreciating in value.** If something depreciates, can we not assume that it is "value" which is taking the plunge?

71.15 **due and payable.** If it is due, it certainly payable.

71.16 **each and every one.** Use *each* or *every*, but not both.

71.17 **end result.** The result has always been the end.

71.18 **endorsed on the back.** *On the back* is redundant.

71.19 **equally as.** The word *as* is not needed.

71.20 **fair and equitable.** If it is fair, is it not equitable? Choose one.

71.21 **falling down.** Why include *down* when that is the only way one can fall?

71.22 **false pretense and false pretext.** Doesn't *pretense* and *pretext* already mean "false." Omit *false.*

71.23 **favorably impressed.** *Favorably* is the only way to be impressed. Omit it.

71.24 **first and foremost** and **first, beginning.** *First* doesn't need the other other two, nor do they need "first."

71.25 **free gratis.** They mean the same thing. Why combine them?

71.26 **gathering together.** Is there another way to gather? Omit *together.*

71.27 **good and.** These two words should not be joined to a word which does not describe someone's nature (e.g., "good and tired" describes someone's *attitude*, not his or nature).

71.28 **great and good friend.** Is not a *great* friend a *good* friend?

71.29 **hale and hearty.** Redundant. Use only one of them.

71.30 **have got to.** What is *got* doing in there?

71.31 **having ways and means.** Might as well write "ways and ways."

71.32 **he is a man who.** Is is necessary to identify *he* as a *man?*

71.33 **honestly and truly.** If one is honest, isn't he or she also true?

71.34 **if, as, and when.** Choose one and omit the other two.

71.35 **in among, in around, in back of, in between,** and **in under.** The addition of the preposition *in* is unnecessary.

71.36 **in regards to.** Change *regards* to *regard.* Also, the preposition *with* sounds better than the preposition *in* when placed at the head of a phrase, but either is acceptable. As an interruptive or add-on phrase where no pause can be detected, the preceding comma is omitted.

71.37 **is when** and **is where.** Never follow these words with a definition (e.g., Recalcitrant *is when* you are somewhat rebellious).

71.38 **kind of** and **sort of.** As leaders of phrases, replace either of these two-word combinations with the word *somewhat* or *rather.* As integral parts of a sentence, consider substituting them with one of these: *seemed, seemingly,* or *seeming to; appeared* or *appearing to; to some degree* or *to some extent; in some measure; rather; apparently.*

71.39 **kith and kin.** The two words mean the same thing. Use only one.

71.40 **last best hope.** If it is one's *last* hope, it certainly one's *best* hope.

71.41 **lo and behold.** Might as well write *behold and behold.*

71.42 **meeting together.** Can you meet someone without coming together?

71.43 **mental telepathy.** It cannot be telepathy unless it is mental. Omit *mental.*

71.44 **near to.** The preposition *to* is an unnecessary addition.

71.45 **not a one.** Eliminate the indefinite article "a."

71.46 **null and void.** Redundant.

71.47 **off from the** and **off of the.** Omit the prepositions *from* and *of.*

71.48 **often accustomed to.** *Accustomed* implies "often," so the word *often* is not needed.

71.49 **one and the same thing.** No reason to include *one and*.

71.50 **out-and-out.** Slang, which is obviously redundant.

71.51 **outside of.** These words must never be used as synonyms for *except for*.

71.52 **over and above.** To be *above* something is to be *over* it.

71.53 **over with.** Omit the preposition *with*. Also, if *with* is preceded by *and done*, eliminate those words as well.

71.54 **part and parcel.** Redundant.

71.55 **planning on.** Drop the preposition *on* and replace it with the preposition *to*.

71.56 **pretending like.** Substitute *to be* or *as if* for the word *like*.

71.57 **raised up.** Ever heard of *raised down?*

71.58 **really and truly.** "Same as honestly and truly." Redundant.

71.59 **self-confessed.** It's impossible to confess for someone else. Omit *self*.

71.60 **settling up.** A bad marriage between two words.

71.61 **she is a woman who.** For her sake, let's hope she *is* a woman.

71.62 **that although, that because, that if, that so long, and that while.** Omit *that*, for there is no need for successive conjunctions.

71.63 **the fact that.** Omit *the fact* and let the word "that" act alone.

71.64 **the one and only.** If there is just *one*, then isn't it the *only* one?

71.65 **the reason is because.** Use *the reason is* or *because*, but not both.

71.66 **unless and until.** Might as well write *unless and unless*.

71.67 **upright and honest.** Being *upright* implies being "honest."

71.68 **well and good.** A bad marriage between two words.

71.69 **you and you alone.** The words *and you alone* are not essential.

Abbreviations

The period (.) is the punctuation mark used in abbreviations, although there are many abbreviations where that is not the case. The abbreviations which follow are grouped under ten separate headings: **Most Frequently Used; Biblical; Degrees (Education); Financial; Footnotes; Measurements & Amounts; Military Rank; Time; Titles; and Miscellanous.** The full words are listed at the left, followed by their abbreviations (in italics, for quick differentiation).

72.1 Frequently Used

and others *et al* 26.2
and so forth *etc.* 26.1
and so on *etc.* 26.4
for example *e.g.* 26.1
that is *i.e.* 26.4

72.2 Biblical

Biblical *Bibl.*
Chronicles *Chron.*
Corinthians *Cor.*
Colossians *Col.*
Daniel *Dan.*
Deuteronomy *Deut.*
Ecclesiastes *Eccles.*
Ephesians *Eph.*
Exodus *Ex.*
Ezekial *Ezek.*
Galathians *Gal.*
Genesis *Gen.*
Habakkuh *Hab.*
Hebrews *Heb.*
Hosea *Hos.*
Isaiah *Is.*
Jeremiah *Jer.*
John *Jn.*
Jonah *Jon.*
Joshua *Josh.*
Judges *Judg.*
Lamentations *Lam.*
Leviticus *Lev.*
Luke *Lk.*
Mark *Mk.*
Matthew *Mat.*
Nehemiah *Neh.*
New Testament *New Test.*
Numbers *Num.*
Obadiah *Obad.*
Old Testament *Old Test.*

Philemon *Philem.*
Philippians *Phil.*
Proverbs *Prov.*
Psalms *Ps.*
Revelations *Rev.*
Romans *Rom.*
Samuel *Sam.*
Scriptures *Scrip.*
Song of Solomon *Song.*
Titus *Tit.*
Zechariah *Zech.*
Zephaniah *Zeph.*

72.3 Degrees (Education)

Bachelor of....
  Agriculture *B. Agr.*
  Applied Science *B.A.S.*
  Architecture *B. Arch.*
  Arts *B.A.*
  Business Admin. *B.B.A.*
  Chemical Science *B.C.S.*
  Chemistry *B.C.*
  Civil Engineering *B.C.E.*
  Civil Law *B.C.L.*
  Commerce *B.C.*
  Dental Surgery *B.D.S.*
  Divinity *B.D.*
  Education *B.E., Ed. B*
  Electrical Eng. *B.E.E.*
  Finance *B.F.*
  Fine Arts *B.F.A.*
  Forestry *B.F.*
  Journalism *B.J.*
  Laws *B.LL., LL.B.*
  Liberal Arts *B.L.A.*
  Library Science *B.L.S.*

Medicine *M.B.*
Mechanical Eng. *B.M.E.*
Pedagogy *B.Pd., B. Pe.*
Pharmacy *B.P.*
Philosophy *B.Phil.*
Physical Educ. *B.P.E.*
Science *B.Sc.*
Science in Educ. *B.S.Ed.*
Social Sciences *B.S.Sc.*
Surgery *B.S.*
Theology *B.Th.*
Doctor of....
  Dental Science *D.D.S.*
  Laws *LL.D.*
  Medicine *M.D.*
  Music *Mus.D., Mus.Dr.*
  Philsophy *D. Phil.*
  Science *D.Sc.*
  Theology *D.Th.*
Master of....
  Agriculture *M. Agr.*
  Business Admin. *M.B.A.*
  Civil Law *M.C.L.*
  Dental Surgery *M.D.S.*
  Education *M.Ed.*
  Laws *LL.M*
  Music *Mus.M.*
  Science *M.Sc.*
  Surgery *M.Ch.*

72.4 Financial

according to value *a.v.*
account *acct.*
account current *a/c*
account of *a/o*
annual *ann.*
balance *bal.*
bank *bk.*

bankrupt *bkpt.*
bill of sale *B/S*
bookkeeping *bkkpg.*
by the year *per ann.*
cash discount *c.d.*
cash on delivery *c.o.d.*
cent(s) *ct(s).*
charge(d) *chg.*
check *ck.*
collateral *collat.*
collect on delivery *c.o.d.*
cost and freight *c.f.*
creditors *crs.*
dealer *dlr.*
debtor *dr.*
demand draft *d.d., D/D*
deposit *dep.*
deposit receipt *D/R*
dollar *dol.*
expenses *exp.*
financial *fin.*
free on board *f.o.b.*
free on rails *f.o.r.*
freight bill *f.b.*
franc *fr.*
interest *int.*
inventory *invt.*
joint account *j.a.*
gross national prod. *GNP*
letter of credit *l/c, L/C*
Mark *Mk*
mortgage *mtge.*
no funds *N.F., n/f*
overdraft *o.d.*
overcharge *o/c*
paid *pd.*
payment *payt., pymt.*
pay on delivery *p.o.d.*
peco *p.*
percent *pct.*
petty cash *p/c, P/C*
postpaid *ppd.*
pound *L.*
prepaid *ppd.*
profit and loss *P and L*
quarter (period) *qtr.*
receipt *rcpt.*
seller's option *s.o.*
ruble *rub.*
yen *Y*

72.5 Footnotes

NOTE: Italics represent Latin equivalents and must remain as you see them.

about (time) *circa.* or *ca.*
addendum — add.
and others — et al
and the following *et. seq.*
anonymous — anon.
appearing earlier — above
archaic — arch.
article — art.
 • later — below
as above *ut sup.*
as if said *q.d.*
at place desired *ad loc.*
at the beginning *ad. init.*
at the end *ad fin.*
at this time *h.t.*
attributive — attrib.
author's mistake — [sic]
biography — biog.
book — bk.
 • more than one — bks.
chapter — chap. or ch.
 • more than one — chaps.
column — col.
 • more than one — cols.
compare *cf.*
date of death — d.
dialect — dial.
dissertation — diss.
document — doc.
document signed — d.s.
doesn't follow *non seq.*
edited by — ed.
edition — edit.
editor — ed.
English version — E.V.
epilogue — pil.
epitaph — epit.
errors excepted — e.e.
especially — esp.
figure — fig.
 • more than one — figs.
from beginning *ab init.*
frontpiece (book) — front.
forward — fwd.
folios — ff.
following — ff., fol.

glossary — gloss.
in its place — in loc.
in the same place *Ibid.*
inclusive — incl.
handbook — hdbk.
in the work cited *op. cit.*
incorrect— incorr.
introduction— introd.
it doesn't follow *non seq.*
italics — ital.
journal — jour.
Latin — Lat.
line — l.
 • more than one — ll.
location — loc.
manuscript — ms. or MS
manuscripts — mss. or MSS
new edition — n.e.
no publication date — n.d.
no page number — n.p.
notes — nn.
not published — ined.
number— No.
obituary — obit.
obscure —obs.
out of print —O.P., o.p.
page — p
pages — pp
pamphlet — pph
paragraph — par.
 ° more than one — pp.
plate — pl.
 • more than one — pls.
pseudonym — pseud.
same article *op.cit.*
same book *op.cit.*
series — ser.
specifically — specif.
spelling — sp.
the same *id.*
the same as *i.q.*
translation — trans.
unknown *ign.*
unpaged — unp.
unpublished — unpub.
volume — vol.
which is *q.e.*
without date — s.d.
without name — s.n.
year of death — d.

72.6 Measurements and Amounts

acre *a.*
actual weight *A/W* altitude *alt.*
amount *amt.*
atomic weight *at. wt.*
barometic *bar.*
barrel *bbl.*
barrels per day *b.p.d.*
board feet *bd. ft.*
board measure *b.m.*
bushel *bu.*
calorie *cal.*
car load *c.l.*
carat *c., kt.*
centigrade *C., c.*
centimeter *cc.*
cubic *cu., cm*
cubic centimeters *cc.*
cubic foot *cu. ft.*
cubic inches *cu.in.*
cubic yard *cu.yd.*
cycles *cy.*
cycles per second *cps.*
dead weight tons *d.w.t.*
decibel *db*
diameter *diam.*
dimension *dim.*
double *dbl.*
dozen *doz., dz.*
dram *dr.*
degree *deg.*
Fahrenheit *F.*
fathom *fath.*
feet *ft.*
feet per minute *fpm*
feet per second *fps*
five hundred *D*
fluid ounce *fl. oz.*
foot *ft.*
freezing point *f.p., fp*
furlong(s) *fur.*
gallon *gal.*
gallons per min. *g.p.m.*
gram *g., gm.*
gram calorie *g. cal.*
grammar *gram.*
gross *gr.*
gross weight *gr. wt.*
hundred weight *cwt.*
height *ht.*
horsepower *HP, h.p.*

hour(s) *hr(s).*
inch *in.*
inner diameter *i.d.*
kilo *k.*
kilowatt hour *kw. hr.*
kilocycle *kc.*
kilogram *kg., kilog.*
kiloliter *kl., kilol.*
kilometer *km., kilom.*
kilovolt *kv., kw*
kilowatt *kw., kw*
kilowatt hour *kw. hr.*
knot *k.*
length *lgth.*
liquid quart *liq. qt.*
liter *l.*
latitude *lat.*
longitude *long.*
megacycle *mc.*
melting point *m.p., mp*
megaton *mt.*
meter *m.*
metric ton *m.t.*
mile *mi.*
miles per gallon *m.p.g.*
miles per hr. *m.p.h.*
milligram *mg.*
milliliter *ml., ml*
millimeter *mm.*
minute *min.*
molecular wt. *mol. wt.*
net weight *nt. wt.*
ohm *o.*
one thousand *k.*
ounce *oz.*
ounce *ozs.*
parts per million *p.p.m.*
pint *pt.*
pound *lb.*
quart *qt.*
revolutions per min. *r.p.m*
revolutions per sec. *r.p.s.*
second(s) *sec(s).*
square foot *sq. ft.*
square inch *sq. in.*
square mile *sq. mi.*
square yard *sq. yd.*
tablespoon *tbsp.*
teaspoon *tsp.*
ton *t., tn.*
volt *v.*
weight *wt.*
watt-hour(s) *watt-hr(s).*
wattmeter *wm.*

wave length *w.l.*
width *w.*
yard *yd.*

72.7 Military Rank

Adjutant *Adjt.*
Captain *Capt.*
Colonel Col.
Commandant *Comdt.*
Commander *Cmdr.*
commanding officer *C.O.*
Corporal *Cpl.*
Field Marshal *F.M.*
field officer *F.O.*
flying officer *F.O.*
General *Gen.*
junior grade *jg., j.g.*
Lieutenant *Lieut., Lt.*
Lieutenant General *Lt. Gen.*
Major *Maj.*
Major General *Maj. Gen.*
Master Sergeant *M.Sgt.*
medical officer *M.O.*
officer *off.*
Officer of the Day *O.D.*
Private *Pvt.*
Rear Admiral *R.A.*
Sergeant *Sgt.*
Staff Sergeant *S/Sgt.*
Techical Sergeant *T/Sgt.*

72.8 Time

after date *a.d.*
after death (Christ) *A.D.*
afternoon *P.M., p.m.*
before Christ *B.C.*
daylight saving *d.s.*
Friday *Fri.*
Greenwich mean time *GMT*
indefinitely *s.d.*
Monday *Mon.*
month/monthly *mo.*
months *mos.*
mountain time *m.t.*
morning *A.M., a.m.*
quarter *qr.*
quarterly *qr., qrtly.*
Saturday *Sat.*
Sunday *Sun.*
Tuesday *Tues.*
Thursday *Thur.*

313

Wednesday *Wed.*
week *wk.*
weekly *wkly.*
year/yearly *yr.*
years *yrs.*

72.9 Titles
Archbishop *Archbp.*
architect *archt.*
artist *art.*
assistant *Asst.*
attorney *atty.*
auditor *aud.*
author *auth.*
baritone *barit.*
chairman *chm., chmn.*
chaplain *ch.*
Chemical Engineer *Ch. E.*
chemist *chem.*
Chief Justice *Ch. J.*
clergyman *cl.*
clerk *cl.*
Constable *Const.*
cook *ck.*
Commissioner *Comr.*
delegate *del.*
director *Dir.*
doctor *Dr.*
diplomat *dipl.*
engineer *engr.*
Excellency *Exc.*
Ensign *Ens.*
Foreign Office *F.O.*
general manager *G.M.*
general practitioner *G.P.*
governor *Gov.*
General Secretary *G.S.*
Grand Master *G.M.*
His Eminence *H.E.*
His Excellency *H.E.*
Honorable *Hon.*
inspector *insp.*
Judge Advocate *JA*
Justice of the Peace *J.P.*
manager *Mgr.*
Most Reverend *Mt. Rev.*
navigator *navig.*
notary public *N.P.*
petroleum engineer *P.E.*
physician *phys.*
photographer *photog.*
President *Pres.*
principal *prin.*

professor *prof.*
proprietor *propr.*
referee *ref.*
Representative *Rep.*
Reverend *Rev.*
Right Reverend *Rt. Rev.*
scholar *schol.*
secretary *sec., secy.*
Senator *Sen.*
soprano *sop.*
speaker *spkr.*
teacher *tchr.*
Superintendent *Supt.*
treasurer *treas.*
Vice President *V.P.*

72.10 Misc.
about *ca.*
absent *abs.*
absent without leave
AWOL
academy *acad.*
acceptance *acpt.*
acting *actg.*
advertisement *advt.*
aeronautics *aeron.*
against *vs., con.*
agency *agcy.*
agreement *Agt.*
agriculture *agri.*
acknowledge *ack.*
aeronautics *aero.*
algebra *alg.*
also known as *a.k.a.*
alternating current *AC*
alternate *alt.*
America *Amer.*
analogy *anal.*
anatomy *anat.*
and so forth *etc.*
and so on *etc.*
annual *ann.*
answer *ans.*
antiquity *antiq.*
apparatus *appar.*
apartment(s) *apt(s).*
appointment *apmt.*
approximately *approx.*
arrival *ar.*
assigned *asgd.*
associate *assoc.*
association *assn.*
astrology *astrol.*

astronomy *astron.*
atmosphere *atm.*
attention *attn.*
automatic *auto.*
auxiliary *auxil.*
avenue *ave.*
average *avg.*
bachelor *bach.*
back order *b.o.*
bibliography *bibliog.*
biochemistry *biochem.*
biology *biol.*
born *b., n.*
botony *bot.*
boulevard *blvd.*
box *bx.*
Brigade *Brig.*
brothers *bros.*
building *bldg.*
bulletin *bul.*
cancel/cancelled *canc.*
capital *cap.*
capital letters *caps.*
care of *c/o, C/O*
carbon copy *c.c.*
Catholic *Cath.*
center *ctr.*
certificate *certif.*
charter *char.*
Chicago *Chi.*
chronological *chron.*
citation *cit.*
claim *cl.*
clarinet *clar.*
class *cl.*
classic *class.*
classified *class.*
clerical *cler.*
clinic *clin.*
collect *coll.*
column *clm., col.*
combination *comb.*
commercial *cml.*
Commission *Com.*
Committee *Com.*
comparative *compar.*
compartment *compt.*
condition *cond.*
Confederation *Confed.*
confer *cf.*
consecrated *cons.*
consigned *cons.*
Constitution *Const.*
construction *constr.*

contemporary *contemp.*
continue *cont.*
continued *contd.*
contributor *contrib.*
control *contr.*
cooperative *co-op.*
copyright *cop.*
correlative *correl.*
correct *corr.*
correspondence *corres.*
county *Co.*
cross reference *x-ref.*
current *cur.*
daughter *dau.*
deceased *decd.*
decimeter *decim.*
dedication *ded.*
delivered *d/d*
Democrat *Dem.*
department *dept.*
descendent *desc.*
derivation *deriv.*
development *devel.*
diagram *diag.*
died *d.*
direct current *DC*
discharged *disch.*
distributor *distr.*
divorced *div.*
doing business as *d.b.a.*
duplicate *dupl.*
each *ea.*
Earth *E.*
East *E.*
ecclesiastical *eccl.*
ecology *ecol.*
economic *econ.*
electric *elec.*
elevation *elev.*
enclosure *encl.*
engine *eng.*
engineering *engin.*
English *Eng.*
engraved *engr.*
Eskimo *Esk.*
especially *esp.*
Esquire *Esq.*
established *estab.*
estimated *est.*
et cetera *etc.*
Europe/European *Eur.*
evacuation *evac.*
Evangelical *Evang.*
evangelist *evang.*

evaporation *evap.*
excellent *exc.*
exchange *exch.*
exclusive *excl.*
expiration *exp.*
export *exp.*
express *exp.*
extension *ext.*
external *ext.*
extinct *ext.*
facsimile *fac.*
federal *fed.*
federation *fed.*
feminine *f., fem.*
fiction *fict.*
figure *fig.*
first in, first out *FIFO*
first in, last out *FILO*
flourished *fl.*
for example *e.g.*
Fort *Ft.*
forward *fwd.*
freight *frt.*
French *Fr.*
frequency *freq.*
from *fr.*
furnished *furn.*
general *genl.*
General Headquarters *GHQ*
general issue *GI*
general orders *GO*
general post office *G.P.O.*
general quarters *G.Q., GQ*
genitive *gen.*
geographical *geog.*
geologic *geol.*
geometry *geom.*
German *G.*
goods *gds.*
good till cancelled *G.T.C.*
government *govt.*
government issue *GI*
graduate *grad.*
grain(s) *gr.*
granddaughter *g.d.*
grand old party *G.O.P.*
grandson *g.s.*
Greek *Gk.*
guaranteed *guar., gtd.*
gymnasium *gym.*
harbor *h.*
have the body *hab. corp.*
head office *H.O.*
headquarters *hdqrs.*

Hebrew *Heb.*
here lies buried *H.J.S.*
high explosive *H.E., HE*
high frequency *h.f., HF*
high water *h.w.*
historical *hist.*
home office *H.O.*
horizon *hor.*
horticulture *hort.*
hospital *hosp.*
husband *h.*
hydraulic *hydraul.*
hygiene *hyg.*
identification *i.d.*
illustration *illus., illust.*
imported *imp.*
inclosure *incl.*
including *incl., inc.*
incognito *incog.*
Incorporated *Inc.*
increase *inc., incr.*
indefinite *indef.*
individual *individ.*
Infantry *Inf.*
inorganic *inorg.*
inspected *insp.*
insurance *insur.*
intelligence quotient *I.Q.*
international *internat.*
irregularly *irreg.*
Island(s) *I.*
Isle(s) *I.*
journalism *journ.*
Junior *Jr.*
jurisprudence *juris.*
juvenile *juv.*
kingdom *kingd.*
knockout *k.o., KO, K.O.*
laboratory *lab.*
large *lg.*
last in, first out *LIFO*
last in, last out *LILO*
lecture *lect.*
library *lib.*
limited *ltd.*
limited *Ltd.*
low frequency *l.f., L.F.*
low water mark *l.w.m.*
lyric *lyr.*
machinery *mach.*
madame *Mme.*
mademoiselle *Mlle.*
majority *maj.*
management *mgt.*

manufactured *manuf.*
manufacturer *mfr.*
manufacturing *mfg.*
market *mkt.*
married *m.*
masculine *m., masc.*
material *matl., mtl.*
mathematics *math.*
maximum *max.*
measure *meas.*
mechanical *mech.*
meeting *mtg.*
member *mem.*
memorandum *memo*
memorial *mem.*
merchandise *mdse.*
message *msg.*
messieurs *MM.*
metallurgical *metall.*
meteorology *meteorol.*
military *mil.*
miscellaneous *misc.*
Mister *Mr.*
Misters *Messrs.*
Mistress *Mrs.*
mixture *mixt.*
modern *mod.*
molecule(s) *mol.*
monastery *mon.*
Mount *Mt.*
mountains *mts.*
music *mus.*
mythology *mythol.*
namely *viz.*
nautical *naut.*
near *nr.*
negative *neg.*
no good *n.g., N.G.*
normal *norm.*
north *N., N, n.*
northeast *NE*
north-northeast *NNE*
northwest *NW*
number(s) *num*
obsolete *obs.*
occasionally *occ.*
occidental *occ.*
ocean *oc.*
official *off.*
operating room *OR, O.R.*
oppose *opp.*
orchestra *orch.*
ordained *ord.*
ordnance *ordn.*

organic *org.*
original *orig.*
orthopedic *orth.*
overdose of drugs *o.d.*
overtime *O.T.*
package *pkg.*
pair *pr.*
pairs *prs.*
parallel *par.*
paragraph *para.*
patent *pat.*
patented *patd.*
pertaining *pert.*
pharmacy *phar.*
philosophy *philos.*
physics *phys.*
physical training *p.t.*
place *pl.*
plaintiff *plff.*
platoon *plat.*
please reply *R.S.V.P*
plural *pl.*
Police Department *P.D.*
population *pop.*
post exchange *PX*
postmarked *pmkd.*
post mortem *P.M., p.m.*
post office *P.O.*
postscript *P.S.*
prehistoric *prehist.*
preliminary *prelim.*
present *pres.*
principle *prin.*
printed *prtd.*
Prisoner of War *P.O.W.*
private *priv.*
proceedings *proc.*
professional *pro.*
province *prov.*
provisional *prov.*
psychology *psychol.*
pseudonym *pseud.*
quality *qlty.*
query *qy.*
question *qu., ques.*
Railroad *R.R.*
Railway *Ry.*
received *rcd.*
reciprocal *recip.*
record *rec.*
referred *ref.*
refrigeration *refrig.*
regular *reg.*
relative *rel.*

religion *rel.*
report *rpt.*
Republican *Repub.*
requisition *req.*
restaurant *restr.*
retired *ret.*
returned *ret., retd.*
river *riv.*
road *rd.*
room *rm.*
rooms *rms.*
Russian *Russ.*
Saint *St., Ste.*
Saints *SS.*
sealed *sld.*
scheduled *sched.*
school *sch.*
section *sect.*
seminary *sem.*
Senior *Sr.*
sequel *seq.*
serial *ser.*
series *s., ser.*
share(s) *shr(s).*
shipment *shpt.*
shortage *shtg.*
signature *Sig.*
signed *sd., sgd.*
sirs *MM.*
sister *sist.*
small *sm.*
sociological *sociol.*
son *s.*
south *So.*
South Africa *S. Afr.*
South America *S. Amer.*
south-southwest *S.S.W.*
southeast *SE*
southwest *SW*
sovereign *sov.*
special *sp.*
species *spp.*
spring *spg.*
square *sq.*
station *sta.*
standard *std.*
standing room *S.R.O.*
station *sta.*
statistics *stat.*
steamship *s.s.*
storage *stge., stor.*
subject *subj.*
subsidiary *subs.*
substitute *sub., subst.*

316

suggested *sug.*, *sugg.*
supreme supr.
supplement *suppl.*
suspended *susp.*
syndicate *synd.*
synopsis *synop.*
synonymous *syn.*
system *syst.*
target tgt.
technical knockout *TKO*
technology *technol.*
telegram *tel.*
telephone *tel.*
Territory *terr.*, *Ty.*
that is *i.e.*,
theology *theol.*
three times daily *t.i.d.*
title *tit.*
to infinity *ad. inf.*
tonnage *tonn.*
topography *topog.*
township *twp.*
training *tng.*
transfer(red) *transf.*
translation *transl.*
transportation *transp.*
traveler *trav.*
triplicate *tripl.*
Troop *Tr.*
tropical *trop.*
ultimate *ult.*
unabridged *unabr.*
under consideration *s.j.*
undersigned *undsgd.*
University *Univ.*
unlimited *unl.*
unofficial *unof.*
vacuum *vac.*
Vatican *Vat.*
vegetable *veg.*
versus *vs.*, *v.*
veteran *vet.*
veterinary *vet.*
vice versa *v.v.*
vocabulary *vocab.*
warrant *war.*, *wrnt.*
warranty *warrty.*
watt *w.*
when issued *w.i.*
wife *w.*
without interest *ex int.*
youngest *y.*
zoology *zool.*

General Index

...which also includes prefixes, common expressions, familiar phrases, adverbs, conjunctions, interjections, pronouns, prepositions, erroneous word combinations, accented words, nonwords, and words which are frequently followed by hyphens.

a 14.1—2, 29.1

abbreviation
Amounts 72.6
Biblical 72.2
Degrees (educ.) 72.3
Financial 72.4
Footnotes 72.5
Frequently used 72.1
Measurements 72.6
Military rank 72.7
Miscellaneous 72.10
Preceded by number 48.7
Time 72.8
Titles 72.9

about 17.2
About face 67.1—6
above 17.2
above all 28.1
above everything 28.2
Abschied (Ger.) 35.24

accent (´)
Rule 61.1

accept 29.2
accordingly 3.6, 12.1—4
accused 10.1
across 17.2
act your age 27.1—2
A.D. 42.12

adage
Follows...
 • Noun or pronoun 34.1
 • Verb 34.2
Interrupts sentence 34.3

adapt 29.3

addressing someone
Rules 16.2, 35.23

adieu (Fr.) 35.24
addio (Ital.) 35.24

adjective
Rules 11.1—7
Begins...
 • sentence 11.1
 • add-on phrase 22.1
City and state 11.7
Ends a sentence 11.3
Midsentence 11.2
Series 4.9
 • follows series 4.11
Three-word adjective 11.5
Two-word adjective 11.4
Two pairs 11.6
 • *good cop bad cop*
 • *nice cop tough cop*

adopt 39.3
advance 15.1—2

adverb
Rules 12.1—6
Begins
 • a sentence 12.1
 • add-on phrase 22.1
Ending in "ly" 2.1, 12.5
Ends a sentence 12.3
Follows series 4.11
Hyphened 12.6

Midsentence 12.2
Stands alone 12.4

adverbial clause
Rule 20.1

aero 63.1
affect 29.4
affirm 29.5
Afro 62.1
after 10.2, 17.2
after a while 28.3
afternoon 35.24
again 12.1—4
against 17.2

age
After one's name 53.10

aggravate 29.6
agro 63.2
ah 35.28
aha (a-ha) 15.1—2
ahem 35.28
ahoy 15.1—2
aiding and abetting 71.2
ain't 44.3
ain't it the truth 27.1—2
air 63.3
alas 15.1—2
albeit 7.1, 10.3
alias 10.4
all 18.1—8, 64.1
all along 28.4
all clear 27.1—2
all of a sudden 28.5
all the better 28.6

all right 27.1—2
all right already 27.1—2
all together now 28.7
allege 29.5
all's well 27.1—2
aloha 35.24
along 17.2
alongside 17.2

alphabetic letter

Acts as...
- noun 6.1
- prefix 6.2

Before items in list 47.1
Capitalization 68.8
Highlighting 6.1
Omitted from word
- combining words 35.18
- dialect 35.14—17
- first letters 7.9
- first & last 7.12
- middle letters 7.10
- last letter 7.11

also 3.6, 10.5, 12.1—4
although 7.1, 10.6, 13.1
Always 69.1
am 44.3
amen 10.7
amid 17.2
amidst 17.2
among 17.2

amounts

Abbreviations 72.6

amscray 15.1—2
an 14.1—2
an afterthought 27.7
an explanation 27.7
an idea 27.7

and 7.1, 4.7, 10.8
- begins several complex sentences 33.7
- joins...
  - simple sentence 31.1, 31.3, 32.1, 33.2

- simple and complex sentences 31.9, 32.8—9
- complex sentences 31.12;
- omitted between two words 3.4
- repeated 32.4

and doubtless will 28.8
and finally 28.9
and first to go out of 28.10
and how 27.1—2
and naturally 28.9
and/or 10.9
and so 28.9
and with that 28.9
Anglo 62.2
angry at 28.11
angry with 28.11
another 18.1—8
Another thing 27.7
answer 28.7
ante 62.3
anti 62.4
any 18.1—8
any more 28.12
anyone 18.1—8
anyway 3.6, 12.1—4
apértif 61.1

apostrophe (')

Rule 61.2
Combining words 35.18
Contracting *not* 19.9
Joining a verb to a...
- noun 16.8
- pronoun 18.12
Plural number 53.2
Replacing letters 7.9—12
- dialect 35.13—19
Replacing numbers 43.3
Showing ownership
- author 54.3—4
- noun 16.7
- pronoun 18.11
- time 42.3

arch 62.5
are 44.3
aren't 44.3
arguably 2.1
around 17.2

article, magazine

Rule 32.1
Creating headline 7.7—8
Creating bibliography 55.2
In footnote 56.5—6
Referring to 65.4

artwork

Rule 58.1

as 7.1, 10.10, 29.7
- joins sentences 31.2
- precedes indirect quote 37.2
- precedes question 44.8

as best as 71.3
as compared with 28.13
as follows 47.3
as likely as not 28.14
as per your inquiry 70.1
as well 28.15
as you were 67.1—6
assume 29.8

asterisk (*)

Rule 56.1
Curse word substitute 9.2
Footnote 56.2—3
List 47.1, 47.6
Successive quotes 36.18

at 17.2
at a glance 28.16
at all costs 28.17
at ease 67.1—6
at every turn 28.18
at last 27.1—2
at long last 27.1—2
at the present writing 70.1
attaboy 15.1—2, 27.1—2
attaché 61.1
attached hereto 70.1
attached herewith 70.1
attack 15.1—2
attention 15.1—2, 67.1—6

auf Wiedersehen (Ger.)
35.24
au revoir (Fr.) 35.24
auto 63.4
auto-da-fé 61.1
autumn 42.9
avast 15.1—2
away 15.1—2
aweigh anchor 67.1—6
aw shucks 27.1—2

axiom
Rules 39.1—5

back off 27.1—2
bag and baggage 28.19
bah 35.28
baloney 15.1—2
bam 35.28
bang 15.1—2
bank on it 27.1—2
baptized 6.7
barely had 28.20
barring 17.2
basically 3.6, 12.1—4
B.C. 42.12
<u>be</u> 62.6
be careful 27.1—2
bearing the name of 28.21
beats me 27.1—2
because 7.1, 10.11
beep-beep 35.28
before 10.12
begging the question
28.22
begone 15.1—2
behind 17.2
behold 15.1—2
<u>being</u> 28.23, 29.9
being as 28.23
being as how 28.23
being as though 28.23
being that 28.23
below 17.2
beneath 17.2
beside(s) 3.6, 12.1—4
<u>best</u> 64.2
best regards 69.1
best wishes 69.1
better 64.3
between 17.2
beware 15.1—2
<u>beyond</u> 17.2

beyond me 27.1—2
bi 62.7

Bible, books
See "abbreviations"

Biblical abbreviations
Rule 72.2

bibliography
Articles 55.2
Books 55.3—6
• separate, same author
55.4
• more than one author
55.5
• unindentifiable author
55.6
General info 55.1
Speeches 55.7

bienenu (Fr.) 35.24
bingo 15.1—2
bio 62.8
black 64.4
blasé 61.1
blazes 15.1—2
blood 64.5
blow me down 27.1—2
boy oh boy 27.1—2
blue 64.6
bon jour (Fr.) 35.24
bon soir (Fr.) 35.24
boo 35.28
book 64.7

book
See "title (book)"
Bibliography 55.3—6
Referring to 65.3

boom 15.1—2
bosh 15.1—2
<u>both</u> 18.1—8
both alike 71.4

both together 71.4
botheration 15.1—2
bottoms up 27.3

brackets
Rule 61.3
Encasing...
• direct quote 36.10,
36.21
• exclamation mark
2.10
• question mark 2.10,
6.9
• word 2.10
Noting error in quote
36.12
Spelled-out word 2.6
Stage directions 35.26
Within...
• dialogue 35.12,
35.25
• direct quote 36.10

bravissimo 15.1—2
bravo 15.1—2
break it up 27.1—2
bug off 27.1—2

bullets
In a list 47.6

bully 15.1—2
buoyed up 71.5
<u>but</u> 7.1, 10.13, 29.10
• begins contrasting
sentence 31.7
but even at that 26.14
but even here 26.14
but even so 26.14
but for that 26.14
but hey 26.14
but not exactly of 26.14
but of course 26.14
but one thing for sure
26.14
butt out 27.1—2
<u>by</u> 17.2, 29.11, 63.5
• measurement 52.1
by golly 27.1—2
by gosh 27.1—2
by jingo 27.1—2
by leaps and bounds 71.6

by no means 27.1—2
by their very nature 28.24
bye-bye 35.24

by-word
With phrase 28.2
With word 6.4
cachunk 35.28
café 61.1
called 6.7
<u>can</u> 44.3
can it be 27.1—2
can such things be 27.1
canapés 61.1
can't 44.3

capitalization
Rules 68.1—9
After...
• colon 68.1
• opening series 4.12
All letters of word 6.10,
6.12
Alphabetic letter 68.8
Changes in legal
document 68.8
Geographical areas &
directions 68.5
In a list
• phrases 47.1
• sentences 47.1
• words 47.2
In a parentheses 68.2
Literary title 54.2
Nouns/legal document
6.12
One-letter prefix 6.2
Person's title 68.4
Poetry 68.3
Proverb, principle 39.2
Signs & notices 68.9
Trade name 60.1

captions
Rule 66.2

careful 15.1—2
carry on 27.1—2
Case in point 27.7
caution 15.1—2
cease 15.1—2

cent sign
Rule 51.4

centering 10.14

century
Rule 42.12

certainly 3.6, 12.1—4
certified 6.7
Champ Élysées 61.1
chapter and verse 28.25
charge 15.1—2
chargé d' affairs 61.1
cheers 27.3
cheer up 27.1—2
cherrio 35.24
chin up 27.1—2
chop-chop 27.1—2
Christened 6.7
cinéma 61.1

cipher (')
Rule 61.4
Dimensions 52.2
Height, length, width
52.3

city, state
After person's name 21.6
As an adjective 11.7
In a list 46.6, 46.8
Linked to person 59.8

clang 35.28
clang-clang 35.28
classified 6.7
clear 64.8
clearly 3.6, 12.1—4

cliché
Rules 38.1—2

climbing up 71.7
close 64.9

closings, in letters
Business letter 69.1
Personal letter 69.2

co 62.9

colon (:)
Rule 61.5
After...
• com. expression 27.1
• dialogue 35.22
• first word 1.8, 16.2
• introductory sentence
31.11, 32.5, 33.5,
33.10
• opening phrase 20.13
• pairs of word 4.4
• quote 36.2
• series of words 4.12
Before...
• add-on phrase 22.10
• add-on word 18.8
• hello/good-bye 35.24
• last of three sentences
32.6
• last word 3.2, 16.4
• list 46.1, 46.3, 47.3,
47.7—8, 48.2—3
• motto, epitaph 34.1
• preposition 17.7
• proverb, principle
39.4
• question 44.11
• quote 36.2
• series of words 4.17,
48.2
Between...
• numbers in ratio 53.3
• sentences 31.8,
31.15, 32.5—6,
33.3, 33.10
• time elements 42.2
• title and publisher
55.6
• verse numbers 65.2

<u>come</u> again? 27.10
come in 35.24
come off it 27.1—2
come on 27.1—2

comma (,)
Rule 61.6
Before/after...
• direct quote 36.1

324

different than 28.27

dimension
Rules 52.1—3

ding 35.28
ding-dong 35.28
disgtengué 61.1

ditto marks ("")
Rules 61.8
Dimensions 52.2
Height, length, width
52.3
Recipe ingredients 47.9

divorcé 61.1
divorcée 61.1
<u>do</u> 44.3
do tell 27.1—2

doctrine
Rules 39.1—5

does 44.3
doesn't 44.3

donations
Vertical list 47.10

dong 35.28
<u>don't</u> 44.3
don't be absurd 27.1—2
don't be foolish 27.1—2
don't be funny 27.1—2
don't be like that 27.1—2
don't be silly 27.1—2
don't I know it 27.1—2
don't knock it 27.1—2
don't mention it 27.1—2
double 63.7

doubt (showing)
Rule 2.10

<u>down</u> 10.39
down the hatch 27.3
do your worst 27.1—2
drat 15.1—2
dubbed 6.7
duck 15.1—2
<u>due</u> and payable 71.15
due to 28.28

duplicate words
See "identical words"

during 17.2
<u>dying</u> by 28.29
dying from 28.29
dying of 28.29
<u>each</u> 18.1—8
each and every one 71.16
east 10.18
easy 1.7, 3.3, 15.1—2
éclat 61.1
éclair 61.1
eeeee-yiiiii 35.28
effect 29.4
e.g. 46.2
eh 35.28
either 3.6, 10.19
eliciting 29.15

ellipsis (...)
Rule 61.9
Direct quote 36.8
In dialogue 35.7, 35.9

else 7.1, 10.20
emerge 29.16
<u>enclosed</u> herewith 70.1
enclosed please find 70.1
encore 15.1—2
end result 71.17
endorsed on the back
71.18
enigma 44.9
entitled 6.7
entreé 61.1

epitaph
Rules 34.1—3

<u>equally</u> alike 71.4
equally as 71.19
equally together 71.4
ergo 10.21
eureka 15.1—2
eventually 3.6, 12.1—4
ever 63.8
<u>every</u> 11.1—3,
28.30
every now and again 28.30
every now and then 28.30
every once in a while
28.30
every so often 28.30
everybody 18.1—8
everyone 18.1—8
ex 62.11
except 29.2

exclamation mark (!)
Rule 61.10
After...
• common expression
24.4—5
• curse word 18.13
• expression 27.4
• *hello, good-bye*
35.24
• midsentence word
15.2, 18.5
• military command
67.1—6
• pronoun 18.1
• question mark 27.7
• quote 36.13
• stand-alone...
  - phrase 24.1
  - sentence 30.6, 30.9
  - word 5.1—2
Between successive
common expressions
27.5
Showing...
• doubt 2.10
• sarcasm 2.10, 6.9

<u>excuse</u> 10.22
excuse me 27.1—2
exist 29.17

exposé 61.1

expression
See "common expression"

extra 64.13
fair and equitable 71.20
fair enough 27.1—2
Faithfully 69.1
fall 42.9
falling down 71.21
false pretense 71.22
false pretext 71.23
fancy 10.23

farewells
Rule 35.24

farewell 35.24
far out 27.1—2

"feet" sign
Rule 61.4
Dimensions 52.2
Height, length, width
  52.3

fellow 64.14
few 18.1—8
fiancé 61.1
fiancée 61.1
filed 6.7
fiddlesticks 15.1—2
finally 3.6, 12.1—4, 15.1

financial abbreviations
Rule 72.4

fine 2.3, 3.3
Fine business 27.1—2
fire 15.1—2, 64.15
fire away 27.1—2
first 64.16
first and foremost 71.24
first, beginning 71.24
First things first 27.7
fish or cut bait 27.1—2
fold 64.17
folk 64.18
following 46.1, 47.3

follows 46.1, 47.3
foot 64.19

footnotes
Explained 56.1
Bottom of page 56.3
Book 56.4
Article in a book 56.5
Article in a magazine 56.6
Citing authors
  • four or more 56.11
  • group is author 56.12
  • three authors 56.10
  • two authors 56.9
In the text 56.2
List & abbreviations 72
Personal comment 56.13
Same work, another page
  56.8
Two, same work 56.7

for 7.1, 10.24, 17.2
for a fact 28.31
for crying out loud
  27.1—2
for example 28.34, 46.2
for instance 28.34, 46.2
for mercy's sake 27.1—2
for pity's sake 27.1—2
for shame 27.1—2
for short 28.35
for sure 27.1—2
for that matter 28.32
for the life of me 27.1—2
for the love of... 27.1—2
for the most part 28.33
for this reason 28.36

foreign word
Direct quote 36.17
Highlighted 6.13
Slang 8.3

fore 15.1—2, 62.12
forget it 27.1—2
Forgive me 27.1—2
Forward 67.1—6
foster 64.20
fourth(s) 64.21

fraction
Rule 50.1

Decimal fraction 50.2

frankly 3.6, 12.1—4
Fraternally 69.1
free 64.22
free gratis 71.25
from 17.2
furthermore 3.6, 12.1—4
gadzooks 35.28
gangway 15.1—2
gathering together 71.26
gee willikers 27.1—2
gee whiz 27.1—2
gee willikers 27.1—2
geez 35.28
generally 3.6, 12.1—4
get a life 27.1—2
get a move on 27.1—2
get cracking 27.1—2
get going 27.1—2
get lost 27.1—2
get real 27.1—2
get the lead out 27.1—2
get the picture? 27.10
give'em hell 27.1—2
give thought to 44.8
glass 63.9
glad to do it 27.1—2
glad to have met you
  35.24
glad to see you 35.24
Glory be 27.1—2
Glory be to God 27.1—2
God bless me 27.1—2
God bless you 27.4
God forbid 27.1—2
God help us 27.1—2
God knows 27.1—2
God willing 27.1—2
godalmighty 15.1—2
Godspeed 35.24
go in peace 27.1—2
going by the name of
  28.21
golly 15.1—2
good 15.1—2, 64.23
good afternoon 35.24
good and 71.27
good-bye 35.24
good cop bad cop 11.6
good day 35.24
Good enough 27.1—2
good evening 35.24

Good for you 27.1—2
good golly 27.1—2
good heavens 27.1—2
good luck 27.3, 35.24
good morning 35.24
good night 35.24
goodness 15.1—2
goody 15.1—2
goody, goody 27.1—2
gosh 15.1—2
got 10.25
gracias 15.1—2
gracious 15.1—2
graded 6.7
granted 10.26
granting 7.1
gratefully 69.1
great 15.1—2
great and good friend 71.28
grow up 27.1—2
Greek to me 27.1—2

greetings
Rule 35.24

ha 35.28
habitué 61.1
had 10.27, 30.2—3, 44.3
hadn't 44.3
Hah 35.28
ha-ha 35.28
half 64.24
hail 35.24
hale and hearty 71.29
hallellujah 15.1—2
hand 64.25
hands down 28.37
hands off 27.1—2
hanged 29.18
hard 64.26
hardly 26.30
hardly had 28.20
has 44.3
hasn't 44.3
have 26.69, 44.3
have a nice day 35.24
have a safe trip 35.24
have got to 71.30
have mercy 27.1—2
haven't 44.3
having 29.19
having laid 28.39

having lain 28.39
having ways and means 71.31
he 18.1—8
he is a man who 71.32

headings
Rule 66.1
Vertical list 47.3

headline
Rules 7.7—8

heads will roll 27.1—2
hear 10.28
Hear, hear 27.1—2
heart 63.10
Heaven be praised 27.1—2
Heaven forbid 27.1—2
Heaven knows 27.1—2
Heaven knows why 27.1—2
Heavens 15.1—2

height
Rule 52.3

hello 35.24
hells bells 27.1—2
her 18.1—8
here's good luck 27.3
here's how 27.3
here's mud in your eye 27.3
here's to you 27.3
hers 18.11
herself 18.1—8
hey 1.2, 1.4, 3.3, 35.28
hi 35.24
hic 35.28
high 64.27

highlighting
Alphabetic letter 6.1
Direct question 44.5
Phrase 25.1—3
Showing irony 6.8
Showing sarcasm 6.8
Word 6.4, 6.10—12
  • direct quote 36.16

him 18.1—8
himself 18.1—8
hint 29.20
his 18.11
hiss 35.28
hmmm 35.28
ho 35.28
hold 15.1—2
holy cats 27.1—2
holy cow 27.1—2
Holy Moses 27.1—2
home 63.11
honestly 3.6, 12.1—4
honestly and truly 71.33
hooray 35.28
horse apples 27.1—2
hot damn 27.1—2
hot dog 27.1—2
hot doggy 27.1—2
hot ziggety 27.1—2

hours & minutes
Rule 42.2
Elapsed time 42.2
Military time 42.2
Span of 43.1

how 30.5
How about that 27.1—2
how are you 35.24
how come 27.1—2
how do you do 35.24
how ever 27.1—2
how goes it 27.1—2
how should I know 27.1
How so 27.1—2
howdy 35.24
however 3.6, 10.29
huh 35.28
hung 29.18
hurrah 15.1—2
hurry up 27.1—2
hush 15.1—2
hyper 62.13

hyphen (-)
Rule 61.11
Adjective 11.4—5
Adverb 12.6
Between numbers
  • consecutive 53.6

- verses 65.2
Fraction 50.1
Hyphemes 63.1—25
Measurement 52.1
Nouns 16.5—6
- with numbers 48.1
Odds 53.1
Prefixes 62.1—39
Noun 16.6
Ratio 53.3
Rounding off figure 51.5
Score 53.4
Temperature 53.9
Terms of payment 51.6
Time period 42.2, 43.3

hypo 62.14
L 18.1—8, 31.10
- precedes *not* 44.10
I assure you 27.14
I beg you 27.14
I beg your pardon 27.1—2
I believe 27.14
I dare say 27.14
I dare you 27.1—2
I declare 27.14
I don't know 27.14
I feel 27.14
I feel sure 27.14
I gather 27.14
I give up 27.14
I grant you 27.14
I guess 27.14
I heard 27.14
I heard them say 27.14
I kid you not 27.14
I know 27.14
I mean 27.14
I must say 27.14
I promise you 27.14
I rather imagine 27.14
I reckon 27.14
I say 27.14
I say to you 27.14
I should worry 27.14
I suppose 27.14
I suspect 27.14
I swear 27.14
I think 27.14
I thank you 27.14
I told you before 27.14
I understand 27.14
I wonder 27.14

Ibid. 56.7
I'd say 27.14
identical 26.33
identical to 28.40
identical with 28.40

identical words
First two words 1.7
Midsentence 2.5
- pronouns 2.7, 18.10
- simple sentence 30.2
End of sentence 3.3
In a series 4.8

identification
Midsentence 2.3

i.e. 46.2
if 7.1, 10.30, 28.41
if any 28.41
if, as, and when 71.34
if ever 28.41
if not at all 28.41
if not better than 28.42
if only 27.1—2
ill 63.12
I'll be 27.1—2
I'll be jiggered 27.1—2
I'll be hanged 27.14
I'll bet you 27.14
I'll tell you that 27.14
I'll tell you what 27.14
I'll warrant you 27.14
illicit 29.15
I'm sure 27.14
I'm telling you 27.14
imagine 10.31
immerge 29.16
immerse 29.16
implying 29.20
in 17.2
in a word 28.43
in a position to 70.1
in alphabetical order 28.44
in among 71.35
in around 71.35
in back of 71.35
in behalf of 26.45
in due course 70.1
in fact 28.46

in less than 28.49
in no way 28.47
in order 28.48
in regards to 71.36
in reply to yours of 70.1
in reviewing our files 70.1
in terms of 28.50
in that case 28.51
in the event that 70.1
in this case 28.51
in your dreams 27.1—2
in your hat 27.1—2
inasmuch 7.1, 10.32

"inch" sign (")
Rule 61.8
Dimensions 52.2
Height, length, width 52.3

incidentally 3.6, 12.1—4
indeed 3.6, 12.1—4, 15.1

indef. article
Begins...
- add-on phrase 22.1
- sentence 14.1
- phrase 14.2

indicating 29.20
Indo 62.15
inferring 29.20
infra 62.16
inquire 44.8
inscribed 6.7

inscription
Rules 34.1—3

inside 28.49
inside of 28.49
insinuating 29.20
insomuch 7.1, 10.33
instead 3.6, 10.34, 28.67
inter 62.17

interjection
Rules 15.1—2
First word 1.4

Midsentence 2.4, 15.2
Stands alone 5.1—2,
   15.1

into 17.2
intra 62.18

irony (showing)
Rule 6.8

irritate 29.6
is 44.3
is when 71.37
is where 71.37
isn't 44.3
issue 44.9
it 18.1—8, 31.12
it all seems clear 27.7
it appears to me 27.14
it is our belief 70.1
it is said 27.14
it is true 27.14
it seems to me 27.14
it so happens 28.52
it was a bad scene 27.14

italics
Follows *word* 6.6
Foreign word 6.13
Indirect question 45.1
Literary titles 54.1
Show irony 6.8
Show sarcasm 6.9
So-called is implied 6.5
Technical word 6.11
The word "see" 65.1
Word combination 6.15

its—it's 10.35, 18.11
it's Katie bar the... 27.14
It's no use 27.1—2
it's said 27.14
itself 18.1—8
I've heard 27.14
jeez 35.28
jeepers 15.1—2
jet 64.28
jiggers 15.1—2

job title
Rules 57.1—4
In a list 46.7
Military rank in a list
   57.4
With person's name
   • before/after 21.6

just 26.44
just so 28.53
just you wait 27.1—2
ka-poohey 35.28
keep at it 27.1—2
keep it up 27.1—2
kerbam 35.28

kilocycles
Rule 49.4

kind of 71.38
kindest regards 69.1
kith and kin 71.39
knock it off 27.1—2
know what I mean 27.10
known as 6.7
known by the name 28.21
labeled 6.7
laid 29.21
lamé 61.1
land knows 27.1—2
last best hope 71.40
laying 29.21
leaping lizards 27.1—2
leastwise 10.36
left 10.37
Left face 67.1—6

legal document
Defining nouns 6.12

lending 29.22
lest 7.1, 10.38
let me go 27.1—2

letter, alphabetic
See "alphabetic letter"

letter, (closing)
See "closing"

life span
Rule 43.4

like 10.10, 64.29
   • precedes indirect
     quote 37.2
like fun I will 27.1—2
like hell 28.54
likewise 10.40

list (paragraph)
After...
   • *following* 46.1
   • *namely,* etc. 46.2
   • strong pause 46.3
Cities & states 46.8
Dates 46.9
People and...
   • associations 46.4
   • donations 46.5
   • hometowns 46.6
   • job titles 46.7
Phrase or sentence follows
   46.10

list (vertical)
Guidelines 47.1
Capitalization 47.1
Dates 47.11
Doesn't follow verb 47.3
Donations 47.10
Follows a verb 47.2
Indentation 47.1
Major headings 47.4
One list leads to another
   47.5
Parentheses 47.1
Phrases 47.1
Recipes 47.9
Sentences
   • full 47.1, 47.7
   • partial 47.8
Showing relationship
   between items 47.6
Spacing 47.1

Words 47.7

listen 10.41
listen up 27.1—2
literally 3.6, 12.1—4
little 64.30
lo 15.1—2
lo and behold 71.41
loaning 29.22
lock, stock, & barrel 28.55
long 63.13
look 10.41
Look at it this way 27.7
look lively 27.1—2
look out 27.1—2
look sharp 27.1—2
low 64.31
lying 29.21
macro 63.14
majority 29.23
make haste 27.1—2
make it snappy 27.1—2
make my day 27 2
make no mistake 27.1—2
mal 62.19
malarky 15.1—2
man 63.15
man oh man 27.1—2
man overboard 27.1—2
many 18.1—8
many thanks 27.1—2
mark my words 27.1—2
marked 6.7
may 44.3

maxim
Rules 39.1—5

me 18.1—8

measurements
Abbreviations 72.6
Using "by" 52.1
Using "x" 52.2

meeting together 71.42
mega 63.16
mélange 61.1
mental telepathy 71.43
merci 15.1—2
merci beaucoup 27.1—2

meta 62.20
micro 62.21
mid 63.17
might 10.43, 44.3

military command
Counting cadence 67.4
Dramatic pause 67.2
Followed by a noun 67.3
Lengthening a word 67.5
"March" is shortened 67.5
Stands alone 67.1

military rank
Abbreviations 72.7
In a vertical list 57.4

milli 63.18
mine 18.11
mini 62.22
minus 10.44, 17.2
mis 62.23
misnamed 6.7
Mmmm 35.28
Monday 27.8
momentarily 3.6, 12.1—4

money
Rules 51.1—6
Donations in a list
• paragraph 46.5
• vertical 47.10

month
Rule 42.6
Time span 43.2

more or less 28.56
most 29.23
Most gratefully 69.1
Most respectfully 69.1
Most sincerely 69.1

motto
Rules 34.1—3

much obliged 27.1—2
multi 63.19

music, title
Rule 58.2

my eye 27.1—2
my God 27.1—2
my goodness 27.1—2
my land 27.1—2
my stars 27.1—2
my word 27.1—2
myself 18.1—8
naaahhh 35.28
naïveté 61.1

name
Company name
• Followed by *Inc.* 60.2
• Trade name 60.1
Person's name
• By-name 59.2
• Death notice 59.12
• Followed by *of* 59.6
• Identified 59.5
• *Junior* 59.13
• Linked to…
  - group 59.7
  - city 59.8
  - name 59.9
• Milestone 59.11
• Nickname 59.1
• Omitting…
  - first name 59.3
  - last name 59.4
• Question follows 59.10

named 6.7
namely 10.45, 46.2, 47.3
naturally 3.6, 12.1—4
near to 71.44
neither 10.46
neo 62.24
never fear 27.1—2
never mind 27.1—2
never say die 27.1—2
nevertheless 10.47
next 17.2
nice cop tough cop 11.6
nice going 27.1—2

Interrupts sentence 34.3

on 17.2, 26.53—4
on account of 28.59
on average 28.60
on behalf of 28.45
on the double 27.1—2
once 10.57
one 18.1—8
one and the same thing
  71.49
one more time 27.7
one thing for sure 27.7
one's 18.11
oneself 18.1—8
onto 17.2
oomph 35.28
oops 35.28
open fire 27.1—2
or 10.58, 21.10, 29.27
- Between...
  - words in series 4.7
  - sentences 43.11
- Midsentence option
  21.10
- Joining simple sen-
  tences 31.1, 31.3,
  32.1, 32.4, 33.2; be-
  tween simple and
  complex sentences
  31.9, 32.8—9;
  joining complex
  sentences 31.12
or adjacent to 28.61
or else 28.62
or how about this 27.7
otherwise 10.59
other(s) 18.1—8
ouch 35.28
ought 10.60, 44.3
oughtn't 10.60
our 18.11
ours 18.11
ourselves 18.1—8
out-and-out 71.50
outside of 71.51
outside of that 71.51
over 17.2, 63.20
over and above 71.52
over with 71.53
owing to 28.63

page numbers
Bibliography 55.2—3

pairs of words
Adjective 11.6—7
Descriptive 4.2
Identical 4.1, 30.2
Successive 4.3
The verb *had* 30.3

Pan 62.26
papier maché 61.1
para 62.27
Parade rest 67.1—6
pardon 10.61
pardon me 27.1—2

parentheses
Rule 61.12
Around numbers in
series...
- partial sentences 48.4
- phrases 23.5, 48.5
- sentences 48.3
- words 4.18, 48.2
Bibliography 55.2, 55.7
Capitalized word 68.2
Duplicate numbers 53.7
Footnote 56.3—8
Life span 43.4
Midsentence phrase 21.3
Midsentence word 2.3,
12.2
Person's age 53.10
Question 44.5
Sentence interruption
  18.2, 21.7, 31.6,
  31.10, 32.7, 32.11,
  33.8
Source of quote 36.14

part and parcel 71.54

parts of speech
adjective 11.1—7
adverb 12.1—6
conjunction 13.1—4
indefinite article 14.1—2
interjection 15.1—2
noun 6.1—9

preposition 17.1—7
pronoun 18.1—13
verb 19.1—11

passé 61.1
past, present. & future
28.64

patent number
Rule 49.3

pause
After...
- dialogue 35.22
- first word 1.2, 1.8
- introductory sentence
  31.11, 32.5, 33.3
- military command
  67.2
- preposition 17.7
- proverb, principle
  39.4
- phrase 20.12—13
- series 4.4, 4.12
Before...
- last word 3.1—2
- list 46.3
- midsentence word
  2.1, 2.9
- phrase 22.10
- question 44.11
- proverb, etc. 39.5
- question 44.10
- series 4.17
Between
- sentences 31.8,
  31.15, 32.5—6,
  33.4, 33.10, 35.23
Forcing pause 22.9
Within
- dialogue 35.6—8

peace be with you 27.1—2
per 17.2

percentage
Rule 50.3
Terms of payment 51.6

period (.)
Rule 61.13

sans cérémonie 61.1
Santé Fe 61.1

sarcasm
Rules 2.10, 6.9, 15.1,
44.4

sauté 61.1
save us 27.1—2
saving 17.2

say 10.69
say uncle 27.1—2
Say what? 27.10
says you 27.1—2
Says who 27.1—2
scarcely had 28.20
scat 15.1—2

score
Rule 53.4

scram 15.1—2
search me 27.1—2

season
Rule 42.9

seconds
Rule 42.2
Elapsed time 42.2

see 10.41, 65.1
see what I mean? 27.10
see you 35.24
seemingly 3.6, 12.1—4
self 63.23
self-confessed 71.59
semi 62.32

semicolon
Rule 61.17
Before a list 46.2
Between sentences
- before prep.17.6
- before verb 19.8
- complex 31.12
- different subject &
  verb 20.11
- in a series 48.3
- long, related 31.4

- simple 31.8, 32.3—
  4, 33.1—2, 33.4—6
- simple & complex
  31.9, 32.8—11,
  33.10
Between
- authors' names 55.5,
  56.10—11
- partial sentences
  48.4
- quotes 36.7
- words 48.2
In a list 46.3—10

sentence
Follows a list 46.10
In a vertical list 47.7
Interrupts another 18.4
With phrases
- introduced 20.1—17
- midsentence 21.1—
  13
- at end 22.1—11
Words omitted 7.1—6,
30.1
Duplicate 7.6
Within another sentence
18.4

sentence (simple)
Contains contrast 30.6
Duplicate words 30.2
Had appears twice 30.3
Quoting a familiar one
30.7
Verb ends in "ing" 30.4
Who, what, where, when,
or *how* appears 30.5
Words omitted 30.1

sentence (joining two)
Conjunction
- leads off 31.5
- omitted 31.8
- separates simple sen-
  tence from compound
  sentence 31.9

In dialogue 35.21
Joined by...
- *and, or, but* 31.1,
  31.9, 31.12
- *as* 31.2
Long, heavily related 31.4
One sentence...
- interrupts the other
  31.6, 31.10, 31.13
- acts as a contrast 31.7
Share same subject 31.3
Strong pause between
31.11

sentence (joining three)
Adverbial conjunction
used 32.2
Begins with same words
32.4
Contains complex
sentences
- two 32.9
- three 32.10
No conjunctions used 32.3
One sentence...
- interrupts 32.7,
  32.11
- is complex 32.8
Separated by *and, or, but,*
etc. 32.1
Strong pause...
- follows first one 32.5
- precedes last one 32.6

sentence (joining 4+)
Conjunction repeated 33.7
Different lead-in words
33.1
Paragraph interrupts 33.8
One is emphasized 33.9
Simple sentences 33.2
Strong pause follows first
one 33.3, 33.10
With same...
- lead in words 33.4,
  33.6
- verb 33.5

336

338

to the left flank 67.1—6
to the rear 67.1—6
to the rescue 27.1—2
to the right flank 67.1—6
to wit 10.47, 46.2
to you and yours 27.3
today 42.4
tomorrow 42.4
too 3.6, 10.91
too bad 27.1—2
tops 16.4
toward 17.1

trade name
Rule 60.1
trans 62.35
tri 62.36

trite word combinations
Rule 70.1

truism
Rules 39.1—5

trust me 27.2, 27.7
tsk-tsk 35.28
tst-tst 35.28
tush 35.28
tut 35.28
typically 3.6, 12.1—4
ugh 35.28
uh-huh 35.28
ultimately 3.6, 12.1—4
ultra 62.37
u-mmm 35.28
un 62.38
under 17.2, 63.25
• begins job title 57.3

underlining
Curse word substitute 9.1
Replaces name
• author's 55.4
• first name 59.3
• last name 59.4

under the name of 28.21
unless 7.1, 10.92

unless and until 71.66
until 7.1, 10.93
until now 28.73
until then 28.73
up 10.39
upon 17.2
upright and honest 71.67
urgent 15.1—2
us 18.1—8
used 10.95
Uuuuu 35.28
vamoose 15.1—2
varoom 35.28
va-voom 35.28
va-va-voom 35.28

verb
Begins...
• sentence 19.1
• introduct. phrase 19.2
• interrupting phrase 19.4
• add-on phrase 19.5, 22.1
• related sentences 19.8
Contracting 18.12, 19.9
Ends a sentence 19.6
Ends in "ing" 30.4
Follows dialogue 35.1
Hyphened 19.10
Interrupts sentence 19.3
Part of a series 19.7
Omitted in sentence 7.4—6
Precedes
• dialogue 35.1
• list 47.3
• motto, epitaph 34.2
Two in a row 2.8
With dialogue 35.2

Very respectfully 69.1
Very sincerely 69.1
Very truly yours 69.1
very well 27.1—2
vice 57.2

virgule (/)
Rule 61.18
And/or 10.9
Fraction 50.1

Quoting poetry 40.2
Represents preposition 7.2
Word combinations 11.6

viva 15.1—2
vice 62.39
visé 61.1
vroom 35.28
wait and see 27.2, 27.7
wait up 27.1—2
want to know 44.8
was 44.3
wasn't 44.3
watch out 27.1—2
watch your step 27.1—2
way to go 27.2
we 18.1—8
Wednesday 27.8

week
Rule 42.5

welcome 35.24
well 10.96, 64.36
well and good 71.68
well done 27.1—2
Well I never 27.1—2
were 44.3
weren't 44.3
west 10.18
wham 35.28
whap 35.28
what 10.98, 10.125, 30.5
what a life 27.1—2
what a pity 27.1—2
what does it matter 27.1
what do you know 27.1—2
what ever 27.1—2
what gives 27.1—2
what in the world 27.1—2
what of it 27.1—2
what on earth 27.1—2
what the heck 27.1—2
what the hell 27.1—2
what the hey 27.1—2
what the Sam Hill 27.1
what then 28.74
what's cooking 27.1—2
what's the use 27.1—2
what's up 27.1—2
what's with him 27.1—2
whatever 18.5

341

Got a Question about Punctuation?

And you can't find the answer in this book? Give us the opportunity to help you solve it. If we do not know the answer, we will find someone who does. Simply send your question, *along with a self-addressed stamped envelope*, to Branden Publishing Company, Inc; Attention: Punctuation Answer Department; 17 Station Street; Box 843; Brookline Village; Boston, MA 02147. Upon receiving your inquiry, we will attempt to respond within twenty-four (24) hours.

Or Would You Like to Contribute?

Branden is interested in learning about all types of punctuation situations, because we want *The Punctuation Thesaurus* to provide as many answers as possible. Perhaps you know of one or more which would make excellent additions to the book. Or while reading, you might see a unique situation where punctuation is used. In either case, we would like to hear from you. If we decide to add it to our new edition in the future, we will rewrite it and list your name in the book as one of our contributors.

We are also interested in receiving information regarding incorrect or trite word combinations, capitalization, headings, captions, and the hyphenation of prefixes and words.

If you want a response concerning whether or not your contribution was the first to be received by our company on that specific punctuation situation, *you must send along a self-addressed stamped envelope.* Use the same address as shown above.

BRANDEN PUBLISHING COMPANY, INC.